Electronic Public Relations

UNIVERSITY
LIBRARIES

FLORIDA·STATE·UNIVERSITY·
VIRES ARTES MORES
1857

Tallahassee

From the Wadsworth Series in Mass Communication and Journalism

GENERAL MASS COMMUNICATION

Communications Law: Liberties, Restraints, and the Modern Media, by John D. Zelezny
Communications Media in the Information Society, by Joseph Straubhaar and Robert LaRose
Ethics in Media Communications: Cases and Controversies, by Louis Day
International Communications: History, Conflict, and Control of the Global Metropolis,
    by Robert S. Fortner
The Interplay of Influence, 3rd Ed, by Kathleen Hall Jamieson and Karlyn Kohrs Campbell
Media/Impact: An Introduction to Mass Media, 3rd Ed, by Shirley Biagi
Media/Reader: Perspectives on Media Industries, Effects, and Issues, 3rd Ed, by Shirley Biagi
Mediamerica, Mediaworld: Form, Content, and Consequence of Mass Communication, Updated 5th
    Ed, by Edward Jay Whetmore
Women and Media: Content, Careers, and Criticism, by Cynthia Lont

JOURNALISM

Crafting News for Electronic Media: Writing, Reporting, and Production, by Carl Hausman
Creative Editing for Print Media, by Dorothy Bowles, Diane L. Borden, and William Rivers
Free-Lancer and Staff Writer, 5th Ed, by William Rivers
Interviews that Work: A Practical Guide for Journalists, 2nd Ed, by Shirley Biagi
News Writing, by Peter Berkow
The Search: Information Gathering for the Mass Media, by Lauren Kessler and
    Duncan McDonald
When Words Collide: A Media Writer's Guide to Grammar and Style, 4th Ed, by Lauren Kessler
    and Duncan McDonald
Writing and Reporting News: A Coaching Method, by Carole Rich

PHOTOGRAPHY & DESIGN

Design Principles for Desktop Publishers, 2nd Ed, by Tom Lichty
Desktop Computing Workbook, by Paul Martin Lester
Introduction to Photography, 4th Ed, by Marvin J. Rosen and David L. DeVries
Visual Communication: Images with Messages, by Paul Martin Lester

PUBLIC RELATIONS AND ADVERTISING

Advertising and Marketing to the New Majority: A Case Study Approach, by Gail Baker Woods
Creative Strategy in Advertising, 5th Ed, by A. Jerome Jewler
Electronic Public Relations, by Eugene Marlow
International Advertising: Communicating Across Cultures, by Barbara Mueller
Public Relations Cases, 3rd Ed, by Jerry A. Hendrix
Public Relations Writing: Form and Style, 4th Ed, by Doug Newsom and Bob Carrell
This Is PR: The Realities of Public Relations, 6th Ed, by Doug Newsom, Judy VanSlyke Turk, and
    Dean Kruckeberg

RESEARCH AND THEORY

Communication Research: Strategies and Sources, 4th Ed, by Rebecca B. Rubin, Alan M. Rubin,
    and Linda J. Piele
Contemporary Communication Research Methods, by Mary John Smith
Mass Communication Theory: Foundations, Ferment and Future, by Stanley Baran and
    Dennis Davis
Mass Media Research: An Introduction, 4th Ed, by Roger D. Wimmer and Joseph R. Dominick
The Practice of Social Research, 7th Ed, by Earl Babbie
Surveying Public Opinion, by Sondra Miller Rubenstein

Electronic Public Relations

Eugene Marlow, Ph.D.
Baruch College

Janice Sileo
Research Associate

Wadsworth Publishing Company
I(T)P® An International Thomson Publishing Company

Belmont • Albany • Bonn • Boston • Cincinnati • Detroit • London • Madrid • Melbourne •
Mexico City • New York • Paris • San Francisco • Singapore • Tokyo • Toronto • Washington

Communication Studies Editor: Todd R. Armstrong
Editorial Assistant: Michael Gillespie
Production Services Coordinator: Debby Kramer
Production: Vicki Moran, Publishing Support Services
Designer: Robin Gold, Forbes Mill Press
Print Buyer: Barbara Britton
Permissions Editor: Robert Kauser
Copy Editor: Victoria Nelson
Cover Design: Ross Carron
Composition: Vicki Moran, Publishing Support Services
Printer: Malloy Lithographing, Inc.

Printed in the United States of America
1 2 3 4 5 6 7 8 9 10

For more information, contact Wadsworth Publishing Company:

Wadsworth Publishing Company
10 Davis Drive
Belmont, California 94002, USA

International Thomson Editores
Campos Eliseos 385, Piso 7
Col. Polanco
11560 México D.F. México

International Thomson Publishing Europe
Berkshire House 168-173
High Holborn
London, WC1V 7AA, England

International Thomson Publishing GmbH
Königswinterer Strasse 418
53227 Bonn, Germany

Thomas Nelson Australia
102 Dodds Street
South Melbourne 3205
Victoria, Australia

International Thomson Publishing Asia
221 Henderson Road
#05-10 Henderson Building
Singapore 0315

Nelson Canada
1120 Birchmount Road
Scarborough, Ontario
Canada M1K 5G4

International Thomson Publishing Japan
Hirakawacho Kyowa Building, 3F
2-2-1 Hirakawacho
Chiyoda-ku, Tokyo 102, Japan

 Printed on recycled paper

Library of Congress Cataloging-in-Publication Data
Marlow. Eugene
        Electronic public relations / Eugene Marlow. Janice Sileo.
                p.   cm
        Includes bibliographical references (p.   ) and index.
        ISBN: 0-534-26244-9 (pbk.)
             1. Public relations--Technological innovations.   2. Information
technology. I. Sileo. Janice.   II. Title.
        HD59.M27   1996   95–26411
        659.2'0285--dc20

Contents

Foreword

This book was written to provide readers with an overview of electronic public relations applications, vehicles, and distribution channels as well as guidelines for using electronic technologies for public relations purposes. *Electronic Public Relations* is also about the evolution of electronic media in this century: their impact on print media and the changes that have taken place in the public relations profession, journalism, press relations, and consumer and community relations as a consequence.

The book's organizing principle is "audiences"—the general public, the media, communities, organizations, government officials, consumers, investors, employees, managers, individuals. The reality of commerce today is that businesses must pay attention to the consumer, regardless of community: ours is a consumer-driven economy. Ignore the needs of the consumer and your product and service will go unheeded!

Not so coincidentally, *Electronic Public Relations* is also organized historically. The book begins with applications that address relatively large audiences and ends with electronic media that can reach the consumer on a one-on-one basis. Early chapters deal with the more mature electronic technologies, such as radio and television (both broadcast and cable). Later chapters discuss more recent electronic media (such as linear videotape, satellite communications, interactive videodisc, and multimedia). A closing chapter describes the most recent electronic communication medium: the Internet.

During the course of the 158-year development of electronic media, the opportunity for targeting audiences for public relations (as well as for marketing) messages has increased dramatically. Public service announcements (PSAs) distributed through radio and television channels provide public relations practitioners with unprecedented means to reach the general public on a national or a regional scale; the same is true for video news releases and, more recently, satellite media tours.

Linear video, satellite communications, interactive videodisc, and multimedia outlets allow public relations professionals to target various audiences in more highly specific ways—in public exhibits, educational institutions, trade shows, government offices. These same technologies—particularly linear video and satellite communications—have given rise to organizational video networks, so-called corporate video or business television. E-mail technology has increased the ability of employees to communicate with one another and has changed the shape of organizational communications in the process.

The Internet has pushed public relations communications to an even higher magnitude. Today public relations professionals can reach virtually every audience—consumers, the press, government officials, community officials—as individuals all over the world.

This book can serve as a supplemental text for college courses in public relations or corporate video communications; in the professional market, it can serve as a stand-alone reference. It can be incorporated into such courses as introduction to public relations, writing for public relations, public relations campaigns, public relations case histories, public relations or communications research, public affairs, public relations management, public relations law/ethics, and public relations techniques. Public relations professors and students (graduate and undergraduate), professionals working in public relations firms, and public relations managers working in for profit and not-for-profit organizations may all find this book useful.

Electronic Public Relations uses several techniques to deliver its content. At the core of several chapters are interviews with subject experts, practitioners who use electronic media. Many chapters also contain examples of each application and a brief history of the application to give the reader the context for the development of the application.

The book is divided into twelve chapters: Chapter 1 briefly surveys the history of public relations in both print and electronic media. Chapter 2 focuses on the range of electronic media from radio through television, cable, video, multimedia, and on-line vehicles. Chapter 3 examines public service announcements as a means of reaching large general audiences, and Chapter 4 looks at video news releases, both broadcast and cable, as a means of reaching the same audience. Chapter 5 examines satellite media tours; Chapter 6 explores satellite news conferences, electronic media kits, and E-mail as ways of reaching the news media. Chapter 7 focuses on the use of linear videos as well as linear and interactive exhibits with targeted community and government audiences. Chapter 8 looks at ways to communicate on an individual basis with consumers in their own homes: by telephone, home VCR, CD-ROM, or cable television. Chapter 9 discusses the use of electronic media for internal communications within organizations, both for profit and nonprofit, and Chapter 10 examines the use of electronic media for management communications. Chapter 11 explores the electronic frontier—the array of commercial on-line and Internet services that now connect individuals around the globe. Chapter 12, finally, looks at some of the implications of the electronic revolution for the future of the public relations field.

As an epilogue, readers are provided with a recent case study involving a turning point in the history of electronic public relations: the story of Intel's pentium chip debut on the market, as related by James Baar and Theodore Baar. Appendixes list the public relations experts interviewed for this book, organizations that specialize in each electronic public relations application, and specialized professional associations and publication.

Acknowledgments

It is almost impossible to write a book like *Electronic Public Relations* without borrowing some insights from one's previous work.

The genesis for this book was an article on video news releases written in 1994 especially for the journal of the Public Relations Society of America. This material (plus new material dealing with the history and evolution of VNRs) forms the basis for Chapter 4. Portions of Chapter 2 have been borrowed from *Winners! Producing Effective Electronic Media* (Marlow, 1994), specifically those sections dealing with interactive videodisc, multimedia, and satellites and teleconferencing. The cases "Children Are Too Young to Die," "Discover Your Own Song," "Motorola: The Simulated Exploration of Electronic Knowledge," and "American Abstraction, 1930–1945: The Artists Speak" that appear in Chapter 7 also come from this book. The section on videotape and organizational video networks in Chapter 2, the case study "Metro Toronto Community Services" in Chapter 7, and portions of Chapter 9 and Chapter 10 have been adapted from my previous book *Corporate Television Programming* (1992). Finally, sections of Chapter 10 originally appeared in "The Electrovisual Manager," an article published in *Business Horizons,* in 1994.

I am indebted to many people for their comments, observations, and contacts. They are: Nick Peters, Medialink (New York); Judy Lyn Prince, Mobil; Dennis Wigent, K-mart; Kevin Kimball, Siemens Corp. (New York); Marie Gentile, West Glen; Farrell Fitch, National Alliance for the Mentally Ill; Tony Esposito, Bozell (Chicago); Tim Price, Medialink; Elyse Rabinowitz, NTV International; Ed Goldstein, Ruder Finn; Ed Peters, SVP National Satellite Services; Mona Brown, Advertising Council; Michael Lissauer, Public Relations Services Council; Alan Andreasen, Georgetown University; Sally Jewett, On the Screen Productions (Los Angeles); Radio and TV Reports; Karen Kalish, Kalish

Communications; Steve Cook, Cook Public Relations; Kevin Foley, KEF Media Associates; Susan Silk; Kristie Scott, Association Services, International Satellite Communications Association; Suzanne Rothenberg, Suzanne Rothenberg Communications; the Museum of Television and Radio; Phillip O. Keirstead, Florida A & M Tallahassee; Steve Matthis, Montgomery College; Norman Goldstein, Federal Communications Commission; Karen Amster-Young; Christine Kent, Bulldog Reporter (InfoComm Group); Jarlath Connolly, MediaMap; Michael Nikolich, Tech Image; Nancy Collins, CBS/FM Radio; Lynn Cox, Digital Express; Debbie Barnett, National Broadcast Association of Community Affairs; Joe Vecchionne, Prudential Insurance; John Beardsley, Public Relations Society of America; Joe Tiernan, Radio and Television News Directors Association; Bridgett Scott, National Association of Broadcasters; Lori Miller, PRSA Journal Library; Tom Appelman and Dick Hackenberg, Chiat/Day; Jim Olson, CONUS; Lee Stral, PR Forum Mailing List; Bill Lutholtz, Indianapolis Power and Light; Ed Swanson, Video Placement Worldwide; Ginnel Radke, Center for Communication Strategy; Susan Williamson, Annenberg Library; Dave Conway and Bob Treuber, Modern Talking Pictures; Peter Harris, Brouillard Communications; Richard Brooks, BMW; Kathryn Buan, Oracle; Larry Ralph, Museum of Science, Boston; Lawrence Fisher, Maritime Center of East Norwalk; Elizabeth Persichetty, American Association of Museums; Diane Zorich, National Association for Museum Exhibitions; Judy Pomerantz, Exhibit Builder Magazine; Meredith Hunt, Resource Center, Trade Show Bureau; Donna Washington, Convention Liaison Council; Dick Bray, American Society of Association Executives; Dick Jones, New York chapter, International Interactive Communications Society; Kim LaSalle, LaSalle Communications; Judy Pirani, BIS Strategic Decisions; and Luana Lewis, The Advertising Council, Inc.

I am particularly grateful to colleague Neil Ruggles for his content and critique contributions to Chapter 11; his depth of knowledge of the on-line world was invaluable.

My thanks also to Janice Sileo for her editing of the many interviews contained in this volume, for finding research materials essential for the completion of the text, and for her usual good counsel in editing the manuscript drafts.

Special thanks to reviewers Erica Austin of Washington State Univeristy; Don Bates, Executive Vice President of Sumner Rider & Associates, Inc.; Thomas Bowers of University of North Carolina-Chapel Hill; Timothy Coombs of Illinois State University; LuEtt Hanson of Kent State University; Todd Hunt of Rutgers University; Barbara Mueller of San Diego State University; and Maria Russell of Syracuse University for their careful scrutiny and comments on early drafts of the current volume. Their critique in no small way added to the focus and structure of this book.

Last, appreciation to Todd Armstrong, Wadsworth Communication Studies Editor, for his enthusiasm and faith in this book's viability, and to the production and editing staff at Wadsworth for their deft handling of this volume.

—EM

Chapter 1

Public Relations: A Brief History

The practice of modern public relations is virtually a century old. Scott M. Cutlip, Dean Emeritus of the University of Georgia, writes in his exhaustive *The Unseen Power: Public Relations. A History:* "We somewhat arbitrarily place the beginnings of the public relations vocation with the establishment of The Publicity Bureau in Boston in mid-1900, on the eve of the twentieth century" (1994, xvi). Even Cutlip, however, is quick to point out that "all history, including that of public relations, moves in a seamless web. The history of public relations cannot be fully told by simply saying that it grew out of press agentry" (1994, xvi–xvii). Cutlip goes on to observe that in various ways the history of public relations is a reflection of America's social, political, and economic development and has evolved in tandem with these various cultural facets. Today we can add unequivocally that the practice of public relations has also evolved as a direct result of rapid technological developments during the last fifteen years.

Almost a hundred years after its modern initiation, public relations has become a complex and varied field. The Public Relations Society of America (PRSA), itself formed in 1948 as a merger between two other extant groups, defines public relations as:

> *counseling, research, media relations, publicity, employee/member relations, community relations, public affairs, government affairs, issues management, financial relations, industry relations, development/fund raising, minority relations and multi-cultural affairs, special events and public participation, and marketing communications. (1991, pp. 3–4)*

An Industry Overview

Public relations as a practice and a profession has come a long way. According to the *U.S. Industrial Outlook 1994*, receipts for management and public relations establishments reached an estimated $72 billion in 1993, an increase of 5.9 percent from 1992. The sector had a payroll of 680,000 in 1993, up 3.8 percent from the previous year. For 1994, the *Outlook* predicted, increased demand for management and public relations services would result in higher receipts and employment. Receipts were expected to reach $77 billion, or 6.9 percent above the 1993 levels. Employment was forecast to rise 4.4 percent to 710,000.

O'Dwyer's *Directory of Public Relations Firms* lists approximately 660 national and international public relations firms working in 58 foreign countries. The Bureau of Labor Statistics lists 155,000 public relations practitioners as of 1993.

One hundred and eighty-one (181) student chapters at college campuses are accredited by the PRSA. To be accredited, an eligible school must offer five public relations courses. The *New York Times* (1994, pp. B1, B5) reported that 18,220 students were majoring in public relations in the fall of 1992. This is according to a census of 413 higher education programs conducted by Lee Becker of Ohio State University.

From Print to Electronic

For most of its nearly 100-year history, public relations in the United States has had a "print" foundation. But that orientation has begun to change. The concept of electronic public relations did not exist fifteen years ago. While public service announcements did play on broadcast radio in the 1940s and later on broadcast television, video news releases were virtually unheard of at the time; videotape was not commercially introduced until 1956. Organizations began to use videotape networks for internal communications in the early 1970s; interactive videodisc, cable television and satellite technology first became available for public relations purposes in the 1980s. It was not until the late 1980s that the multimedia revolution began.

On the other hand, in the 1990s the distribution of video news releases appears to be expanding and organizational use of teleconferencing and satellite technology for public relations is increasing. Today the Internet is making its way into the public relations practitioner's toolkit. There is every reason to believe this trend will continue for the next several years as electronic technologies (such as cable television and on-line services) continue to evolve on a global scale.

When this book was conceived in mid-1994, we thought we were writing a basic book about electronic public relations vehicles and distribution channels, such as public service announcements, video news releases, satellite media tours and news conferences, and the like. Once a novel concept, electronic public relations in various forms is now standard fare in the public relations practitioner's cornucopia of tools. The major thrust of this volume is that electronic public relations is not just an interesting notion, a novel way of doing things in the 1990s, or an adjunct to print media.

We are in the middle of a revolution. Electronic public relations may be *the* way public relations gets done as we move toward the millennium. It is not a matter of whether public relations professionals use electronic media or not in the future, it will be a matter of *how well* they use these media. Pushing this electronic evolution is the struggle between on-line services (such as the Internet) and the growing glut of "paper" information.

Another central theme of this book is the evolving relationship between public relations practitioners and journalists. As the growth of electronic technologies increasingly forces public relations professionals to communicate via E-mail, the days (or at least the years) of the print news release may be numbered.

If public relations professionals are going to be successful in the future, they must go where the audience is to get their client's message across. Increasingly, that audience is reachable via electronic means. And by audience we mean:

> print and electronic journalists, local, state, regional, federal, and international government officials (legislative, regulatory, executive, judicial), community leaders, chambers of commerce, neighborhood coalitions, community organizations, employees, managers, employee families, customers, distributors, jobbers, wholesalers, retailers, suppliers, teaming partners, subcontractors, professional societies, trade associations, academic faculty and staff, trustees, financial supporters, students, securities analysts, institutional holders, shareholders, bankers, stockbrokers, portfolio managers, potential investors, and special interest groups (environmentalists, the handicapped or disabled, minorities, think tanks, consumer groups, health groups, senior citizens, religious organizations)

—potentially on a global scale.

In the Beginning

In early 1838, Samuel Finley Breese Morse—artist, daguerrotypist, a so-called "American Leonardo"—gave a series of public demonstrations of the first practical electromagnetic telegraph. In 1844, after receiving a $30,000 grant to construct a telegraph line between Baltimore and Washington, D.C. the year before, Morse finally opened the nation's first commercial telegraph line on May 24 with the now famous query, "What hath God wrought?" (Czitrom, 1982, pp. 4–6) On that day the electronic communications age was born.

Seventy-eight years later, the basis for modern network broadcasting was created in the United States by the American Telephone & Telegraph Company (AT&T). In February 1922, the company proposed that thirty-eight radio broadcasting stations be linked by AT&T long-distance telephone lines. The stations would each be charged a fee by AT&T and would be encouraged, in turn, to sell for commercial purposes the air time they had available. The commercial aspects of the proposal were condemned by many in the press, some of whom may have been anticipating unwanted competition for advertisers' dollars (Marlow & Secunda, 1991, pp. 25–26).

In 1922, AT&T opened radio station WEAF in New York based on a novel concept—toll broadcasting. AT&T saw WEAF's service as parallel to telephone service. The company would provide no programs, only facilities. Whoever wished to address a message to the radio audience would pay a tool or fee to use the station, which was to be a kind of telephone booth of the air. Of course, the telephone company soon found that it had to provide programming on a sustaining (unsponsored) basis when there were no messages. On August 28, 1922 at 5 P.M., WEAF aired its first toll broadcast. A Mr. Blackwell of the Queensboro Corporation spoke for 10 minutes about Hawthorne Court, a condominium in the Jackson Heights section of Long Island, New York. The toll was $50. On August 28, 1922, the first commercial had been broadcast (Smith, 1985, p. 20), and the electronic marketing (and public relations) era was born.

Between 1838 and the mid-1990s, a plethora of electronic media outlets have been created, and sooner or later public relations professionals have figured out how to use every one of them to reach a variety of audiences on a local, regional, national, and global scale.

Vehicles, Channels, and Applications

Today, public relations practitioners have a vast array of electronic media vehicles and channels to choose from, depending on their communications objectives, message, and audience:

- *Vehicles:* radio and television public service advertising spots, video news releases, satellite news conferences, satellite media tours, product or service linear videos, interactive videodiscs, multimedia, E-mail messages, Internet Gopher sites, Internet websites

- *Distribution channels:* local radio stations, network radio stations, ad hoc audio conferences, network and local broadcast television news operations, network and local cable television news operations, home video outlets, internal organizational videotape networks, internal two-way videoconferencing systems, internal one-way video, two-way audio organ-izational teleconferencing networks, public exhibits, local area networks (LANs), fax networks, 800 and 900 toll numbers, and on-line information systems (see Table 1)

These vehicles and distribution channels can be used for:

- *Applications:* reaching the general public, reaching print and electronic journalists, reaching communities, reaching the consumer at home, reaching employees, reaching managers, and reaching individuals on a global scale (see Table 2)

Table 1

Electronic Media Channels		
Radio	11,700+ stations	500 million radios
Commercial broadcast TV	1,145 stations	95+ million TV - households
Cable TV	11,351 cable systems	59+ million TV - households
Organizational video networks	12,000 organizations	
Organizations with VCRs	5 million	
Home video (VCRs)	76 million television households	135 million VCRs
Teleconferencing rooms	15,000 video rooms	
Interactive videodisc	100,000	
Multimedia players	17 million	
Faxes	3.2 million (U.S.)	
Online information systems	Three major purveyors: CompuServe, Prodigy, America Online	7.5 million subscribers
Internet	118,000 domain names	5–30 million users

Table 2

Electronic Media Channels: Applications

Radio	Public service advertising
	Media tours
Commercial broadcast TV	Public service advertising
	Video news releases
	Media tours
Cable TV	Public service advertising
	Video news releases
	Media tours
	Community relations (via access channels)
	Employee communications (via access channels)
Organizational video networks	Employee communications
	Management communications
	Internal marketing communications
Teleconferencing	Media relations
	Customer relations
	Government relations
	Employee recruiting
VCRs	Product marketing/public relations
	Service marketing/public relations
	Employee communications
	Investor relations
	Government relations
	Trade shows
	Consumer shows
Interactive videodisc	Community relations (exhibits)
	Trade shows
	Consumer shows
Multimedia	Employee communications
	Media relations
	Government relations
	Investor relations
	Trade shows
	Consumer shows
Faxes	Media relations
	Government relations
	Investor relations

Faxes, cont.	Investor relations Customer relations Community relations
E-mail	Employee communications Media relations Community relations Government relations Peer-peer communications Customer relations Research and intelligence gathering
Online information systems	Customer relations
800 and 900 toll numbers	Media relations Government relations Investor relations Customer relations Community relations

General Programming Guidelines

In *Corporate Television Programming* (Marlow, 1992), I identified several rules that cut across various organizational electronic media programming applications. These rules also apply to many of the electronic public relations applications described in this volume. They are:

Rule 1: Define objectives. If you don't know where you're going, you won't get there.

Rule 2: Consider using various electronic media for effective public relations. No one medium can effectively communicate everything. This is a multimedia world. You need various media to get the communications job done.

Rule 3: Let the production style grow out of the content. Let the form fit the function. The choice of production styles should be organic to the content.

Rule 4: Let the location of the shoot grow out of the content. Same as rule 3.

Rule 5: Use professionals and nonprofessionals as appropriate. Similar to rules 3 and 4. The choice of who appears in front of the camera should grow out of program objectives, content, and intended audience.

Rule 6: A program's length depends on what has to be said. Say what has to be said and get off the stage. This might take one minute or one hour.

Rule 7: Ensure the use of the program in the field. Even if the programming is great, if it's not distributed and used in the field, it will be worthless.

Rule 8: Control the viewing environment as much as possible. Same as for rule 7. This will be difficult. A public relations practitioner cannot have absolute control over when, where, and how a program gets shown. But you must make the attempt anyway.

Rule 9: Measure the effectiveness of the program. So you've just produced a spectacular, highly cost-effective program. How do you know this? If you don't attempt to measure effectiveness in some way (even if it means just asking the client) you'll never know if you've satisfied your client's objectives.

Rule 10: The production quality of the program should be a reflection of executives appearing in it. Nonprofessional corporate executives deserve every break they can get. Just because they're not professionals doesn't mean they shouldn't get professional treatment.

Rule 11: Prepare talent before shooting begins. Everything in life is just one big preparation for something. Ditto with talent before a shoot. The more they know about what is going to happen, the better the chances for success on the set.

Rule 12: Provide an adequate distribution system. So you've got great programming. If you can't get it to your intended audience, the programming will die on the vine.

Rule 13: Quality is the only rule that counts. Strive for as much quality as possible, always. For survival in the 1990s, there is no such thing as less quality for one program and more quality for another.

Rule 14: Promote, promote, promote. Marketing and publicizing programming enhances its effective use in the field.

In *Winners! Producing Effective Electronic Media,* three themes emerged from interviews with electronic media producers. These were:

1. Highly effective programs are ones in which the program's concept is either highly unique or reaches creatively to execute a concept that no one else has challenged.
2. Highly effective programs deal with the human drama, or so-called "people" issues.
3. To produce an effective electronic media program requires a high level of pre-production planning, planning, planning. (Marlow, 1994, pp. 2–3)

Like any other communication form, electronic media must be used strategically: How does the electronic application fit with the overall public relations (and marketing) plan? Who is the audience? Where is the audience? In what environment will the audience receive this electrovisualized message? How will the effectiveness of the presentation be measured? Was the presentation effective, and why? Students of public relations and practicing professionals are encouraged to keep these rules, themes, and guidelines in mind as they move through this volume.

Chapter 2

Electronic Media: The Technologies

It is important to step back and view the technological context in which the practice of electronic public relations takes place. To make full effective and efficient use of electronic media, we need to understand how these technologies developed and what they can do.

The consistent developmental theme over time is an evolution from media that reach many people at one time (such as broadcast radio and television) to media that can reach a few people at any time (such as CD-ROM, the Internet, and the World Wide Web). In effect, as the twentieth century has progressed, electronic communications media have become more accessible to more people on a global scale. Geographic, physical, and political boundaries have been transcended. Time, similarly, has been transcended. The dissemination of news, for example, is no longer time dependent; it can be accessed 24 hours a day. A corollary to this rule is that over time electronic communications media have moved from linear (one-way) communications to interactive (two-way) communications. Starting with radio, let's examine the historical development of the electronic technologies.

Radio

As reported in Chapter 1, when AT&T's WEAF aired its first toll broadcast in 1922, the first "electronic" commercial had been broadcast. AT&T was ultimately pressured by the federal government to divest itself of its radio network, which had rapidly grown to twenty-six stations. In 1926, the stations were sold to RCA, which formed a subsidiary, the National Broadcasting Corporation, to operate the chain (Marlow & Secunda, 1991, p. 26).

Soon after network radio emerged as a mass medium, advertisers and their advertising agencies began to shape the networks' growth as programmers as well as providing financial support. By the mid-1940s, network radio had become a primary advertising medium for national advertisers. Programming was largely a product of the advertising industry. By 1950, 95 percent of all American families owned a radio (Marlow & Secunda, 1991, p. 27).

In 1994, there were more than 11,000 AM and FM radio stations in the United States. The average U.S. household had 5.6 radio receivers, totalling about 576,500,000. Radio reached 96 percent of persons twelve years and older weekly (National Association of Broadcasters, 1994, p. 34).

Broadcast Television Networks

Commercial television broadcasting began in a limited way in 1941 but was temporarily abandoned at the start of World War II. Plans to launch the new medium in the United States were resumed following the end of hostilities in 1945. Less than a year later, television broadcasting in America began.

Only 6,000 television sets were sold to Americans in 1946. The following year, the number jumped to 179,000. Four networks emerged to provide programming: NBC, CBS, DuMont, and ABC. In 1948, generally regarded as the year when commercial broadcast television emerged as a major mass medium in the United States, only seventeen stations were broadcasting. Within a year, there were 51 (Marlow & Secunda, 1991, p. 30). Today over 1,100 television stations are broadcasting commercially sponsored programming to over 98 million television households (Adweek Magazines, 1994, p. 20).

Cable Television

According to some accounts, the first cable television system was constructed in 1949 in Astoria, Oregon by the owner of a local radio station. In 1972, the Federal Communications Commission launched a cable access experiment requiring cable system operators, in certain locations, to provide the public sector with access channels and 5 minutes of free production time (Hollowell, 1980–1981, pp. 3, 102). From these modest beginnings, various technological developments—not the least of which is satellite technology—have spawned a formidable entertainment and information delivery system: cable television.

The cable television industry, as of the end of 1994, was a $23 billion industry (basic and pay revenues) taking in an additional $4.6 billion in advertising revenues. (National Cable Television Association, spring 1995, pp. 8a, 9a). In 1994, there were 11,351 cable television systems in communities throughout the United States, compared to only 2,490 in 1970. These cable television systems boasted 57 and 60 million subscribers (depending on whether you read A. C. Nielsen or Paul Kagan Associates). When we consider that there are more than 95 million television households in the United States, cable television (basic and/or pay) reaches between 62 to 64 percent of the television viewing households in America (National Cable Television Association, spring 1995, p. 1A).

Cable television has, inherently, launched dozens (potentially hundreds) of so-called basic and pay channels. Many of these channels—such as ESPN, Cable News Network, C-SPAN, The Weather Channel, Headline News, CNBC, even MTV—are founded on news, or include news programming as part of their formats.

Since September 1990, cable television has also given rise to a half dozen or so local 24-hour, seven-day all-news channels, including:

ChicagoLand Television News (since January 1992)

New England Cable News (since March 1992)

Newschannel 8 (since October 1991)

New York 1 News (since September 1992)

Orange County Newschannel (since September 1990)

Pittsburgh Cable News Channel (since January 1994)

These local, all-news cable television channels are precursors of a trend. We will probably see the creation of such operations in many major television markets across the country in five years or so as the world becomes even more global and our sense of immediate community becomes more pronounced. These network and local cable news channels offer opportunities for public relations campaigns (such as public service announcements and video news release material) to be distributed electronically.

The vertical market programming channels that have been created as a result of cable television's growth have also created electronic public relations opportunities. The examples are numerous. In fact, vertical cable television programming channels appear to have many of the characteristics of vertical audience magazines. One planned cable television channel (as of this writing), the Home and Garden Network, is founded on the various publications of Meredith Publishing, publishers of *House & Garden*.

Videotape and Organizational Video Networks

At the National Association of Radio and Television Broadcasters (NARTB) trade show held in Chicago in April 1956, Ampex introduced a commercially viable 900-pound quadraplex videotape recorder using 2-inch wide tape manufactured by 3M. The recorder sold initially for $75,000 per unit and functioned only in black and white (Marlow & Secunda, 1991, p. 6). Just a few years later, by the late 1950s, a handful of so-called "nonbroadcast" organizations—including the U.S. Air Force, the University of Texas, Buick, and Ford—had adopted the videotape medium for a variety of programming purposes. In 1971, the Sony Corporation introduced the first three-quarter inch U-Matic videocassette to the American market and in 1975, the half-inch Betamax format (Marlow & Secunda, 1991, p. 19).

In the early stages a handful of individuals and organizations enthusiastically adopted the medium, while most others either could not afford it or were askance to try it. And even with the advent of the videocassette in the 1970s, there was still resistance to the medium in the corporate world, at least.

By the 1990s, in contrast, tens of thousands of corporate, medical, legal, educational, religious and governmental organizations use linear videotape technology for a wide variety of internal and external communications applications. Clearly, in forty years the use of videotape has gone far beyond original expectations in the broadcast, then nonbroadcast, contexts.

Linear videotape probably reached its zenith in the late 1980s as an electrovisual technology in the nonbroadcast context, at least. Over the next decade or so, this technology, which gave birth to a cornucopia of management communications channels, will slowly but surely give way to other electrovisual technologies, such as the CD-ROM, and, ultimately, to an integrated system that combines the computer with a compact disc and desktop teleconferencing capability.

The upcoming change from videotape to video compact disc will be invisible to viewers, just as it is invisible to home television viewers when they watch a film that is actually being played back from a videotape. In the years to come, this "film" will increasingly be played back from videodisc technology. Moreover, when a standard for high definition television (HDTV) is agreed on and ultimately becomes commercially available, film, too, may start to wane as a communications technology.

The communications door that will be opened by the encroachment of CD/videodisc (or multimedia) technology is the increased capacity for interactivity, which will increase participation of corporate members throughout an organization and allow greater access to information by lower-level employees.

The increasing use of electrovisual technologies—such as videotape, teleconferencing, and computer networks—has had and will have meaningful impacts on the structure of organizations and the role of top and middle managers. Organizations have already become flatter, and middle managers fewer, as a consequence of this technology.

Regardless of extant and emerging communications technologies, however, employees will still need to know how to communicate effectively and efficiently in speaking, in writing, and in the electrovisual medium.

Interactive Videodisc

From the perspective of the 1990s, it is easy to assume that multimedia technology had interactive videodisc technology—first commercially introduced in 1978—as its technological precursor. But as Emmy award-winning engineer Mark Schubin points out, "the three major forms of television storage—disks, magnetic tape, and film—all had their origins in…1927" (Schubin, 1980, p. 7). Schubin recounts how a means of television signal storage was found in a patent application filed by Boris Rtcheouloff on January 4, 1927 in Britain. His proposal would have applied the magnetic recording techniques developed by Valdemar Poulsen at the end of the last century to television. However, two scientists—R. V. L. Hartley and H. E. Ives of Electrical Research Products—felt that both the lighting problem and the dim, tiny image problem of very early television might be solved by interposing film at the imaging and display points. On September 14, 1927, they publicly announced their method of intermediate film television. In the same year a third proposal for video recording was put forth by John Logie Baird, generally considered the first person to achieve recognizable television pictures. Baird's system was called "Phonovision" (Schubin, 1991, p. 9).

Almost thirty years later, Ampex introduced its quadraplex videotape recorder at the NARTB show. This television storage technology was partly based on the pioneering work of the Germans, who had developed audio magnetic recording during World War II. Nine years later, Magnetic Video Recording "provided a magnetic disc for video recording that provided stop action and instant replay for a CBS football pickup on July 8, 1965" (Schubin, 1991, p. 13). It is interesting to note that CBS was also the first broadcaster to purchase the Ampex manufactured Quadraplex videotape recording machines.

In 1978, Philips and MCA introduced the first interactive multimedia format—the analog laser videodisc—to the North American market (Banet, 1992, p. 11). The laserdisc provided a full-screen, full-motion video, two tracks of good audio, and up to 108,000 still color images. IBM and Pioneer brought out laserdisc players in various combinations (e.g., DiscoVision) that could be interfaced with the microcomputers of the day as well as players that were manufactured with internal microprocessors. As Bernard Banet points out, these devices "made it possible to link the computer's text files, structured databases, computer graphics, and logic with the laserdiscs' audiovisual sights and sounds" (1992, p. 11). Presently, Banet adds, "the videodisc is alive and well in training and education, where developers have learned that a little interactivity goes a long way, and that Level I can often be quite effective in the classroom" (1991, p. 13).

According to a Forrester Research report, the Electronic Industries Association reported that sales of laserdisc players with interactive capabilities were up 23 percent in 1992 (October 1992, p. 5). More than 1,000 interactive videodisc applications exist in museums across the country. And there are at least 5,000 highly interactive public access information kiosks where information seekers find practical answers to everyday questions. Add to that an installed base of more than 100,000 laserdisc players in education in 1992, most shared among many classrooms. *Electronic Media* (1991, p. 28) reported 80,000 videodisc players in U.S. schools in late 1991, and apparently that figure was double the number of players from just a year earlier.

Clearly, the example of video technology demonstrates that one major requisite for a technology to attract a significant number of adopters is standardization. It is also true—particularly if we look at the development of videotape and computer technology—that portability is another.

Multimedia

While there are certainly similarities between interactive videodisc and multimedia, multimedia is a distinct medium. Robert E. Bergman and Thomas V. Moore, writing in *Managing Interactive Video/Multimedia Projects*, have this to say:

> *For several years, the videodisc was the only source of motion video segments that could be accessed rapidly enough to support effective interactivity. Hence, the term applied to these applications came to be "interactive videodisc," or more commonly, "IVD." Recently, however, digital technology has made it possible to provide motion video using other devices, especially the small optical disks called CD-ROM....Another factor has been the development of image-based applications that use graphic pictures and digital audio, and no motion video at all....The term "multimedia" has been adapted as a generic reference to all such image-based applications (1990, p. 5).*

Thomas Reeves and Stephan Harmon, writing in *Interact,* take matters a step further when they define multimedia as "an interactive database that allows users to access information in multiple forms, including text, graphics, video, and audio" (1991, p. 29). They further define *hypermedia,* a subset of multimedia, as "an interactive database that allows users to access multiple forms of information, but is specifically designed with linked nodes of information to allow that access in any manner of the users' choosing" (1991, p. 29).

The Microsoft Corporation defines computer-based multimedia as "the integration of text, graphics, audio, video and other types of information into a single seamless whole" (1993, p. 2). Clearly, multimedia has evolved from an integration of various digital, electronic aural, and visual technologies into an interactive medium for use in the home and the office.

Multimedia—which we may now define as the simultaneous use of motion video, audio and data requiring the use of a computer, CD-ROM, and a videodisc player—may be the future medium of choice, if a CD-ROM product is distinguished by its accessibility, ease of use, and creative visualization. (*CD-ROM* stands for compact disc–read only memory.) There are two choices critical to creating a superior CD-ROM product: (1) an interface that makes a user's search intuitive, and (2) a search engine (i.e., searching tool) that enables the user to get anywhere easily, to browse at will, and to find and aggregate information in any way desired.

It is the interface between the user and the information on the CD-ROM that determines whether the user feels trapped inside a PC screen and goes fleeing to the nearest book, or feels in control of searching through masses of material in a way that no print index can ever allow. If an electronic product does not make the search easy and effective, then it is little more than a method for saving library shelf space, and the user will soon determine that he or she is better off browsing through a book.

A quality search engine and interface will allow the user the following capabilities:

- *Searching:* User-defined searches, nested searching, fuzzy searching, thesaurus synonym searching, query saving, storing search results.
- *Proximity searching:* Within number of words, within sentence, within paragraph, order-dependent.
- *Links:* Interdocument links, searches on selected words in a document, book marks, attachment of notes to text, generation of tables of contents based on text.

A search interface and engine also allow the user to:

- browse the CD-ROM expertly.
- browse a full text article in the database.
- copy information to a printer.
- copy material to a disk.

The adoption of interactive multimedia technology, particularly CD-ROM, is growing in both nonprofit and for-profit organizations. According to software giant Microsoft: "Over the past three years, the multimedia market has nearly doubled in total revenues from $2.9 billion to $5 billion [in 1992]. Forecasters project a tripling of the market to $15.4 billion just two years from now, with total revenues nearing $24 billion by the end of the decade" (1993, p. 2). Microsoft points to a range of factors fueling this growth, including:

- More powerful microprocessors capable of handling large, complex files needed for multimedia information
- Advances in computer software, from new graphical user interfaces to object-oriented programming, that make electronic systems faster, easier, and more efficient
- Emerging standards around digital audio, video, and multimedia systems
- New computers and consumer electronics products including these new components and standards
- Increasing affordability and prevalence of multimedia-oriented peripherals, such as CD-ROM drives and audio boards. CD-ROM disks can hold more than 650MB of data, enough for delivering an entire encyclopedia plus thousands of graphics and audio files (1993, p. 2)

In 1992, the state of Florida determined that all of its students could benefit from exposure to the interactive learning potential of multimedia. The compelling reason? AIDS prevention. Multimedia technology was chosen as the delivery method because only multimedia can deliver the impact, immediacy, and selectivity the message warrants. California and Texas were planning to follow Florida's lead in recommending integrating multimedia into its education system.

In April 1993, the National Association of Broadcasters (NAB) added NAB Multimedia World to its annual conference. This recognition confirms what most people using multimedia already know: the broadcast and multimedia worlds are becoming increasingly intertwined, especially in areas of post-production and animation.

According to Hank Evers, of the Pioneer Corporation Multimedia System Division, multimedia's benefits have also persuaded many print-based publishers to reevaluate their businesses. Publishers are learning to identify their business in terms of content (intellectual and artistic) that they own and to separate it from the medium in which it appears. This also holds true in network television. ABC News and the Discovery Channel find themselves in the same camp as *The Encyclopedia Britannica*—they are "content owners."

Why has multimedia technology, particularly CD-ROM, received wider acceptance, not only in educational and medical institutions, but in a growing number of business organizations as well? Dataware Technologies identifies two reasons: "First, technological developments have substantially lowered the barriers to cost-effective use of CD-ROM....A technology that was once only potentially beneficial is now affordable, easy to use, and widely employed. Second, CD-ROM has demonstrated clear benefits....More than 5,000 CD-ROM titles are now in print in a broad range of applications, including over 3,000 commercial products" (1993, p. 1). One CD-ROM, Dataware points out, can hold the equivalent of 1,500 floppy disks, 250,000 pages of text, or 12,000 scanned images at an incremental media cost of $2 per disk.

InfoTech, an international consulting and research firm specializing in optical disk and information technology markets, estimates that "the commercial market shipped 3,256 titles valued at nearly $2 billion in 1992 and forecasts growth to nearly 8,000 titles valued at over $4 billion by 1995" (Dataware, 1993, p. 29). But there is a long way to go before everything converts from print to optical. According to Dataware, estimates put print publishing at more than 90 percent of the publishing universe, with electronic at 10 percent. Optical publishing represents about 5 percent of the electronic publishing share, or 0.5 percent (Dataware, 1993, p. 28).

While governmental, educational and medical institutions seem to be embracing multimedia technology, this does not appear to be true of corporate America. As reported in *Interactive Media Business,* a survey by Cambridge, Massachusetts–based Forrester Research of sixty-four Fortune 1000 MIS executives revealed a uniform uncertainty about multimedia's benefits. However, the report also predicts that "within three years multimedia will be widely accepted and implemented." The report also indicated that while "it took ten years for ...videoconferencing to become accepted...one of the more promising uses for desktop video is desktop–based videoconferencing" (December 1992, p. 13). Forrester Research estimates that desktop videoconferencing will grow to a $835 million market by 1997. The report also underscores that multimedia will continue to enjoy widespread popularity in education and training.

Publishers' sales of multimedia titles were projected to reach $394 million in 1994, according to *Economics of Multimedia Title Publishing*, a study published by SIMBA Information (1994, p. 2). The 1994 revenue would represent a 77 percent increase over sales of $222 million in 1993. The report adds that there will be more than 17 million multimedia-capable personal computers with CD-ROM drives by the end of 1995, and the number will increase by approximately 5 million in each of the next two years.

On the other side of the ledger, the report points out that "while the multimedia market continues to develop, there are still many more multimedia-capable computers without CD-ROM drives than with one." At the end of 1993, there were 20–22 million multimedia-capable PCs—an estimated 10 million IBM compatibles and another 10–12 million Apple Macintoshes (SIMBA, 1994, p. 3).

Satellites and Teleconferencing

In 1945, Arthur C. Clark (best known for his short story upon which the movie *2001: A Space Odyssey* is based) suggested in the British academic journal *Wireless World* the concept of a geosynchronous satellite positioned 22,300 miles above the equator as the perfect platform for television broadcasting (Rogers, 1986, p. 58). In 1957, Russia launched Sputnik, the first space satellite.

Over thirty-five years later, according to the International Teleconferencing Association (ITCA), a clearinghouse for the teleconferencing industry with national headquarters located in McLean, Virginia, satellite-based teleconferencing in its various forms was expected to post revenues that broke the $3.0 billion mark in 1994, with total revenues reported of $3.098 billion for the year. This figure compares to the $2.3 billion in total revenues in 1993, the $1.75 billion in 1992, and the 1991 revenues of $1.43 billion. In effect, the teleconferencing business virtually doubled in four years. (ITCA news release, June 1995; June 14, 1993). According to the ITCA, videoconferencing edged past conference calls in 1994 as the largest revenue generator, producing revenues of $1.530 billion. Revenues were fueled by the more than 23,000 two-way interactive videoconferencing rooms operational in North America by the end of 1994. This installed base of video rooms was up nearly 8,000 over the count at the end of 1993.

These figures compare dramatically to the teleconferencing activity of little more than a decade ago. In a 1983 research report, Quantum Science Corporation estimated that the number of business meetings held via motion video, freeze frame, or audiographic teleconferencing would increase from 89,400 in 1981 to 1.8 million in 1986, creating a $580 million market for suppliers of equipment and particularly transmission services (1983, p. 40).

Teleconferencing has clearly become an accepted means of business communication. Technological advancements coupled with inherent efficiencies will probably continue to spur the growth of teleconferencing; eventually it will become a household feature much like the telephone. Frank Knott, ITCA president, stated: "The H.320 standard is having its long awaited impact on the videoconferencing field in North America and throughout the world. With standards-compliant videoconferencing now available from the desktop to the conference room, we are seeing the interoperability necessary for the market to skyrocket." To demonstrate interoperability through standards, the ITCA staged *Interoperability V,* 20 hours of live videoconferences tying more than a dozen equipment manufacturers and carriers at its 1995 conference and trade show.

Teleconferencing is a generic form of pulling together various technologies and applications while using electronic channels to facilitate real-time communication among a group of people at various locations. Teleconferencing encompasses various subcategories that include audioconferencing, audiographics conferencing, videoconferencing, business television, and distance learning or distance education. Audioconferencing employs voice communications by telephone lines.

The greatest change in the industry are the end users. Teleconferencing users were once solely Fortune 500 companies that were financially in a position to purchase the necessary technology as well as gaining the expertise to use it. Today, users now include virtually everyone—from the medical profession to business organizations. In the medical field, medical groups use audioconferencing to discuss patients and to obtain long-distance opinions of X rays while using audiographics; business organizations use audioconferencing to bring their executives together by phone.

Teleconferencing seems to work best when it fills some unique human need or a unique application. As a corollary to this rule, it is important, users say, to define that critical need. Further, teleconferencing managers need to take their audiences into consideration—in effect, to ask the question: "What are our audience's needs?" Paralleling this consideration are the requirements for a high degree of advance planning, rehearsal of teleconferencing participants, and high production values, particularly in video teleconferences.

Teleconferencing managers interviewed for *Winners! Producing Effective Electronic Media* (Marlow, 1994) also urge other users to make the content of teleconferences about "real people" and "real stories." In one case, users were advised to develop systems that are "humanizing, require participation, provide feedback and have style." Finally, users are advised to create a conferencing system that has flexibility. It is curious to observe that while teleconferencing deals with an electronic technology, the advice offered by users centers on "people" considerations. While the users, for the most part, are concerned with the so-called software, or people, elements of the technology, they are rarely concerned with the operational effectiveness of the technology. In effect, the technology appears invisible. And while users are certainly aware of technical considerations, their main production challenges center on human factors rather than technical factors.

It is perhaps a sign that a technology is coming of age when users can be more concerned with human rather than technological factors. In the videotape technology arena of the 1960s, for example, technological problems were abundant, particularly in standardization issues. As we have already seen, it was not until the early 1970s, with the advent of the standardized and highly portable three-quarter inch U-Matic videocassette, commercially introduced by Sony, that the videocassette took off.

According to several sources, teleconferencing was already taking off as an internal and external communications tool in the 1980s as various corporate, medical, educational, and governmental institutions explored the possibilities. In the 1990s, therefore, excellence is not so dependent on technological prowess as it is on managerial expertise and the awareness of users of the technology's "people" communications potential.

Further, the concept of teleconferencing—whether audio only, or full-blown two-way video, two-way audio—is the reality expression of the "global village" concept articulated by Marshall McLuhan in *Understanding Media: The Extensions of Man* (1964). With the flowering of global telecommunications networks, the promise of networked multimedia communications, as John S. Mayo, president of AT&T Bell Laboratories put it in a 1993 symposium, is fast becoming a reality.

Trends in microelectronics, photonics, speech processing, video, computing, telecommunications and information network architecture, wireless communications, software, and terminals are all creating vast opportunities for highly interactive information-sharing systems on a global basis. Ironically, these same electronic technologies will also have the effect of creating more "physical travel"—what John Naisbitt refers to as "high tech/high touch." In other words, as we gain more and more capacity for traveling electronically, the more we will want real person-to-person contact.

Teleconferencing has the potential for encompassing all the other electronic technologies—at the office and in the home. The personal computer will become the central communication device. Sooner or later, it will all become standardized on a global basis, and highly portable. Dick Tracy's wristwatch, with its two-way radio and TV, could become a common technological reality!

Computers, LANs, and E-Mail

In 1946, the first mainframe computer (ENIAC) with 70,000 resistors and 18,000 vacuum tubes (weighing 30 tons) was developed at the Moore School of Electrical Engineering in the University of Pennsylvania (Forester, 1987, p. 17). In 1971, the microprocessor, a computer-control unit on a semiconductor chip, was invented by Ted Hoff at Intel Corporation, a Silicon Valley microelectronics company (Rogers, 1986, p. 25). A mere twenty-four years later, personal computers and computer networks are ubiquitous in tens of thousands of organizations.

Lawrence G. Tesler, graphing the relative cost of computation from 1950 into the 1990s, indicates that computing cost has been halved approximately every three years in the most powerful commercial machines, starting with the IBM 650 to the more recent CRAY Y-MP/864 (1991, p. 88). Thomas W. Malone and John F. Rockart, both of M.I.T., point to the effects of computers and computer networks: "The revolution underway today," they say, "will be driven not by changes in production but by changes in coordination....By dramatically reducing the costs of coordination and increasing its speed and quality, these new technologies will enable people to coordinate more effectively, to do much more coordination and to form new, coordination-intensive business structures" (1991, p. 128).

On-Line Information Services

According to John Naisbitt's *Trend Letter*, "More and more consumers who once relied on newspapers, magazines and television for information now tap into thousands of databases. All they need are a computer, a telephone and a modem—and the willingness to sift through (and pay for) an avalanche of information" (1992, p. 1.). The newsletter points out that some 5,000 periodicals are available by computer, and describes Prodigy, the home computer service headquartered in White Plains, New York, followed by Columbus, Ohio–based CompuServe, and America Online. Other on-line services include: Genie, based in Rockville, Maryland; the Public Electronic Network (Santa Monica, California); and Access Atlanta. PR Online, a free database for journalists and a service of Washington, D.C.–based public relations firm Stephen K. Cook & Company—provides a variety of news services, including U.S. Newswire, and the Actuarial Profession in North America, and the Brookings Institution, among others.

Another exponentially growing on-line network providing electronic public relations opportunities is, of course, the Internet. It is probable that on-line services will have a major impact on journalism, publishing, public relations, and—

with the advent of the multimedia capabilities of the World Wide Web on the Internet—the entire information and entertainment industries on a global scale.

It seems that all new communications media begin with one ostensible purpose and gradually evolve into wider applications with an ever-broadening population of users. For example, when videotape was first commercially introduced in April 1956, its original perceived value was to accommodate the simultaneous airing of news programs, such as videotaping an East Coast news program for replay later on the West Coast. Today, however, videotape is used for a multiplicity of applications far beyond that originally intended. On-line information services fit this pattern.

Even though CompuServe, the world's oldest consumer-oriented on-line service is a little over ten years old and has over 2 million subscribers, we are still at the relatively early stages of the expansion of this mode of electronic communication. According to Rosalind Resnick (1994): "Currently, there are 6.5 million consumer online service users nationwide, according to SIMBA, a Wilton, Connecticut, market research firm that tracks the online services industry. Though that number has soared by 33 percent in the first nine months of this year [1994], it still represents only a small percentage of computer users." Resnick reports that the Microsoft Network, "to be launched as part of the new Windows 95 operating system and now in beta testing, conceivably could expand the online market to as many as 60 million Windows users worldwide." Microsoft's new service will be accessible in more than thirty-five countries and its client application will be localized in twenty languages.

The Internet

The development of on-line information services—such as CompuServe, Prodigy, America Online, the Whole Earth Lectronic Link (WELL), Delphi, and Genie, among others—has its probable beginnings with the Internet. What began as a U.S. Department of Defense communications network has now broadened to a worldwide network, and public relations practitioners—as well as electronic marketers—are beginning to find applications for it.

According to John Perry Barlow, "When it was first patched together in 1968, DARPANET, as it was then called, connected machines in the computer-science departments of seven universities at speeds that were geologically deliberate by today's standards" (1994, xvi). Today, the Internet is a worldwide network linking millions of host computers and people. The Internet has grown far beyond its government and university roots to include commercial institutions and individual users around the world; it has become a supernetwork of more than 15,000 networks connecting over 38 million people. An additional 150,000 connect each month for the first time. By 1998, it is projected that 100 million will be using the Internet (Angell & Heslop, 1995, p. 3), and 200 million by the end of the decade (Lewis, 1995, p. C15).

Unlike traditional on-line commercial services, where one computer system serves a single dedicated group of people, the Internet connects computers worldwide using standard sets of hardware and software. Once connected, computer users can then exchange electronic mail and files, share public "news" discussions, search for information, and remotely access other archives and information services worldwide. A user can find many organizations on the Internet, such as computer companies and other high-tech corporations; most government agencies, such as the Defense Department, NASA, EPA, the Library of Congress, the White House, and the House of Representatives; and nearly all universities.

Building on this base, many commercial companies and media organizations are joining the Internet to distribute information, provide customer support, and take product orders. Individuals are tapping into Internet resources to conduct research and keep in touch with people around the country and the world with high-speed links that connect Asia, Latin America, Africa, and all of Europe (Digital Express, 1994).

According to Washington, D.C.–based netResults,

> The futuristic 'information superhighway' touted by Al Gore, John Malone, and Bill Gates and the Internet have a great deal in common. Both are interactive, which means a consumer can both receive and send information. Both rely on sophisticated electronic networks that can send enormous packets of information, at the speed of light, from one corner of the globe to the other. Both represent the future for business in the 21st century. The difference, though, is that the 'information superhighway' is a vision, a plan, a concept. The Internet is here today and will most certainly be incorporated into the 'superhighway' of the future.
>
> [While the Internet dates from the late 1960s] and has been popular within universities for decades. In the last few years, though, interest has surged— mostly due to the proliferation of inexpensive personal computers (netResults, 1994).

The advent of personal computers is clearly a moving force in the evolution of on-line service as well as software. According to Link Resources Corporation, a New York–based research company, in 1989 approximately 22 percent of

American households with children owned a personal computer. By the end of 1994, Link estimated 42 percent of households with children owned a personal computer (Lynn, 1994, pp. D1, D15).

Time magazine estimates that 20 million people explore the "Net" each day and that millions more will log on each month. What attracts new users? Features like electronic mail, discussion groups, and immediate access to items as diverse as airline schedules, lyrics of a Bob Dylan song, the databases of every major academic library in the world (plus the Library of Congress), and thousands of software applications (netResults, 1994).

Yet another name for the Net is *cyberspace,* a term coined by science fiction writer William Gibson in his 1984 novel *Neuromancer:*

> *Cyberspace. A consensual hallucination experienced daily by billions of legitimate operators, in every nation, by children being taught mathematical concepts…A graphic representation of data abstracted from the banks of every computer in the human system. Unthinkable complexity. Lines of light ranged in the nonspace of the mind, clusters and constellations of data. Like city lights receding. (quoted in Rheingold, 1991, p. 16)*

Gibson's description of cyberspace as "lines of light" is not unlike the early descriptions of Samuel B. Morse's telegraph as "lightning lines" (Czitrom, 1982, chap. 1). Further, as Czitrom points out, the concept of communication in terms of light can be found in the Bible (Job 38:35): "Canst thou send lightnings, that they may go, and say unto thee, Here we are?" Czitrom elaborates: "This Biblical quotation, one of the impossibilities enumerated to convince Job of his ignorance and weakness, frequently prefaced nineteenth-century writing on the telegraph" (1982, p. 9). As Czitrom also emphasizes: "Before the telegraph there existed no separation between transportation and communication. Information travelled only as fast as the messenger who carried it. The telegraph dissolved that unity and quickly spread across the land to form the first of the great communication networks" (1982, p. 3). To this we can add that the Internet—a.k.a. the Net, cyberspace, the information superhighway—is the latest of the "great communication networks," linking millions of people around the globe.

In simple terms, the Net can be used to start relationships, publish your own writings, get updates, play games, send and receive electronic mail, search through libraries around the world, trade advice, ask and answer questions, and exchange opinions. To get on the Net requires a personal computer, a modem (preferably one with a 14,400 bits per second capability), and communications software to control the modem.

The World Wide Web

A major relatively recent development in the exponential growth of the so-called Internet is the World Wide Web (WWW). The Web began in March 1989, when Tim Berners-Lee of CERN (the European Laboratory for Particle Physics located in Geneva, Switzerland, a collective of European high-energy physics researchers) proposed the project as a means of transporting research and ideas effectively throughout the organization.

Effective communications was a goal of CERNs for many years because its members were located in a number of countries. The goal of the project was to build a distributed hypermedia system that would allow the exchange of information across the Internet in the form of hypertext documents.

Hypertext is text with pointers to other text, allowing the user to branch off to another document for more information on a given topic and then return to the same location in the original document with ease. To access the Web, users run a browser; the browser reads and retrieves documents from WWW servers. Netscape is the most popular WWW browser.

Information providers establish WWW servers for use by network user with WWW browsers. The browsers can, in addition, access files by file transfer protocol (FTP), Gopher, and an ever-increasing range of other methods. Browsers are available for many computer platforms. WWW browsers and servers also deliver hypermedia documents to network users. *Hypermedia* is a superset of hypertext—it is any medium with pointers to other media. This means that browsers are able to display images, sound, or animations in addition to text.

Kevin Hughes explains hypertext on the World Wide Web in this way:

> *The official description describes the World Wide Web as a "wide-area hypermedia information retrieval initiative aiming to give universal access to a large universe of documents." What the World Wide Web (WWW, W3) project has done is provide users on computer networks with a consistent means to access a variety of media in a simplified fashion. Using a popular software interface to the Web called Mosaic, the Web project has changed the way people view and create information—it has created the first true global hypermedia network.*
>
> *The operation of the Web relies on hypertext as its means of interacting with users. Hypertext is basically the same as regular text—it can be stored, read, searched, or edited—with an important exception: hypertext contains connections within the text to other documents.*
>
> *For instance, suppose you were able to somehow select (with a mouse or with your finger) the word "hypertext" in the sentence before this one. In a hypertext system, you would then have one or more documents related to hypertext appear before you—a history of hypertext, for example, or the*

Webster's definition of hypertext. These new texts would themselves have links and connections to other documents—continually selecting text would take you on a free-associative tour of information. In this way, hypertext links, called hyperlinks, can create a complex virtual web of connections.

Hypermedia is hypertext with a difference—hypermedia documents contain links not only to other pieces of text, but also to other forms of media—sounds, images, and movies. Images themselves can be selected to link to sounds or documents. (Hughes, 1993)

Months after CERN's original proposal, the National Center for Supercomputing Applications (NCSA) began a project to create an interface to the World Wide Web. One of NCSA's missions was to aid the scientific research community by producing widely available noncommercial software. Another of its goals was to investigate new research technologies in the hope that commercial interests will be able to profit from them. In these ways, the Web project was quite appropriate. The NCSA's Software Design Group began work on a versatile, multiplatform interface to the World Wide Web, and called it Mosaic. In the first half of 1993, the first version of NCSA's Web browser was made available to the Internet community. Because earlier beta versions were distributed, Mosaic had already developed a strong yet small following by the time it was officially released.

Because of the number of traditional services it could handle and its easy, point-and-click hypermedia interface, Mosaic soon became the most popular interface to the Web. Currently versions of Mosaic can run on Suns, Silicon Graphics workstations, IBM-compatibles running Microsoft Windows, Macintoshes, and computers running other various forms of UNIX.

By 1995 Netscape, however, had eclipsed all other web browsers and captured at least 75 percent of the market.

Summary

The history of electronic media began with the telegraph (using a series of dots and dashes to represent letters of the alphabet—itself a digitization of sounds of speech)—moved to linear, noninteractive technologies (such as radio and television), and has moved on to interactive technologies (such as multimedia and the Internet).

The instant the telegraph was first used, the concept of "information access" was changed forever. Now information could be "messengered" at the speed of light. Physical boundaries (and subsequently political ones as well) were transcended. Leaping forward to the present day, the meaning of the Internet is that anyone with a computer, modem, telephone line, telecommunications software, and an Internet access provider can communicate with anyone, anywhere in the world, at any time with comparable hardware and software. The Internet user can also access information in seconds without having to go through layers of clerks to get to the information—that is, presuming the information is on line. But increasingly more and more information is accessible via the Internet on a global scale.

The meaning of electronic media is that it is part of the inexorable march towards the externalization and extension of our senses on a global scale. In the proverbial beginning, the elders sat around the campfire telling the stories of the tribe. Everyone in earshot was part of the village communication system. Today, our campfire is electronic and global—we have realized the global village (some even call it the global theater!). In effect, humans (as a species) are in the process of externalizing our senses and extending our ability to communicate at increasingly greater distances in shorter and shorter time spans. It is only a matter of time before the Internet as a communication system can also be used habitually for audio as well as visual communication. (And it will be portable.) All these electronic media will continue to expand, providing public relations practitioners with the ability to reach audiences individually, locally, regionally, nationally, and internationally in a variety of contexts, as the following chapters describe.

Chapter 3

Reaching the General Public: Public Service Announcements

Messages on the Radio

In March 1942, the War Advertising Council was set up as the official homefront propaganda arm to the Office of War Information. Soon radio audiences heard messages in support of the nation's World War II effort: "Loose Lips Sink Ships," "Keep 'em Rolling" and innumerable variants on "Buy War Bonds," among others.

By the end of World War II, the practice of volunteering free time or advertisements in support of governmental and voluntary sector activities had become a tradition. Pleas in support of the USO and the Red Cross were joined by those in support of a new organization, CARE, brought into being to channel American generosity to war victims (Dessart, 1982, p. 5).

More and more organizations began to use radio stations, and later television, to reach their publics with PSAs. By 1980, it was estimated that among 419 television stations the average number of PSAs run in a typical week was 205. In that same year the U.S. Treasury Department reported there were 846,000 nonprofit distributing organizations with tax-exempt status (Dessart, 1982, p. 6). As of September 30, 1994, the Treasury Department reported there were 1,138,598 tax exempt organizations in the United States, of which 599,745 had 501 (c)(3) nonprofit status. Accordingly, the IRS received 47,000 applications for nonprofit status in 1992, of which it approved 36,000 (U.S. Internal Revenue Service, 1994).

PSAs Defined

Public service advertising (PSA), also referred to as public service announcements, is probably the earliest form of electronic public relations with initial outlets on radio and then broadcast and cable television.

According to the Federal Communications Commission:

A Public Service Announcement (PSA) is any announcement (including network) for which no charge is made and which promotes programs, activities, for services of Federal, State, or local governments (e.g., recruiting, sales of bonds, etc.) of the programs, activities, or services of non-profit organizations…and other announcements regarded as serving community interests, excluding time signals, routine weather announcements, and promotional announcements. (FCC Form 3031V, iii)

As George Dessart wrote in an informative booklet published in 1982 by the still-extant National Broadcast Association for Community Affairs, "Public Service Announcements serve to validate and to promote organizations, their projects, their concerns; to raise funds; to turn out audiences and build constituencies; to serve as a major source of information about the public and voluntary sectors and a major vehicle for their communications to the American public.…And unlike commercial announcements, they do not cost their sponsors a single penny for air time. Rather, they represent a contribution by radio and television stations" (1982, p.1).

Audiences and Outlets

The public relations practitioner has the choice of attempting to disseminate a PSA nationally, regionally, or even locally, depending on the nature of the non-profit organization and the audience targeted. Distribution channels can include local or network radio, local or network television, or cable television news channels.

The Motivation to Air

There is some confusion about whether or not radio and television stations are required to run PSAs as part of their mandate. The reality is that they are not legally required to do so, even though the airing of PSAs has become a common part of the radio and television programming mix.

According to the FCC, "Individual radio and television station licensees are responsible for selecting all broadcast matter and for determining how their stations can best serve their communities (FCC, March 1993, p. 6). Further, "PSAs have never been required by the Commission, and until September 26, 1980 individual stations were given little public service recognition for the airing of them"

(FCC, 1980). And even though there has been some concern that PSAs—by their very nature a commercial with a public service message that is aired free of charge to the sponsoring organization—might be aired at nonproductive times, such as very late evening and early morning, the Commission found that in 1980, at least,

> *(1) Stations averaged more than two hours per week, or about 1 to 1 1/2 minutes per hour of PSAs; (2) the usual PSA ran approximately 30 seconds; and (3) PSAs seemed to be evenly distributed throughout the broadcast day, i.e., they were not generally clustered in the 'graveyard' hours nor during prime audience periods. (Federal Register, p. 13946)*

The airing of PSAs, clearly, is in a radio or television station's self-interest and the interest of the community they serve. This implied mandate is found in an FCC policy statement of 1960:

> *Broadcasting licensees must assume responsibility for all material which is broadcast through their facilities. This includes all programs and advertising material which they present to the public....The diligent and continuing effort in good faith, to determine the tastes, needs and desires of the public in this community and to provide programming to meet those needs and interests. This, again, is a duty personal to the licensee and may not be avoided by delegation of the responsibility to others. (FCC, 1960)*

Guidelines: What Gets on the Air

The radio or television station's department in charge of standards and practices is the office to contact if an organization contemplates airing a PSA. However, based on a random sample of radio and television stations and networks in the New York City area, many stations (network or local) do not have specific PSA guidelines.

WNBC Television, though, provides the following guidelines to prospective qualifying organizations:

> *WNBC New York is pleased to provide free air time for public service announcements to promote and serve the interests of our viewers and non-profit organizations.*
>
> *If you are submitting a PSA, send in on 1" format; make sure that the title of the PSA, length, and the name/address/telephone no. of the non-profit organization is clearly noted on the tape box and tape.*
>
> *If this is your first time submitting a spot make sure that you send evidence of your 501(c)(3) proof of your tax exempt status and background information on your organization.*

*If you want to know whether or not your spot is on the air, please call the
second week of every month or for a quicker response, you can fax a request
to 212 956-6029.*

We do not produce PSAs.

*We do not schedule date restricted PSAs promoting events. PSAs are aired on
a three monthly rotation. (WNBC, 1994)*

WCBS Newsradio 88 in New York provides a similar set of guidelines for
radio PSAs:

*WCBS-AM will consider public service announcements from any local
non-profit–charitable organization and government entity in the tri-state area.
In order to conform with the station's long-standing practices, these messages
should be of a noncontroversial and nonpolitical nature.*

*The PSA message must offer a specific ongoing service to the community,
such as a telephone number to call for further information about a service, or
offer free educational material to listeners.*

*You should submit your PSA request one month in advance from the date
that you would like to air it. Send us your correspondence on letterhead paper
listing your board of directors with a copy of the organization's Internal
Revenue Service's 501(c)(3) tax exempt letter. In your correspondence include
your organization's statement of purpose. Without proof of your 501(c)(3)
status we cannot air your PSAs.*

*Messages must be 25 seconds in length—the equivalent of 8 typewritten
lines, so that WCBS can add a 5-second station identification. They should be
mailed (not faxed) in the form of a script or on a reel-to-reel tape. The majority of PSAs aired by our station come to us in the form of scripts. All recorded
messages must be accompanied by a script. Each PSA's message must include
and clearly identify the name of the submitting organization.*

*WCBS will air PSAs for small and large organizations that provide services
applicable to a large segment of our audience. It should be clear that due to
limited air time for PSAs, we will not be able to accommodate every organization that submits a request. WCBS reserves the right to edit PSAs scripts before
they are broadcast.*

*WCBS airs dated PSAs promoting annual events such as benefits or semi-
nars only when the station is invited to consider supporting your activity early
on. If you would like WCBS to promote your annual event, please contact us
while you are in the planning stages and not just before the event takes place.
(WCBS, undated)*

True to its "annual events" policy, partnership with two local nonprofit organizations WCBS published a 160-page accessibility guide for people with dis-
abilities to New York City's cultural institutions in 1992. And in collaboration

with the Columbia School of Public Health, WCBS produced a four-month, on-air public health campaign that included publishing and distributing, free of charge, a personal health guide.

Are PSAs Effective?

The Advertising Council's Advertising Research Committee and the Advertising Research Foundation conducted a two-year study to determine the effectiveness of PSAs in the competitive media marketplace. The study itself was worth about $1 million in all, with most resources donated; in addition, several major advertisers donated television time worth a total of $74.6 million to the effort."

> *Each year, more and more local, national and media-produced public service advertising (PSA) campaigns compete for media time and space. This has put pressure on the media to run fewer ad placements per campaign. It has also led to the media requesting more guidance from The Advertising Council in scheduling PSAs for maximum impact. (Advertising Council, 1991, p. 3)*

The objectives of the study were to:

- measure the effects of public service advertising on the awareness, beliefs, and actions of the target audience
- measure the effects of both average and above-average media schedules over time
- create a research model to aid in evaluating future public service advertising campaigns. (Advertising Council, 1991, p. 3)

The campaign chosen for the study was the American Cancer Society's Colon Cancer Early Detection campaign featuring the tag line "Colon Cancer: Don't find out about it too late in life." This campaign was chosen because: (1) it was a relatively new campaign dealing with an issue that had not received recent media attention; (2) it was a health-related campaign, the largest category of Ad Council campaigns; (3) the creative execution was strong; (4) the campaign called upon the target audience to take specific measurable action; and (5) it had the potential for saving thousands of lives each year (Advertising Council, 1991, p. 4).

According to the study, each year colon cancer strikes about 155,000 adults over the age of forty in the United States. It strikes men and women equally and kills them equally—about 61,000 a year. The current survival rate is 50 percent, but if this cancer were detected early—by a simple set of tests—the survival rate could be 90 percent. That translates into 50,000 lives that could be saved each year by one public service advertising campaign (Advertising Council, 1991, p. 4).

The 30-second television spot, created pro bono by Calet, Hirsh, & Spector Inc of New York, opens on a poignant graveside scene as a family mourns the death of a middle-aged man. Flashbacks to his life and his illness in the hospital lead to the endline, "Colon Cancer: Don't find out about it too late in life" (Advertising Council, 1991, pp. 2–3).

The campaign ran and research was conducted within four BehaviorScan test markets—Eau Claire, Wisconsin; Marion, Indiana; Grand Junction, Colorado; and Pittsfield, Massachusetts. An equal number of target households—including the target audience of adults aged forty to sixty-nine—were chosen in each market. Each market's split cable facilities were used to deliver the PSA to those households and to control the level of advertising received by each household (Advertising Council, 1991, p. 6).

The campaign ad tested consisted of one 30-second television PSA which ran from July 31, 1989 to July 23, 1990, with three waves of research being conducted: (1) benchmark wave in July 1989 prior to the campaign; (2) wave 1 in January 1990, six months into the campaign; and wave 2 in July 1990, twelve months into the campaign. The sample size for each research wave was: 757 households for the benchmark wave; 1,511 households for wave 1; and 1,500 households for wave 2 (Advertising Council, p. 6). The test provided five major findings:

Finding 1: Public service advertising is very effective in building awareness.

According to the study, if the major goal of a public service advertising campaign is to build awareness, this study showed that an average level of advertising can accomplish this goal. It also showed that consistency and targeted media placement are important in increasing awareness. The longer a public service advertising campaign runs, the more awareness can be expected to increase. The more targeted the media placement, the more awareness will increase among the target audience.

Proven/related awareness among those exposed to an average level of advertising increased from 11 percent prior to advertising to 29 percent after six months. Awareness continued to build throughout the 12-month campaign, reaching 40 percent of target households at the end of that time.

The most dramatic increase in awareness came among men, where advertising awareness increased from 6 percent before media exposure to 35 percent at the end of the campaign. Although women's awareness started out higher than men's and did increase, men's awareness increased twice as fast as women's. This finding is in keeping with the fact that the content of the campaign placed more emphasis on colon cancer as a problem for men. It also reflects the fact that a concerted effort was made to target men by placing more PSAs than usual in sports, prime time, and early news programming (Advertising Council, 1991, pp. 10–11).

Finding 2: Public service advertising can be used effectively to reinforce positive beliefs which lead to action.

Two separate belief statements were measured. Agreement with belief statement 1, "If colon cancer is diagnosed in its early stage, it can be cured 90 percent of the time," showed an increase from 69 percent to 75 percent in six months among those exposed to an average level of advertising, and then leveled off at 73 percent at the end of twelve months. Those expressing disbelief in this statement also decreased during that period (Advertising Council, 1991, p. 12).

Agreement with belief statement 2, "Everyone over 40 should have an annual exam for colon cancer," showed a small increase from 62 percent to 64 percent in six months, and then increased to 67 percent at the end of twelve months among those holding the statement to be "definitely and/or very likely true." Looking at those who held that statement to be "definitely true," it is clear that the intensity of belief in the value of an annual exam increased significantly as well (Advertising Council, 1991, p. 13).

Finding 3: To increase personal concern about health issues, it's important to maximize advertising exposure among your target audience.

In measuring personal concern about "the possibility that you or someone from your family might have colon cancer in the future," this study found a direct correlation between the number of advertising exposure opportunities—the number of PSAs that actually ran while a target household's TV set was turned on and tuned to the channel—and both an increase in concern and in the intensity of that concern.

Personal concern increased most among those households exposed to the highest number of PSAs—that is, thirty-one or more PSAs over the course of the year. In addition, the most consistent increase in concern occurred among those expressing the highest level of concern—those saying they were "extremely concerned about the issue" (Advertising Council, 1991, p. 14).

Finding 4: Public service advertising has a positive impact on a person's decision to take action.

In the study's words: Action first requires intent. To determine public service advertising's effect on people's decision to take action, the study measured the target audience's intent to talk to their doctor about colon cancer on their next visit. The study found that an average level of advertising produced a statistically significant increase in the intention to take action. It also raised questions about advertising wearout. The study found there was no increase in the intention to act in the first six months. It took a full twelve months to show an incremental increase in intention—from 16 percent to 18 percent. While this increase may not seem significant, it translates into a 12.5 percent increase in intention over twelve months—enough to be statistically significant and to save lives (Advertising Council, 1991, p. 15).

The study also found that the intention to act peaked at from sixteen to thirty exposure opportunities among total respondents, men and women. The researchers surmised "this may be due in large part to the fact that only one 30-second creative execution was run during the length of the campaign, eventually invoking the law of diminishing returns and creating advertising wearout" (Advertising Council, 1991, p. 16).

Finding 5: Public service advertising can move people to action—in this case, life-saving action.

The study found that public service advertising can move people to action with an average level of advertising. It also showed that consistency and targeted media placement are critical in maximizing the effectiveness of public service advertising. It took a full year for this campaign to begin saving lives, and it generated the most action among men—that audience segment deliberately targeted in media placement. Among total respondents, it took a full year to see an increase in those who recalled speaking to their doctor about colon cancer—from 7 percent to 9 percent. This translates into a statistically significant 28.6 percent increase in the number of people taking action—life-saving action (Advertising Council, 1991, p. 17).

All the long-term increases in those who took action happened among men—from 7 percent to 12 percent (a 71.4% increase) among those exposed to average levels of advertising, and from 7 percent to 15 percent (a 114.3% increase) among those exposed to above average levels of advertising. As the study states: Based on these results, if this campaign were duplicated nationally for a year, we could expect an additional 1.7 to 2.7 million men over 40 to consult their doctor about colon cancer. In the process, we could also expect to save thousands of lives by early detection. The high motivation for action among men can be attributed to several factors. First...the content of the PSA placed more emphasis on colon cancer as a problem among men rather than women. Second, there was a concerted effort to target men by placing more PSAs than usual in sports, prime-time and news programming. Finally, there may be a two-tiered effect at work. The campaign may have motivated women—who were as likely as men to have increased awareness of the advertising—to motivate men to take action, which is not unusual with regard to health-related behavior (Advertising Council, 1991, p. 18).

The Advertising Council's evaluative effort underscores the effectiveness of PSAs. Moreover, it is always reassuring to have some quantitative proof that a PSA has a chance not only of reaching its intended audience, but also of having an impact. Clearly, if a PSA has a penetrating concept, it has a chance of being aired and serving its purpose, as reflected by the numerous PSAs—whose images have become part of American popular culture—that are listed in the following section.

Successful PSA Campaigns

There have been numerous successful public service announcement campaigns, among them:

Only You Can Prevent Forest Fires (Smokey Bear/Forest Fire Prevention)

Take a Bite Out of Crime (McGruff the Crime Dog/Crime Prevention)

Pollution Is a Crying Shame (The Crying Indian/Keep America Beautiful)

Cross at the Green, Not In Between (Children's Safety)

A Mind Is a Terrible Thing to Waste (United Negro College Fund)

Be a Hero...Volunteer (Breaking the Cycle of the Disadvantaged)

You Could Learn a Lot from a Dummy. Buckle Your Safety Belt. (Crash Dummies/Drunk Driving Prevention)

It's a Congested World. Do Your Share. (Earth Share /Ecology)

Don't Be Afraid, Be a Friend (Leadership Conference Education Fund)

There's No Excuse. (Domestic Violence Prevention)

Get High, Get Stupid, Get AIDS (Drug Abuse and AIDS Prevention)

Be a Teacher. Be a Hero. (Recruiting New Teachers)

Not all PSA campaigns receive national attention. Many, though, are successful and get the job done given their objectives. Tony Esposito (group manager of Bozell Public Relations in Chicago) described some of his work with PSAs: "We were in a project working with the National Stroke Association, the American College of Chest Physicians, the Alliance for Aging Research, and the

American Association of Retired Persons. This program began two years ago and stems from a consensus report published by the American College of Chest Physicians (ACCP) that showed that people with a common heart ailment called arterial fibrillation, or AF, which is an irregular heart beat, are at a greater risk of a stroke than the general population. The consensus report stated that when given anti-coagulation therapy these patients can greatly reduce that risk of stroke."

Bozell Public Relations set out to create a public education campaign to alert the general populace to the fact that a person can have AF without even knowing it. They also wanted to let those people who may have been diagnosed with AF in the past know that they should probably see their physician again to determine if they are a good candidate for anti-coagulation therapy.

Esposito explained that one of the primary methods Bozell used to educate the general public was a series of public service announcements for radio and television: "We did four different spots. One was with Louis Gossett, Jr., the actor, primarily targeting the African-American community. We did two spots with Edward James Olmos aimed at the Hispanic population—one in English and one in Spanish. We did a spot with Hakeem Olajuwon, the center for the Houston Rockets, who himself suffers from AF. And we did one with Hume Cronin and the late Jessica Tandy—both of whom have AF—obviously targeted at the older community."

The program did not rely solely on PSAs to get the message out. Along with the release of these PSAs, they also did a staggered release with traditional print media relations as well as video news releases and satellite media tours. They released the first set of PSAs, the ones featuring Gossett and Olmos, in December 1993. The satellite media tours were done two weeks apart in January 1994. We focused on the top 100 markets. More than 150 television stations ran the first set of public service announcements for approximately 50,000 air plays, including broadcast and cable. There were 42,000 air plays on radio.

Producing PSAs: Some Guidelines

Control costs. Esposito offered several budget parameters as guidelines for producing a PSA:

> On the distribution end, you can figure $20,000–$30,000. That should cover all of your tape duplication, tracking all the reports they issue back to you, sending out the tapes and a good deal of the hand-holding that goes along with it. I

hate to give guesstimates on production because it turns people off, and they say, 'We can't afford to do that,' so we have to look somewhere else. You can do some amazing things on a much lower budget today then you could do five years ago on a much higher budget, if that makes any sense. For $5,000 you can produce some pretty fantastic video for 30-second PSAs.

For probably between $20,000 and $30,000 you can produce on to film, that's not including talent fees. Obviously, when you use a celebrity, you're going to pay a higher talent fee than if you use actors. Then you get into union and non-union situations and everything else.

If you're lucky enough where you can get celebrities to donate their time, that's ideal. But even if the celebrities volunteer their time, I would recommend budgeting some kind of stipend because when they're doing it gratis, you are at their mercy. And if they want to do one take, there's not a whole lot you can do about it. But the minute you involve any amount of money, you're going to involve some kind of contract and they are at least obligated to give you what you need.

Create visibility. Esposito also had the following advice for producing a PSA that would get aired: "You're competing with a lot of other people for the time. TV means it's got to be fairly visual. You are much better off with somebody who is very visible, a celebrity or a known or would-be known, in our case, a physician. For example, most people would not be able to name the president of the National Stroke Association, but his status certainly carries a lot of weight."

Produce for quality. Esposito commented on the need for quality: "People tend to skim in the worst possible places and that is in the production values. You are going to far increase your chances of airing a PSA if you produce one in the highest-quality way that you can, even if you don't have a celebrity. A well-produced piece is going to be used over something that looks like it was thrown together on the fly."

Select a competent distributor. Regarding distribution, Esposito strongly recommended "using a service that distributes PSAs and has a prior track record. Such a service already has a relationship or those station's it contacts have a history of using PSAs. Some distribution houses primarily distribute public service announcements."

Deliver a mix of PSA lengths. New York–based Medialink (1994) adds some other advice about PSAs that electronic public relations professionals should heed. First, there have been changes in the manner in which PSAs are produced and distributed. Spots run shorter than ever, reflecting the increasing competition for air time between local and national groups. This means, says Medialink, that PSA producers must deliver a mix of increasingly popular 10-second and 30-second spots, as well as less frequently used 60-second spots, to give the broadcaster the widest possible options.

Stress current events. Medialink also points out that decreased lead time required for distribution means that mailing is being replaced by satellite delivery. "The most effective distribution technique," says Medialink, "combines two separate satellite transmissions per PSA: computerized notification to stations, personalized PSA alert mailings to individual public service directors, limited targeted cassette distribution to key stations, and electronic encoding of the PSA for exact, detailed reports on confirmed airings (more on encoding in the chapter on video news releases)" (Medialink, 1994, p. 8).

Contact stations ahead of distribution. Finally, public relations practitioners must plan ahead and go through the sometimes tedious task of contacting stations (whether the PSA is destined for radio or television) to find out in what form the station wants the PSA (script only, reel-to-reel, cassette, BetaSP, three-quarter inch videocassette, satellite transmission). This step provides an opportunity to connect with the key contact at the radio or television station, which, in turn, could successfully lead to the airing of the PSA.

Chapter 4

Reaching the General Public: Video News Releases

VNRs Defined

Video news releases, or VNRs, are stories 90–120 seconds in length that provide useful public information but incorporate a reference to an organization's specific product or service. The VNR serves several mutual purposes. On one hand, it provides local television news programmers with soft news segments that can often be localized. For the organizational programmer, it is a way to generate public relations for a product or service on a national or regional scale. Handled properly, the VNR can be tied into an overall public relations and marketing campaign for the product or service.

Audiences and Outlets

As an electronic public relations vehicle, a video news release must first meet the approval of the news director or a producer in a broadcast or cable television news department. From this perspective, the VNR differs from a public service announcement, which must meet certain standards of acceptability from a radio or television station's standards department.

When it is aired, a PSA is aired as the producing organization created it. A video news release, however, will probably not get on the air exactly as the producing organization created it—for a variety of reasons. First, a VNR is not a public service announcement (although there may be elements of public interest in the material). A VNR is about a product or service that has news interest value and interest to the community served by the broadcast or cable television outlet. Second, the material will be used by the television outlet's news department. PSAs are not necessarily news, and they get on the air in time slots that may have nothing to do with news. Because they are specifically news oriented, VNRs will be shaped by the news department, if the material is going to get on the air.

A Brief History

Because a VNR is primarily a news vehicle with an underlying profit or advertising motivation, its history has been somewhat rocky and, in certain cases, downright volatile. Larry Moskowitz, president of New York-based Medialink, points to several milestones in the early days: the years 1948, when the first time public relations films were delivered to television stations, and 1958, when Nelson Rockefeller hired a television crew to cover his gubernatorial campaign speeches and his staff handed films to television stations along the campaign trail.

Several electronic technological developments helped spur the video news release business. In 1956, Ampex and Minnesota Mining and Manufacturing (3M) introduced commercially viable videotape players and tape stock. By 1960, one inch helical scan technology made duplication easy, and in 1971 Sony introduced the three-quarter inch U-Matic videocassette to the United States. This standard and highly portable videotape format not only exponentially increased the development of organizational video networks, it also helped spawn more portable so-called electronic field production (EFP) as well as editing. By 1978, Moskowitz also points out, large public relations firms had begun to use video news releases on a regular basis. And by the early 1980s, satellite technology had reached sufficient critical mass that it had become the dominant technological form of television distribution, including the distribution of video news releases.

During the 1980s, though, video news releases had a bumpy history. Two themes emerged as the video news release business evolved in this decade: (1) the credibility of VNRs as "news"; and (2) gauging the viewership of VNRs in quantitative terms. In December 1989, for example, the *Public Relations Journal* reported that "the industry is still plagued by some suppliers who grossly exaggerate the numbers of VNRs they distribute to impress potential clients." Also, those polled for the 1989 survey commented that "VNRs that are of poor technical quality or lack a real news or feature angle also damage the industry by undermining credibility with news organizations." Many of the two dozen VNR producers/distributors surveyed expressed a need for an industry code of ethics that would address usage monitoring methods and quality standards and help minimize practices that threatened the gradually improving image of the industry ("VNR Update," p. 23).

A year later, the *Public Relations Journal* reported:

Technical quality and content is improving, due mainly to the growing number of TV journalists who have defected from low-paying news jobs to become VNR producers. Surveys show that news directors short on staff and money are increasing their use of VNR's. International markets are opening up. In addition, satellite distribution has spawned a host of new producers, making VNRs a public relations tool available to virtually any size client. (Public Relations Journal, *December 1990, p. 28)*

The major problem reported in 1990 was that clients had too high expectations in terms of number of viewers.

In 1991, however, VNRs, particularly those produced and distributed by pharmaceutical companies, came under congressional scrutiny, specifically by Senator Edward Kennedy's Senate Labor and Human Resources Committee. Some of the conclusions drawn from the deliberations—why powerful, synergistic forces drive TV stations to use drug industry VNRs—included: (1) the weakening economics of local television, which enhances the desire for slick news segments with designer features, but not designer prices; (2) the strong appeal of VNRs to marketers as an almost ideal alternative to paid commercials; (3) the huge payoffs for the drug industry in stimulating public demand for its products (Taylor & Mintz, 1991, p. 484). The center of the debate focused on the apparent guile and deception of the VNRs—which featured white-coated, confidence-inspiring physicians paid by the manufacturers as well as lead-ins and closings suggested by the manufacturers public relations firms—which had the cumulative effect of "trick[ing] viewers into assuming not only that they are hearing and seeing authentic news but it is news produced by their admirably enterprising local station." (Taylor & Mintz, 1991, p. 480).

About a week later, *Variety* reported that Time Warner was taking advantage of its substantial media capabilities to promote a *Time* magazine excerpt from a forthcoming Oliver North autobiography. Time Warner produced a VNR that was picked up by more than fifty stations. Steve Friedman, *NBC News* executive producer, remarked: "What *Time* did was all part of the ongoing video revolution. We wouldn't use any material we wouldn't do ourselves....Of course, the first preference is to do it yourself. But it was the weekend and *Time* was very clever in controlling the material. We didn't have a whole lot of time or access" (Robins, 1991, p. 69).

This case exemplifies the evolving relationship between television news organizations and suppliers of material outside the traditional news mainstream. While in the case of the drug industry VNRs a public relations firm supplied the segment, in the Oliver North case a news organization—*Time*—supplied the material. Nonetheless, in both cases a product was being touted.

Later that year, in December 1991—just in time, it seems, to reinstate the VNR business with some credibility—Nielsen Media Research announced the launch of SIGMA, an electronic VNR monitoring system, which it had been testing since October 1988. The system—an application of a fifteen-year-old technology first used to confirm that affiliate stations were airing network programming—had the impact of providing more empirical information regarding the size of VNR viewing audiences.

The VNR business took its lumps again, though, in February 1992, when *TV Guide* published a damning article entitled "Fake News" (Lieberman, 1992) that undermined the credibility of the VNR format. After the dust had settled, the result was the development of a Code of Good Practice for Video News Releases by a special committee of the Public Relations Service Council (PRSC). The code reads as follows:

- The objective of a VNR is to present information, pictures, and sound that TV journalists can use and rely on for quality, accuracy, and perspective.
- Information contained in a VNR, to the extent possible, must be accurate and verifiable. Intentionally false or misleading information must be avoided.
- A VNR must be clearly identified as such on the video's opening slate and any advisory material and scripts that precede or accompany tape distribution.
- The sponsoring company, organization, or individual must also be clearly identified on the video slate.
- The name and phone number of a responsible party must be provided on the video for journalists to contact.
- Persons interviewed in the VNR must be accurately identified by name, title, and affiliation on the video. (Shell, 1992)

Interestingly, this code from the producers' side of the house appeared some five years *after* the Radio and Television News Directors Association's (RTNDA) adoption of a revised code of ethics that reads in part "[Members] will guard against using audio or video material in a way that deceives the audience" (RTNDA, 1987).

In early 1993, David Bartlett, president of the RTNDA, reaffirmed the association's position on video news releases when he stated: "RTNDA does not endorse the use of so-called 'video news releases,' but neither do we reject their use as long as that use conforms to the association's code of ethics.... Accordingly, RTNDA believes that good journalistic practice calls for clear identification of all material received from outside sources, including material distributed in the form of video or audio news releases."

Semantics and Economics

By mid-1993, the tug of war between news organizations and VNR producers seems to have evolved into two simple questions: "What is a VNR?" and "Should news directors use them or not?"

As for the first question, if a television station uses B–roll footage provided by a VNR producer, is the reedited material now a VNR or just video material provided by a nonnews entity? Or is a VNR a VNR when an A–roll version— completely edited and voiced—is put on the air? (A–roll is video material that has been scripted and edited. B–roll, on the other hand, is raw video material, e. g., action footage that shows what an on-camera interviewee is describing.) David Bartlett commented on this issue in an interview:

> I'm not convinced everyone who talks about VNRs either pro or con is really talking about the same thing. There is some dispute about a precise definition of what constitutes a VNR. For example, everybody understands and I think would accept that those unfortunate, phony news stories that are distributed, or used to be distributed as VNRs, where some PR person masquerades as a reporter and the structure of the package tends to suggest that it's a real news story when, in fact, it's not. Everybody would agree that would not be a VNR.
>
> But what about video from the Space Shuttle, distributed by NASA? What about the famous piece of video from the President of Columbia imploring Americans not to use cocaine and screw up his country? [In August, 1989, a VNR showing Columbia's President, Virgilio Barco, issuing a stiff warning to drug traffickers in his country was reportedly seen by 75 million viewers ("VNR Update," 1989, p. 23)].This was a piece that ran on major network news shows and which was distributed by a public relations firm. It was what it was, and it was self-evident, but it could also, I think, be very easily described and probably was described on the bill as a VNR. The government of Columbia paid for that PR firm.
>
> I think we have to, first of all, be careful, if we can't settle on a definition of VNRs, at least understand we are not always talking about the same thing, and that one type of VNR may come in for greater criticism than another type of a VNR.

The other issue is economics. Should news directors use VNRs at all? The fact is, news organizations need video material from other than their own resources, and video footage providers (including VNR producers) need an outlet for their material (regardless of product or service). On both sides of the aisle there appears to be a difference of perception. VNR producers believe that news organizations benefit from their material in two ways: (1) they provide video footage that news organizations would not normally have the resources to access, and (2) the material supplements the diminishing staff size of news departments.

The first benefit is correct, but the second does not square with the facts. According to the latest research from the RTNDA (Stone, 1994, p. 20), the television news force grew by several hundred again last year. Average gains of about one person per newsroom in middle and small markets more than offset reductions averaging two at stations in the fifty largest markets. The RTNDA-funded research revealed that "the estimated TV news workforce in 1993 was 24,500 (21,800 full-time and 2,700 part-time) people at 740 stations…800 more full-time and 100 less part-time staff than in 1992." These numbers, moreover, reflect a long-term trend: "From 1987 to 1993, the TV news work force increased by 30 percent. If it keeps growing at that rate, 33,000 people will be working in newsrooms at TV stations by the year 2000."

So where does the apparent increased demand come from? According to Joe Tiernan, editor of the RTNDA's *Communicator,*

> *I think the reason why they may be used more is not so much that the news staff has been cut back, but news time has been expanding, especially in the early morning, like 6 in the morning. Many stations have a half-hour or hour newscast before they go into the* Today *show or* Good Morning, America. *A lot of stations are doing 60-second news updates all day long. The early and late time periods that are now being utilized more by news operations create a need for video. You have staffs of thirty or forty at local, small, medium-sized stations, but they are now responsible for producing at least two or three hours or more per day of news, and for the news producers to find interesting stories can sometimes be overwhelming.*

Television journalists, on the other hand, claim officially that they rarely use VNR footage. Steve Coe, however, writes in *Broadcasting & Cable:* "Most news executives at stations say video news releases are used rarely, if ever. But according to the companies that produce and distribute the footage commissioned by corporations and other entities, and research compiled by Nielsen, usage is at an all-time high" (1993, p. 17).

RTNDA's Bartlett observes:

There has always been, since well before the invention of television, something of a symbiotic relationship between public relations people, press agents, what have you, and news organizations. At the very simplest end of the spectrum, public relations firms are professional sources, and news organizations thrive on sources. To the extent that some people have said VNRs provide cheap video to news organizations, I think that's dangerous because it might tempt a news organization to use video that they otherwise wouldn't use, simply because it's video. Or they might accidentally use video not thinking about the implications of the source.

I'm thinking about B–roll here, where a piece of video ends up in the B-roll library and gets pulled out in a totally different connection at some later point. Had you looked at that video more carefully, had you stopped and said, "Okay, I'm going to go shoot this, take this picture, and use this as the B-roll," instead of just pulling something blindly out of the file, you might have shot it a little bit differently or used it a little bit differently, so I think it's dangerous to rely on any crutch, including a VNR, but at the same time I'm not going to tell you that there's anything intrinsically wrong with putting VNR material on the air. There is not.

Neither side seems totally willing to fully accept the other's contribution. Perhaps it is just as well. On one hand, journalists need to maintain their objective stance. Even within news organizations, there is at least an "official" separation between sales and editorial departments, although critics contend the line is blurring. On the other, VNR producers need to satisfy marketing and public relations objectives. Regardless, the explosion of print and electronic information channels and the resulting reorganization of economic relationships among purveyors of so-called "news" have caused some reluctant relationships, including that between television news organizations and VNR producers and their clients.

The Evolving VNR: Guidelines

Its history notwithstanding, in the last few years organizations that create video news releases appear to have evolved their strategic management of this electronic public relations format: they seem more sensitive to the needs of news directors and are taking a far more focused approach to when, where, how, and why they distribute a video news release.

According to various public relations professionals with extensive experience producing video news releases, a successful VNR must have newsworthiness, timeliness, a visual story, entertainment value, and effective content.

Newsworthiness. Lew Allison, a former senior vice president with the public relations firm Hill and Knowlton and now a consultant, points out:

> *If the company's strategy includes efforts to attract attention by the broadcast media, and if the company goes ahead and considers the video news release, first thing it needs to make sure of is that it has news. "News" is the VNRs middle name. It won't get on the air if it isn't newsworthy, and, as a matter of fact, it can be negative.*
>
> *If a company with a good solid reputation puts out a VNR that news editors are going to scorn, that can really be a very bad thing. You've got to have a clear goal in mind, and you need to be sure there is a news angle to what you're offering the newsrooms.*

A visual story. Allison underscored the need for a news story that's visual: "If it's not a television story, a VNR should not be used. For example, a financial institution might have a very big announcement to make. It could be page 1 of the business section of the *New York Times,* but there might not be a single visual aspect to it. Television, of course, needs good strong images, as well as the news angle, so, if your company's message isn't the kind that would appeal to television news editors, then you shouldn't do it."

Most Americans, Allison said, get most of their information on current events from television. Consequently, "the image of the company and the message that it wants to deliver reaches an awful lot of Americans when it is done right. The television image is an effective way to deliver that kind of a message, or to suit that kind of purpose. In other words, people pay attention to television and a good, colorful, newsy image strikes the viewer's mind pretty forcefully, according to most theories about television. So, I think that when it works it reaches large, large numbers of people in a way that is attention getting and memorable."

Timeliness and audience. Elizabeth Parkinson, a producer with Edelman Public Relations Worldwide in Chicago, stressed the need for timeliness:

> *To fit our criteria we usually recommend that the VNR have a timely basis, that it's tied to some kind of announcement or something that's going to be launched or give stations a reason to want to air it at a certain point in time," Parkinson said. "If it doesn't have a timely basis, we usually stay away from it, because there's no reason that you need something as immediate as videotape. Maybe it would be suited just as a straight press release, or maybe as a brochure or something that's a little less immediate.*
>
> *Another criterion is who the audience is. Is what they're trying to communicate for the general public? If they're trying to reach doctors or a very specific base of constituents, then maybe mass broadcast isn't the way to go. We're*

*going into a period when we're going to have 500 channels soon in which mes-
sages get lost, and if you're trying to target a specific audience then maybe a
VNR isn't the way to go. It's better if it's a really broad consumer-based
audience.*

Entertainment value. Universal Studios, Florida uses VNRs for all major
events and usually for the opening of new attractions and additions to the park.
Jim Hampton, manager of Publicity and PR/Universal, explained:

*For the "Flintstones Weekend" we had John Goodman, Rick Moranis, and the
other stars of the Flintstones here. Universal Pictures brought them in to talk
with the entertainment press about the release of the film. So they were here.
We have a new exhibit at Universal called "Backstage with the Flintstones," in
which we brought all the sets from Hollywood. It will be a walk-through exhibit
for summer, so we wanted to incorporate those two, the fact that we had a lot
of the stars from the film and they would be talking about the film, and push
our new exhibit.*

*We melded those two together and did a VNR that was uplinked via satellite
on Monday around the country, and that's the kind of usage that we do more
than any other, although we have all kinds of reasons for uplinking or sending
out VNRs to people. Mostly they are national releases.*

Effective content. Pepsi distributes a dozen or so B–rolls a year (they don't call
them VNRs). They are rarely mass distributed—maybe one or two a year. Most
are earmarked for a particular type of reporter: feature, sports, entertainment,
new products, and so on.

Rebecca Madeira, vice president for public affairs at Pepsi, found the kind of
VNR content that seemed to work best was personality profiles in the entertainment area, because they allowed reporters to look at a celebrity in very different
situations that they might not have access to on their own, either because of time
or location:

*Reporters tend to really like a chance to see a celebrity up close and personal,
and B–roll, especially when it's outtakes, flubs. Jokes off camera are a lot more
fun. They've already seen the finished pieces—that's what commercials are.
This just gives them a chance to come backstage with us and get to know the
person, get to know what it's like to work with them or get to know what they
are thinking about, and a lot of other things.*

VNRs that don't work, in Madeira's opinion, are heavy-handed product messages; selling messages; and overuse of trademarks, logos, or point of view. "The

objectivity is so important," she says. "The distance really helps. A reporter's point of view is going to result in a far more effective piece than something that is prepackaged and looks like an infomercial."

VNRs: A Strategic Choice

These basic VNR characteristics aside, public relations practitioners need to take a strategic stance on VNRs.

To VNR or not to VNR. Edelman's Parkinson positions the VNR as one part of an overall communications plan. Because press releases and various printed materials often lack the same immediacy or visual effect as a broadcast piece does, it's a logical step for companies to use a visual medium for their message or product so that it can reach its intended audience. "We actually counsel a fair amount of our clients not to do VNRs because they are not necessarily appropriate in every single instance," says Parkinson. "The most successes we've had is when a VNR has involved a new product introduction and involves something very visual, a unique event. We also counsel people that it depends on who they are trying to reach. If it's a consumer message, then broadcast is a good way to reach them."

For companies large and not so large. VNRs are not expensive to produce compared to advertising. "Smaller companies," Elizabeth Parkinson says, "if they are interested in the publicity component compared to the advertising component, probably get a much bigger bang for their buck if they do a VNR, as compared to advertising."

Time and place. Pepsi's Madeira explains the need for selectivity when using VNRs as part of the communications mix: "I think VNRs have a time and a place. This is a very visual world nowadays as far as communications is concerned, and I think it's the responsibility of anyone charged with communication for a company, service, product, whatever, to have some good, clear, basic materials that explain how the business works or what the product is and these materials are both visual and written, and that's really what's new about our business."

Madeira believes that the PR person needs to be able to explain how things work visually as well as providing very detailed press kits with backgrounders, fact sheets, and traditional tools. She distinguishes between A–roll and B–roll VNRs, and which works best. B–rolls are not tightly edited and packaged, but consist of a number of segments of materials, scenes, or soundbites presented in an organized fashion with a table of contents. "Because they have not been pieced together, that's something the local producer or reporter is free to do." Madeira says: "Pepsi Cola Company tends to prefer B–roll format to a preproduced, tight 3-minute VNR piece that has already culled through all the material, has a very distinct point of view, and is looking more like some kind of prepackaged announcement rather than raw material that the news show can use and draw from, and put together on their own."

VNRs as community relations. Discount retailer K-mart has also made use of VNRs. Dennis Wigent of K-mart explains: "VNRs are the major way we work with community relations. Around the holidays we do a number of programs. Last year, for example…we had stores involved in something called 'Shop With A Cop.' Local police choose underprivileged kids and K-Mart gives them a major discount on items and the kids come and shop at the Kmart store. Anything that can be a national program works well with a VNR."

Wigent believes such VNRs are effective for a number of reasons, but especially because research shows that fewer people read newspapers and more people are getting their information from television. "That's a fair assessment of our customer," says Wigent. "So television is a medium that's a very good one for us. Also, they're very emotional. They're visual to begin with. A scene of fifty kids and fifty cops going through a K-mart store shopping is pretty impactful. And is more impactful in an electronic means than in newspapers."

Image building. Jim Schwinn, manager of broadcast media relations, at Minnesota Mining and Manufacturing, uses VNRs to push an image: namely, positioning 3M as the most innovative corporation in the world. Says Schwinn: "I might use a product, a new technology, processes, people significant to the moment, whatever the case may be." Schwinn's VNR focus echoes Madeira's—using VNRs for selective markets. His strategy is now targeting public relations efforts "market by market, issue by issue, and product by product."

One 3M VNR concerned a third grade class that sent the company some suggestions for redesigning one of its overhead projectors; coincidentally, a portion of that design had already been used in the new model. The company sent the class a free projector and thanked them for their efforts. Another VNR covered the company's flood relief efforts in 1993, when 3M sent truckloads of relief materials to the Salvation Army and the American Red Cross for St. Louis, Missouri distribution centers in the aftermath of that year's floods.

Schwinn offers this advice about using VNRs:

I think you need to know what is acceptable and what will sell. Most distribution companies will give you a hand in that, but it's good to have somebody internal who has been in the business, somebody who has been in television journalism, and knows what makes a good news story visually, information-wise, and how it flows.

But I think first and foremost you've got to ask yourself, if you know in your mind what this story looks like as a finished piece, is this something you would watch on TV, and say, "Huh, I didn't know that." That would be worthwhile. Or maybe refine it back to if you could put yourself in the position of a news producer or news editor seeing that piece, would you say, "Yeah, we want that in the show," or would you say, "It's hype," "it's fluff"?

Schwinn believes there are more cases in which 3M would not use a VNR than when they would. A VNR is just one way to tell an inherently good story, he stresses, and that story should not be limited just to that telling. A good story can be told in many different formats. A story not worth telling shouldn't be a VNR or anything else.

Fulfilling News Directors' Needs

Elizabeth Parkinson and others underscore the reality that video news releases (when they are actually aired) fulfill not only a client's public relations needs, but also satisfy the news material needs of television stations news directors.

Access to Material

First and foremost, VNRs give a television news department access to newsworthy material. Elizabeth Parkinson gives this example:

We handle the Starkist Dolphin-Safe Tuna. There was an immediate message that had to go out, and the stations needed footage that maybe a lot of people couldn't have gone out and gotten. So we were able to supply footage that a lot of stations don't have the manpower to get.

We interviewed spokespeople who possibly the networks would not have had access to, so we were able to supply, right from the horse's mouth, the message itself. So something like that is very successful. It's immediate, we're giving them access to footage, or to interviews that they wouldn't necessarily have the manpower to go out and get. They can't be everywhere.

At the same time, however, television news departments' goals must be respected. "You have to keep in mind that they have a certain standard of objectivity they have to maintain," says Parkinson. "As long as you respect that level of objectivity and supply them with nonbiased material, then it's really a win-win situation for both parties." It's important, she believes, to be clear about the source of the footage. "It has to be very noncommercial, and that's what we counsel our clients on. And if it's a narrated VNR it has to be very straightforward. It can't be anything that you would not hear an anchor or a reporter say on a daily basis. As long as you supply them with something that they can feel good about using and doesn't infringe on their objectivity, then that's fine—they're doing their job."

Commercialism *Verboten*

Jim Hampton also confirms the need to stay away from being too commercial: "We're trying to give reporters something they can actually use on the news or one of their top programs or entertainment programs. So we find that the *E Entertainments* and *Entertainment Tonights* use a lot of bits and pieces of what we put out because it is just good stuff." Hampton believes that trying to send a blatantly commercial message is a waste of time and trying to sell a product directly using a VNR is a waste of money. "Hardly any news department would even look at it," he says, "and I can't think of a show that would use it. There has to be some meat to the VNR or you're just wasting time and money." Any company that tries to use VNRs in a manipulative fashion on a consistent basis will fail, he adds. Because many people in public relations have a background in news reporting, they know how to make a solid, effective VNR that news departments will want to use.

The News Director's Point of View

Hampton came out of a news background to work at Universal Studios. Greg Albrecht, publicity manager of Walt Disney World, reflects a similar background and hence an in-the-trenches understanding of what news directors need:

> I've been on the other side, publicity and public relations for about three years, especially now that I am head of publicity and press for both Disney Worlds. Before that I was in television news for fifteen years as a news director, reporter and producer.
>
> From that side I viewed VNRs in a very critical manner. I felt they were giant commercial endorsements for products and because of ethics, standards, and things like that, I felt they had very little to offer my news department. I thought there was a lot companies could do, but I didn't feel they were being handled effectively in VNRs. I was very suspect of them.

Now he is on the other side, Albrecht says, knocking on the doors of some news departments. From his previous experience he knows that even the term "VNRs" sends up a red flag for most news directors that says, "This is a commercial, let's not use it."

Creating Special News Programming

Albrecht describes the kind of programming Disney now produces for television news departments: "What we've started to do is actually create news programming. I know that the news department isn't going to run a blatant commercial about a new product, whether it is a new resort, or Splash Mountain, or a character. So what we're looking to do is give something to the news departments they can use, news their viewers can use, but that also helps get our message out."

Albrecht lists the resources he can make available to news departments. One is a series called *The 60-Second Tennis Tip,* a 90-second, 26-piece series in which tennis experts give fun, easy tips to the viewers. The package has a very low Disney ID in it and is sent out free of charge to fifty markets nationwide. Another series, *Animal Talk,* is set in a zoological park called Discovery Island. Each week a zoological expert does a small piece on the animal of the day. The show focuses on endangered species, species preservation, natural habitat, and the like. That 90-second weekly piece runs in seventy markets across the United States. With other series such as *Golf Tips* and *Culinary Tips,* Albrecht hopes to provide news departments with the kind of content that they want to air—attention-getting news that their viewers can use. This format, Albrecht believes, has changed the traditional focus of VNRs to something brand new.

Staying in touch. Albrecht emphasizes the need to stay in touch with news directors: "If a news director calls us and says this is too commercial, we'll pull it and rework it for them. They need quality material....[and] we solicit input. We bring in news directors regularly to talk to us about what kind of material they would like. And a lot of times they'll come down and they'll generate stories on our material, and it may not have a Disney subtitle, but they can use it as a backdrop, or they can use our experts....but again we are very sensitive about making sure that it's not too commercial."

Producing and Distributing VNRs

Medialink offers the following keys to successful VNR production:

1. Shoot on videotape in broadcast news style, emphasizing quick cuts and noncommercial production values.

2. A VNR "package" (full narrated story with announce track) should run 1:30 to 2:00, followed by 3 to 5 minutes of B–roll (supplemental unedited video) to help the television news producer edit the story.

3. A VNR comprised of B–roll only (no narrated package) is effective when the story is self-evident and the television news producer does not need detailed context or the spin of a script to understand it.

4. The package should be produced with split audio channels (separate channels for the announce track and natural sound on tape) or in two versions, one with the announce track and the natural sound combined throughout, followed immediately by the same package with natural sound only. This allows the television news producer maximum flexibility in presenting the story.

5. The subject of interview soundbites in the VNR should be looking at the interviewer slightly off-camera to the right or the left.

6. All supers or Chyrons should be presented on a slate at the start of the VNR rather than on tape during the VNR. This allows stations to recreate the information in their own style. Make sure the sequence of identifications on the slate matches their order and appearance in the VNR.

7. For technical or otherwise complex stories, use graphics and animation to illustrate key points.

8. Never allow your reporter to do a stand-up in the VNR, and never produce a music bed under the package.

9. Do not blatantly hype your organization, product, or service with obvious brand or logo shots. Use soundbites from credible third parties such as consumer groups or trade associations to endorse your product or service.

10. Make sure the VNR has news that lends itself to television. If you can imagine your story on television news, you have the makings of a VNR. (Medialink, 1994, p. 3)

Another important key to a successful VNR distribution that is part of an electronic public relations campaign, adds Medialink, is effective, speedy, and comprehensive notification of broadcast and cable news and specialty programs. The company also stresses the importance of usage monitoring and comprehensive reporting (Medialink, 1994, p. 3).

Karen Kalish of Washington, D.C.–based Kalish Communications points out that often small stations will air a finished VNR as it is, mid-sized stations will replace a narration track with their own reporter's voice before they air it, and large stations will use the video and interviews to put their own piece together. Kalish also underscores the opportunities for leveraging the material shot for a VNR: it can be used again for a fundraising video, a marketing piece, a public service announcement, even airline in-flight programming.

Sally Jewett, President of Los Angeles–based On The Scene Productions, emphasizes the importance of a good distributor:

> *Make sure you work with a company that has a solid background in placement results. Your videos won't get used if no one knows about it. A newsroom is a busy place, so don't rely on wire services or mailers to get results. Generally the most effective way to achieve substantial placement is to use the labor-intensive method of getting on the phone and pitching the material one-on-one to the person who has the power to get your video on the air. Work with a company whose people have solid relationships with reporters and producers, and you have a better chance of having your story catch their attention—and get on the air. (Jewett, 1991)*

Tracking VNRs

At least two systems are in general use for tracking VNRs. The first is the Sigma Tracking system, marketed by Nielsen Media Research. Launched in 1991, Sigma is the leading automated VNR tracking system and works as follows: An invisible code is stamped on a client's video (on lines 20 and 22 of the Vertical Blanking Interval) with an encoding device that is then read 24 hours a day by Nielsen decoders in the nation's top 212 television markets. If any or all of the VNR is aired, the decoder reports the time, date, stations, and second by second use of the coded VNR. The data are then processed by Nielsen computers, which create usage reports (Shell, 1993, p. 15).

Another system, Video Encoded Invisible Light (VEIL) technology, tracks VNRs in the top seventy-five television markets with an accuracy rate of 99 percent. This service is offered by Radio/TV Reports. The encoding process was developed and patented by Beaverton, Oregon–based Interactive Systems.

According to Radio/TV Reports, the VEIL process works by implanting an invisible light directly into the picture, making it impervious to tampering and impossible to remove. The light pulses are modulated to create unique computer readable bits of data—forming a VNR identifier and time counter—which are transmitted back to the collection point in each city, where the time, date, and segment length is recorded and usage reports generated for clients (Shell, 1993, p. 15).

The two tracking systems provide "usage" feedback, information valuable to public relations professionals and their clients. Usage is clearly the quantitative stuff that tells all concerned if the VNR reached its intended audience, in what order of magnitude, and, implicitly, at what level of impact.

Reaching the General Public: Satellite Media Tours

Satellite Media Tours Defined

A satellite media tour is a series of preset interviews conducted via satellite between a spokesperson representing a product or service and radio and/or television station reporters across the country, or around the world. The spokesperson speaks from one location but is switched electronically in sequence from one station interview to another, conducting an on-air, one-on-one discussion either live (usually on noontime shows) or pretaped for use on a later news segment (Medialink, 1994, p. 4).

Satellite media tours are a cost-effective means of generating television exposure, accomplishing in hours what would require days or weeks on the road. More importantly, satellite media tours provide a subject or spokesperson with immediate access to radio or television reporters either during a crisis or to make a time-sensitive announcement (Medialink, 1994, p. 4).

Audiences and Outlets

The audience for a satellite media tour is the general public. As with VNRs, however, the electronic journalist at the local level acts as an intermediary between the interviewee and the general public; the radio and/or television journalist serves as an interlocutor between the person with a product or service to talk about and the radio and television audience.

K-mart: Celebrity Success

Some companies have had a positive long-term experience with this form of electronic public relations. For example, retailer K-mart is heavily into the use of electronic media for internal public relations, including a major business television network. All 2,338 K-mart stores in the United States are wired for television reception. The company produces about 30 to 40 hours of programming internally every month. In addition, K-mart produces investor meetings, video news releases—and satellite media tours. K-mart originates about 90 percent of these productions out of its Troy, Michigan studios, which include a full production facility with a satellite uplink. A significant number of satellite media tours also originate in New York.

Dennis Wigent, K-mart manager for internal electronic communications, says that his company has found this electronic public relations channel extremely effective when the person being showcased is a name, a celebrity, or someone very high in an organization. Satellite media tours are not terribly effective, he believes, for a soft message:

> *What we found with satellite media tours, for example, was that you get fewer usages as you would with a VNR, but you can take more time and it is a very targeted group you are getting because if someone has taken the time to book an interview for a satellite media tour, chances are they're going to use it. Whereas with a VNR you may get usages, but it may be 10 seconds or so.*

One of K-mart's early experiences with satellite media tours was when K-mart changed its logo in 1989-90. That announcement was made live, from a store, as an unveiling and a press conference. The event was broadcast live on satellite to any news organization that wanted to pick it up along with a video news release also distributed via satellite. In the afternoon the chairman of K-mart was available for a satellite media tour to talk to the business press about it. As a result of this coordination, Wigent estimates that they garnered over 12 million viewers.

K-mart's more recent current use of satellite media tours involves model and actress Kathy Ireland promoting a line of exercise wear and swimsuits. As part of a larger media tour, Ireland's satellite media tour booked nineteen stations a week in advance, some live and some taped. A generic interview was also taped and sent to stations requesting it.

K-mart also sponsors Indy cars. According to Wigent:

> *Around Indianapolis 500 time we get one of our drivers for a satellite media tour. This year we have Mario Andretti. It was his last year of racing. That was, again, one where we booked everything we could possibly book. Mario is such a major figure in racing. We had him, I think, for three hours. We did about fifteen interviews. With him you get some of the networks, such as ESPN and CNN.*

The extent to which a satellite media tour can be implemented, says Wigent, is "usually simply a matter of a time constraint. If you book an interview every ten minutes, about the most you can keep somebody is basically three hours. We've got Kathy here with four. Twenty stations is about the most we've gone to with interviews in a satellite media tour environment. What happens is that these tours get legs. They get some generic or stations will take down somebody else's interview and cut their people in." When K-mart gets feedback, he reports, they have as many as thirty to thirty-five stations using a satellite media tour where only fifteen to twenty actually did the interview.

National Stroke Association et al.: Targeting Audiences

A few years ago, a satellite media tour was developed for a program cosponsored by the National Stroke Association, the American College of Chest Physicians, the Alliance for Aging Research, and the American Association of Retired Persons—an alliance of nonprofit organizations.

As reported in Chapter 3, the program stemmed from a consensus report published by the ACCP that showed that people with a common heart ailment—arterial fibrillation (AF), an irregular heartbeat—were at a greater risk of a stroke than the general population. The consensus report stated these patients can greatly reduce that risk of stroke with anti-coagulation therapy.

Tony Esposito, group manager of Bozell Public Relations in Chicago, underscored the importance of celebrities in enhancing the success of this satellite media tour. He also pointed to the necessity of thinking through the tour's timing. "We were targeting stations in large urban areas with large African-American populations. And this obviously gave us a pretty good focus, especially in the top ten markets—the top twenty-five was our focus. We did pretty well. We had eight of the top ten markets, thirteen of the top fifteen, and twenty of the top twenty-five markets, with at least one top station in all of those markets."

The content and structure of the station-by-station interviews, says Esposito, "were generally live interviews, particularly on the East Coast for the noon newscasts. And that seems to be where stations like to use these type of things the most. They generally like to do them live and slate them for the noon newscast because they have time to fill. Some of them will take them live to tape and run them in their early afternoon news casts. Between the two of them we did about 3.5 million in audience."

The cost of a satellite media tour varies depending on the amount of time spent in the studio. Tony Esposito believes a three-hour satellite media tour can be produced for as little as $10,000.

Mobil Oil: On the Road with the Travel Guide

Much of Mobil Oil's public relations activities is done in video: video news releases, marketing tapes, point of sale tapes, corporate identification videos, television commercials, forums, how-to tapes, safety and training tapes.

Judy Lynn Prince, executive television producer with this Fortune 500 company, gave her perspective on the major advantages of the satellite media tour: "It's the intimacy. The immediacy. You can get your story out right now while it's hot. You don't have to take the time to travel to the market. If it's hot news, that's the way to do it. But if it's strictly a soft news, feature news media tour, you still need to go out and do the old fashion media tour."

Prince described the company's use of a satellite media tour to announce the Mobil Travel Guide:

> We do a satellite media tour on the Mobil Travel Guide Five Star Award Winners, and what it takes to be one, how you keep your five stars, what people are looking for when they go to a five star location, and the importance of the five stars. I've done the spokeswoman for the Mobil Travel Guide and the Five Star announcement. We also do a video news release for them. Based on that placement, very often we get requests from television stations in the various five star markets. There are thirty-six Five Star Award Winners, such as in Los Angeles, St. Louis, Miami, New York, Chicago. In those cities, a number of the television stations will ask the people who are doing the VNR placement if there is somebody they can talk to live. That has generated a satellite media tour. It's slightly different than your traditional satellite media tour.

Mobil Oil is organized to provide stations with almost immediate access to high-level corporate executives when the occasion arises. According to Prince: "When CNN wants to talk with our chairman, we have a videotaping room on our premises in Fairfax, Virginia. We take our senior executive down to the videotaping room, put the ear piece in his ear, turn on the camera, and have it all set up when Lou Dobbs or whoever from CNN's *Moneyline* or CNBC ask questions. Ideally, you ask us now for an interview and 20 minutes later we could be doing a television interview with a station."

Guidelines

Like all electronic public relations applications, effective satellite media tours adhere to certain guidelines: a compelling story, a celebrity presence, understanding the news director's needs, and a competent production facility.

A compelling story. For example, like the public service announcement and the video news release, a satellite media tour must have a compelling story to tell. On this aspect, K-mart's Dennis Wigent offered this advice for public relations practitioners contemplating a satellite media tour: "You've got to have a good story to start with. You start with the story and then choose the media. Don't try and force something into a medium that just doesn't work. I think that's number one—have a good story and make sure it fits the medium."

A celebrity presence. Bozell's Tony Esposito reiterated the advantage of having a celebrity as part of the satellite media tour event: "You're competing with a lot of other people for the time. You have to have something that's going to catch the viewer. Television means it has got to be fairly visual. You are much better off with somebody who is very visible, in terms of a celebrity or a known or would-be known, in our case physician. For example, most people would not be able to name the president of the National Stroke Association, but the title certainly carries a lot of weight."

The news director's needs. Esposito also pointed to the necessity of putting yourself in the broadcast journalist's shoes: "The biggest piece of advice on a satellite media tour I would give is you really have to think like a producer. You have to think of all of the potential angles and certainly any local angle you can apply to their particular market. You also have to do all of their leg work and all of their homework and a fair amount of hand-holding. The more you can give them the less they have to do, the better off you are and the higher your chances are of getting a placement that is used and perhaps even used multiple times."

A competent production facility. Choosing a competent television production facility out of which to originate the satellite media tour is a critical decision in the process. "Shop around," Tony Esposito advises.

> *Try and find a production company that specializes in this kind of electronic public relations application and hopefully has its own facilities. If you do this, you're going to get a much better price from them than if you hire an independent producer who goes and hires a studio and crew and everything else for you.*
>
> *You should also look for one that does a lot of satellite media tours, because again they have the relationships with stations, they've worked with them in the past, the producer at the station knows the individual or the organization and knows they're going to get a quality feed and knows that everything will be done for them, essentially.*

New York–based Medialink offers this advice to organizations considering satellite media tours:

1. Define your objective and select a topic with news producers in mind. A compelling news hook, a local angle, and a recognized spokesperson are keys to a successful satellite media tour.

2. Include B–roll of the story with the satellite media tour. Stations often package soundbites from the interview for later use on news programs. Visuals in the B–roll make the satellite media tour more attractive to stations.

3. Most satellite media tours are conducted from a studio set. However, an organization can conduct a satellite media tour from any location, making it more convenient for the spokesperson and increasing the visual impact of the tour.

4. Ensure the spokesperson is informed, media trained and attired appropriately for a television news appearance. The spokesperson should be briefed about how to balance the organization's message with the stations' news interest. (Medialink, 1994, p. 5)

Chapter 6

Reaching the Media

There are three core ways that public relations practitioners can reach print and/or electronic journalists via electronic media: a satellite news conference, an electronic media kit (EMK), or E-mail.

Satellite News Conferences Defined

A satellite news conference allows participants (i.e., interviewees) to interact with journalists, either by satellite or telephone transmission. Logistically, a satellite news conference originates from one location (either a studio, a public location, such as a hotel with television production facilities, or ad hoc at the organization's facility) and is transmitted—via satellite—to numerous locations in the region, nationally, even internationally.

Perhaps the most famous satellite news conference in recent history was the one Johnson & Johnson held shortly after the first deaths from Tylenol package tampering in September 1982. In this instance, top company executives gathered in a single location and met the media both at that location and at many other locations around the country (via satellite and telephone). It is one of the most effective satellite media conferences on record.

Audiences and Outlets

The primary audience for a satellite news conference is the media. Ultimately the information gleaned from a satellite news conference finds its way to the general public. But there is a difference between a satellite media tour and a satellite media conference. First, the satellite media tour may be delivered to the general public "live" as it happens, or the conversation between the spokesperson and the interviewer may be taped and broadcast later.

A satellite news conference, on the other hand, does not necessarily get on the air live or on tape. Rather, the satellite news conference is designed primarily for the benefit of the media—to provide information, to disseminate late-breaking news, and to offer journalists an opportunity to ask questions. There may be times when the satellite news conference is broadcast live, but more often than not this is not the case.

A Siemens Corporation News Conference: With Pictures

Siemens Corporation has had a very positive experience with satellite news conferences. In 1994, Siemens held a "State of the Business" media video conference in New York to announce the launching of some apprenticeship training programs in the United States. The announcement directly followed President Clinton's State of the Union Address emphasizing apprenticeship training and worker training. According to Kevin Kimball, Siemen's director of public relations (New York),

> We used that as part of the theme to one of the messages of our video conference....We also wired in, using a third-party vendor, journalists in those regions where we have a critical mass of companies or businesses as well as major trade publications, or where there's a critical mass of trade publications, such as Boston, Detroit, Chicago. All told, I think the video conference had fifty to sixty participants, some from here in New York watching it live, others plugged in by way of video conference.
>
> The spokesperson was the president of our company, Albert Hoser. He delivered a 5 to 10 minute opening statement that was open to questions and answers via two-way audio. [It lasted] about 45 minutes to an hour and involved trade media, business media, daily media, security analysts wanting research.
>
> At least five of our regional public relations offices in the United States were involved...Boca Raton, Atlanta, Chicago, Cupertino, and Iselin. I think there were some other key locations such as Boston, Los Angeles, wherever they could downlink.

In Kimball's view, the video conference was very effective. Although American journalists on the whole do not favor media conferences, in this case the conference was like an electronic editorial tour or media visit to their offices.

The conference was a convenient way for them to establish dialogue, not necessarily generating news or coming away with a story, but as a way of building eclectic relationships. The other measure was the frequency of contact thereafter.

A Siemens Corporation News Conference: Sans Pictures

Siemens also experimented with a satellite news conference without pictures. Its subsidiary company in Boca Raton, Florida, Siemens, Stromburg Carlson, announced a multimedia alliance with other large U.S. companies. Two partner companies were Scientific Atlanta, in Atlanta and Sun Micro Systems in California. Kimball describes the conference:

> We knew this would be a fairly significant event. Even though it's an alliance, it's an alliance to serve the global multimedia market. Multimedia is a buzz phrase right now—a buzz topic among journalists. Rather than just announcing it in a press release, we wanted to go the extra step, give it the extra impetus to really draw attention to some of our key messages.
>
> We gathered the spokespersons from the three companies, all senior level vice presidents, in a hotel in Orlando. We arranged a teleconference setup with a company called CompuTech that we designated our third-party vendor. Then we staggered interviews throughout the course of the day with the major business media.
>
> For instance, from 8–8:30 the AP guy had one-on-one interviews with the executives from the three companies. Then from 8:30–9 it was Bloomberg; 9–9:30, Reuters; 10:30–11:15, the Wall Street Journal; 11:15–12, two reporters from Business Week, and on and on—the Washington Post, Investors Business Daily, right up to 4 o'clock. All the business media and the key daily media were given one-on-one interview opportunities at the convenience of their desks and not in a competitive environment where there were other reporters asking questions.
>
> This was all audio. Then at 4 o'clock we brought in via teleconference about forty members of the trade media that serve the telephone, computer, and cable TV industries. They all participated in a one-on-many interview.
>
> For us it was a fairly efficient way of not only getting our executives but our alliance partner executives before key members of the media in a very cost-effective and time-efficient manner.

At the same time Siemens was holding a conference in Munich with the same alliance partners to connect with the international and global media. This conference was timed to coincide with the Florida event so that nobody scooped anybody else. Consequently, says Kimball, Siemens got good global coverage— stories in the *New York Times,* the *Wall Street Journal,* the *Washington Post,* and Reuters, as well as CNBC, CNN, and Bloomberg television.

Guidelines

The implicit guideline for all these case studies is planning, planning, planning. Clearly, while a satellite news conference that is organized in a hurry cannot be planned to the nth degree, preparation is paramount. Conversely, when there is ample time between a go-ahead for a satellite news conference and the actual event, there is no excuse for not adequately planning for a smooth execution.

Electronic Media Kits Defined

Electronic media kits (EMKs) can be defined in two ways: (1) the electronic transmittal of a still photo or graphic to television newsroom via satellite, providing stations with a visual that can enhance a news story; or (2) linear or multimedia video material that is included in the traditional media kit provided to the media at a news conference or by mail distribution.

New York–based West Glen Communications defines an electronic media kit as one that consists of "video footage (B–roll) accompanied by printed materials which television news directors can use to develop their own story. These are especially important aids for news directors at stations in major markets who may not accept independently produced video news releases" (West Glen Communications, 1994).

The EMK can also include a videocassette running anywhere from 8 to 10 minutes featuring random shots of visuals relating to the story, soundbites of spokespersons, and printed background information that provides more details about the various components of the story. These printed materials can include a spokesperson bio, product information, focus group or clinical trial information, reprints of published articles, brochures, a fact sheet, bibliography, and/or a list of organizations to contact for further information.

Audiences and Outlets

Clearly, the primary audience for an electronic media kit is print and electronic journalists. This audience can include journalists in print media (such newspapers, magazines, or wire services) or electronic media (radio, broadcast television, cable television). Electronic media kits and B–roll help get a story in front of the broadcast media by grabbing their attention.

Photographic Telefeed

New York–based Medialink offers a service that allows a public relations client to transmit a still photo or graphic to television newsrooms via satellite. This so-called *photographic telefeed* delivers the image of a notable magazine or book cover as an adjunct to a press release. An organization can transmit a new corporate logo, compact disc, videocassette cover, or a graph of a significant financial and economic statistic. This technique is a precursor to the use of Web sites on the Internet as a means of providing print and electronic journalists with visual material for their stories.

Using EMKs to Promote Travel

When the German National Soccer Team toured the United States in 1993, members of the club were enlisted to promote travel to Germany by the German National Tourism Board. Chicago–based KEF Media Associates shot soundbites at a news conference with news tape of popular German destinations. "The footage was edited and packaged into a colorful, self-contained binder," says KEF Media Associates president Kevin Foley. "The kit was delivered to more than 100 international news media at the World Cup Draw in December [1993] in Las Vegas and proved to be a hit" ("'Flexible' B–roll packages," 1994, p. 38).

Using EMKs to Promote Electronic Programming

Suzanne Rothenberg Communications, a New York–based public relations firm, uses EMKs in the form of television publicity for television programming, much of it children's and PBS programming. The company represents the underwriters, the production company, or the station in promoting the programming by garnering reviews and feature stories.

"There are a number of different ways I have occasion to use videos," says Suzanne Rothenberg, company president.

> *With television programming, first, we send out a video of the television program to the critics, so the critics can review them. But another function that comes up often with television programming is that television stations are interested in video about the television programs.*

For example, if we can create a behind-the-scenes video, a making-of video, then that video can be used in a number of different ways. It can be used in clips as B–roll when a star is interviewed on a television program. It is sometimes used in its entirety as an interstitial. Some cable networks (such as Arts & Entertainment) will use programming like that. Mainly it's programming that adds an extra dimension to the program that is going to be aired.

Rothenberg described how video material is used to reach the magazine or television media:

If you want to get your star on the so-called television media, it's like getting your star an interview in a magazine, except there's better exposure. If you want to get your star on Entertainment Tonight *or the* Today Show *or CNN* Showbiz Today—*if you tell them you have B–roll or video or a VNR about your subject or behind the scenes, they're more interested in you than if you just say "Can I bring my star to your studio for an interview?"*

Rothenberg commented on how strategies have changed in publicizing television programming:

It used to be you could have a media conference announcing a television show. Your star would be at the media conference and Entertainment Tonight *would cover it and then show it. They don't want to do that anymore. They don't want to cover media conferences or media events, but they do want to cover behind the scenes happenings.*

Right now we're doing record sessions for the Magic School Bus *second season, an animated show on PBS we represent. We took a video crew to a record session for Lily Tomlin, Tony Randall, and Rita Moreno, who are the voices for a particular show. The reason we did that was now at the beginning of next year, in the fall, I can call up* Entertainment Tonight *or* Extra *or CNN and say, "I have behind the scenes footage for the* Magic School Bus *with these stars in it." Most likely they're going to be interested in it and that will give us publicity for the show and saves the outlet, meaning* Entertainment Tonight *or the others from sending a crew any place.*

In the past we've done dramas, such as a Hallmark Hall of Fame drama on location someplace with a major star in it. We'll sometimes bring a video crew to do what we call "a making-of." The video crew will shoot the film as it's being filmed. The video will include interviews with the director, the producer, the stars and will come out looking like a minidocumentary about the show. It will be called The Making of...*whatever the show is that we're shooting.*

That could be of interest again to a program like Entertainment Tonight. *It could be of interest to a morning show, if it wants to introduce a star and show a little bit of what's going on, on the set. It could be of interest to perhaps a cable channel that may show the whole minidocumentary—a 5-minute piece—between programming or times when they need to fill things in.*

Rothenberg reflected that the budget range for these kinds of so-called electronic media kits that ranged from $10,000 to $30,000. "The costs could run $20,000 to $50,000 or even more for an elaborate production with more shoot locations, voiceovers, and special effects."

A CD-ROM (Interactive) Application: BMW

So far, we have looked at electronic media kits transmitted via satellite and the more traditional linear (noninteractive) form. One company, specifically BMW, has produced an interactive CD-ROM EMK about its products designed especially for members of the media.

Richard Brooks, corporate communications manager at BMW headquarters in New Jersey, explains:

> *We did it for a number of reasons. I don't know if you've ever seen a typical automotive company product media kit, but they typically weigh between 5 and 10 pounds and range from 75 to almost 500 pages of copy. At one of the larger U.S. auto shows a couple years ago, reporters were actually using shopping carts to haul around the media material they would pick up at the various media conferences. There had to be a better way to do it. In fact, there was.*
>
> *Five years ago, putting press materials on a floppy disk was all the rage. You usually put it in a choice of two software packages: one was DOS based and the other one was probably for Apple. We looked at floppy disks and thought that was a good idea. But that was three or four years ago. So what would be the next big step? We wanted to incorporate as many multimedia features as we could.*
>
> *CD-ROM has a lot of space. You have many multimedia features—full motion video, animation, lots of graphics, including high-resolution photography—that can be downloadable, plus pages and pages of text potential.*
>
> *With the help of a company in California, we went about designing a media kit that could take our entire product line, which at that time was eighteen models, with all the specifications and all the photography, and combine that with other elements we weren't able to combine before, including the marketing programs that would be used to support the products. That kind of integrated presentation could never be optimized before.*
>
> *In fact, what BMW was doing for the journalist was creating a context—a context in which we wanted our cars to appear—and from that aspect it's been very successful.*

According to Brooks, BMW's first CD-ROM, issued in March 1994, took about four months to produce. Today, he believes, that time could be compressed to as little as three months and possibly as little as two, depending on much new information they had to add: "Building the architecture of the disk was probably the most difficult and certainly the most expensive. The proprietary piece of software that drove the CD-ROM the vendor [i.e., the software developer] developed on its own."

Brooks reviewed the benefits of producing an electronic media kit in a CD-ROM format:

> *Many of the systems in our cars are very technical, very dynamic and they are very difficult to explain on a piece of paper. They are difficult to explain even when you're looking at a video. But if you combine the text with the video, then you've created an entirely new kind of image. We were able to do that very effectively with the CD-ROM.*
>
> *We were able to take technologies—like antilock brakes, for instance— which are something you can't really understand unless you experience it. If you show how it works using animation and video on the screen and then explain it with a voiceover or with downloadable text, then it becomes much more user friendly. There's probably a total of an hour on the CD-ROM with the various clips. We put an entire 20-minute infomercial on the disk.*

As a direct result of response to the first, BMW is already at work on a second CD-ROM and planned three for 1995:

> *We're on the second disk. The original printing was supposed to be 1,000 and they ended printing 2,500 because of demand. The automotive industry—automotive journalists may be unique in this regard—has many freelancers who are either very into it or not into it at all. You capture the ones who are very into it and you sometimes lose the ones who aren't. There's still a bit of missionary work involved at BMW. Eventually this will become at least part of a standard.*

Many journalists requested that other colleagues be sent the BMW CD-ROM as well. Brooks believes it provides a better archive mechanism than print or video EMKs. "People don't have the space to store ten thousand media kits," he says, "especially in a modern newsroom, where there's virtually no room for anything except people and machines."

The most reassuring feedback, he reports, was that this media kit reflected BMW's image—the high-tech, high-touch, user-friendly, easily understandable but high-performance car that the times demand.

> *I think we got some very positive comments from one of the bureau chiefs from the Associated Press who predicted that this would become one of the standards*

in automotive journalism in the coming years. The reason? The biggest one was that it captured all the information. What he was referring specifically to was the way it treated statistics. One of the biggest necessary evils are these pages and pages of specifications that basically don't change from model to model and year to year—they remain constant. But all those things are easily captured and they can be literally downloaded into an article or some other kind of journalistic thing from the CD-ROM.

Analyzing the costs involved, Brooks predicted a decrease by about 20 percent for each issue. BMW invested $200,000 in the initial architecture and hopes to realize the savings in subsequent disks. "Frankly," Brooks says, "I don't know if I can call it savings because the preproduction costs are constant unless you get to a certain breakeven point. We'll come to a point where we'll be manufacturing enough to make the savings realized, but we haven't reached that point yet."

Brooks suggested that CD-ROM versions of media kits will have an impact on print counterparts: "I think the way that it is delivered will change. I think you will always be able to get a press release on paper. But certainly we were looking to get into other areas—including on-line systems where you would dial a number or access a home page on the Internet (we don't have one yet), where you would be able to access sales for 1994 and things like that. Then you would get a press release faxed back to you or in whatever format you wanted it in—an E-mail message or something like that."

When asked if he saw other companies moving into CD-ROM for their electronic media kits in the next five years, Brooks replied: "Yes. I don't think it's going to be quick. I think we're going to have the lead for a couple of years. I think there's definitely a need for it in journalism. But I think car companies are waiting to see if consumer demand develops for this kind of packaging, because a lot of the information is transferable. We're looking at the same thing, except that we went with the media kit first and the consumer application second."

The new medium, he believes, will alter marketing content: "It depends on if you're talking to a PR guy or a marketing guy. The marketing guy thinks there has to be a large entertainment quotient. [But] all of our surveys for consumers say that a lot of the time all they want is no-nonsense information."

Producing the EMK: Some Guidelines

A great deal has been written about how to produce good, effective television programming. It won't be repeated here.

The elements that go into an effective electronic media kit, however, very much parallel those of the television commercial.

The EMK must convey information concisely. The audience, after all, for an EMK is a journalist who does not have leisure time to spend. At least it should be the public relations professional's assumption at all times that an audience doesn't have any time to waste. Thus, every second of the EMK, whether in linear or interactive form, should have some informational meaning.

The EMK must convince a journalist to take action at some future point—namely, to use some of the information in a story.

The production team brought together to produce the EMK should include, at the very least, a qualified copywriter, art director, producer, and director. Together they can create a program with the right combination of production elements.

The copywriter and the art director play key roles in the development of the script. Inherently, the EMK should be designed to convey information about the product or service as succinctly and visually as possible. The copywriter and art director must develop an immediately accessible visual and/or aural theme.

The visual and aural theme should pervade the entire EMK. It should be immediately understandable. If it takes more than a few seconds for everyone to understand the central idea of the program, another one should be found. The central idea of the program is the way to the video's success: the program's script will grow out of it; all casting, direction, music selection, voiceover and graphic treatment will be guided by it.

An EMK should be highly graphic. Stylistically, it should be understood by a viewer watching the program at a distance with or without the soundtrack. The visual style of the program must be highly telegraphic. The pictures must be designed so that even if the sound were turned off (which has been known to happen), the visual elements can tell the story independently of the sound track.

An EMK should be entertaining as well as informative. It should stand on its own in any context, and its quality should also be immediately recognizable. In the final analysis, the true test of an EMK's quality is the immediate reaction it provokes. Journalists should feel persuaded to seek more information about the product or service.

Do your homework before starting to shoot. This rule more than suggests that the content of an EMK be carefully scrutinized, analyzed, sorted out, and tested before a script is created and production begins. Various parties should become involved. First, of course, is the client or department that wants to produce the EMK. Second is a producer who has the knowledge and skills to convert content and objectives into an effective EMK whether using internal or external production resources, the third element in the creation of the EMK.

Choose a production style appropriate to the audience and environment in which the EMK will be shown. The audiences for an EMK are external to the corporation. More than any other vehicle, this kind of programming will be compared with the techniques and quality of commercial television and theatrical film production.

Knowing the environment the EMK will be viewed in and its audience could have a major impact on the style of the EMK. For example, if it is designed for a small journalism audience, the EMK could contain a personalized trailer by a product manager, depending on the customer involved. The rest of the EMK could use a variety of production techniques, including documentary, dramatizations and demonstrations, and so on, depending on the content to be conveyed.

Measure the effectiveness of the EMK. It is important to know if the EMK succeeded or failed, and why. After all, EMKs would not be produced were it not for the assumption that they help inform journalists. It is imperative to define some baseline against which to measure the EMK's effectiveness. Journalists can provide this feedback. Of course, the major way of gauging feedback is increased number of stories on the organization's product or service or an increase in the quality of story placement.

E-Mail, the Internet, and Journalists

Using on-line services or the Internet for distributing electronic news releases or contacting editors and journalists is increasingly becoming a common daily event for public relations practitioners.

Christina O'Connell has been using both commercial services and the Internet for public relations work for about seven years. She has found two general categories of effective work on the Internet: "E-mail and file transfers are often the handiest means for getting releases and backgrounders to editors—not only fast, but so much simpler to use—editors can cut and paste quotes into their stories directly from E-mail. And often editors who are hard to reach via phone are responsive to E-mail, but, as always, check whether the editor in question likes to work this way" (O'Connell, Internet communique, October 31, 1994).

Kate Caldwell, who does media relations work for Colorado State University, offered several examples of how she has used the Internet for media relations in an academic setting:

> *Profnet provides me with access to media around the world. By responding to desperate reporters specific needs for sources, I can nourish relationships that can lead to placement of future stories.*
>
> *ListServers, such as SPJ On-Line and Journet, provide me with an opportunity to build working relationships with media based on intellectual respect, first, and then professional respect. Using the Internet, I have been able to place*

stories in the New York Times, *on ABC's 20/20 newsmagazine, CNN and the Discovery [cable] Channel, many international magazines, and a wide variety of regional media. These placements would not have been possible without the relationships established through the Internet. (Caldwell, Internet communique, November 3, 1994)*

Tech Image is a midwestern company that promotes high-tech companies and groups, including the Interactive Multimedia Association. Michael Nikolich, president of Tech Image, provided an example of using the Internet for an interactive press conference or on-line press conference somewhat akin to a satellite press conference:

Some of the tools you can use within your website on the Internet is interactive press conferences. The same thing you can do on CompuServe and America Online. In the past you had to gather people into a room to announce a new product or service. This is a way to do it in a digital environment. They seem to be pretty effective.

This really is a way to work off the keyboards where you can direct questions to a CEO. There are press conferences going on everyday. A lot of bands, like the Rolling Stones, have done several interactive press conferences. In fact, the Stones are doing a concert tour that they're going to be broadcasting live via the Internet to people who have access to the Net and they're going to have to have an engine and a piece of software to be able to translate the sound, and a lot of storage. You're also going to have to have a very wide band width. You're going to probably need an ISDN line so that you can actually hear the thing in real time.

The relationship between public relations companies and journalists is also evolving as a result of the Internet and on-line services. Says Nikolich: "One of the things we won't do is bombard people with press releases via the Internet, unless they say to us, 'This is how we want to get it. We don't want a pile of paper coming in anymore. We want to get our piles digitally.' At that point we add them to our media list and maybe they're getting things via the Internet, they're getting things by MCI Mail, by CompuServe, America Online, Prodigy, whatever flavor they want. Now we have a means to do that."

Nikolich describes his company's experience working with a reporter on a story for one of their clients. "We tried to talk to him several times and he was too busy. We tried every conceivable means to link him up with our client. We finally looked up his America Online address and directed things to him that way. He sent us back the nicest note saying he applauds us for our aggressiveness without being obnoxious and that's the way he prefers to correspond with us.

Ever since then, we have a regular dialogue with him now. It's all done electronically. He has to log on to America Online to get it [information], but people do that regularly."

Judy Lynn Prince, executive television producer at Mobil Oil, made it clear that the use of on-line services, particularly for E-mail contact with journalists, is imperative: "I'd hate to be without E-mail. It's changed communication completely. The Internet as it keeps growing will also change the quickness that people can get their news, their information. We send out our press releases by E-mail. We have not been sending out paper news releases for five, six years. It works as well as the old-fashioned paper press release used to work. But that's the way the journalists want to receive it."

When asked why she thought they want to receive it like that, Prince replied:

> *Because that's the way they're writing. It's fitting into their way of doing business. If we want to communicate with them, we have to do it the way their job is handled. We need them as much as they need us, but it's better if we do it their way.*
>
> *And we do it with absolutely every press release we send out. You send them out via PR News Wire or Business News Wire and they just automatically go E-mail. There are several other services. You're getting to the* Wall Street Journal, *Dow Jones, Bloomberg Financial Services. You can tell just by the phone calls that come back within 10 minutes of sending it that they have received it.*
>
> *With the old-fashioned way of mailing out press releases, you felt the need to call and say, "Did you get it? Did you get it?" They don't want to be bothered with phone calls. They got it. You know they got it. They may not want it, they may not use it, they may not care about it, but you know they got it. People read E-mail, people don't read junk mail. That's not to say there's not a lot of junk mail on E-mail.*

As with PSAs and VNRs, success with editors and journalists via E-mail requires public relations practitioners to look before they leap: You must contact the editor or journalist in advance to make sure that E-mail is the way they want to receive the material. Take nothing for granted. The adoption of new media takes time. Some journalists will only accept material via E-mail. Some refuse to do so. And there are lots of people still in transition.

Chapter 7

Reaching Community and Government Audiences

Audiences and Outlets

While PSAs, VNRs, and satellite media tours can effectively reach the general public, and targeting the print and electronic media can effectively garner time and space to tell a client's product or service story, public relations practitioners also have an opportunity to reach community groups and government bodies with electronic media.

These audiences might include:

local, state, regional, federal, and international government officials (legislative, regulatory, executive, judicial)

community leaders

chambers of commerce

neighborhood coalitions

community organizations

professional societies

trade associations

academic faculty and staff, trustees, and students

special interest groups (environmentalists, the handicapped or disabled, minorities, think tanks, consumer groups, health groups, senior citizens, religious organizations)

Organizations and public relations practitioners can communicate to community groups and government organizations through a variety of electronic media:

1. Sponsored linear video programs distributed to educational institutions

2. Linear video programs shown to community groups and government organizations for either large-group, small-group, or one-on-one presentations

3. Linear and interactive video programs in public exhibit environments

4. Videoconferences to educational and medical institutions

5. Telecommunications (FAX, 800/900 numbers) to government and community groups

Sponsored Videos

In 1937, Western Electric founded a company to introduce sound-on-film technology for the classroom. That company was called the Modern Talking Picture Service ("Modern Talking Pictures," 1994). Today, Modern Talking Pictures is a major distributor of sponsored videos to the education market.

Ed Swanson, executive vice president of Video Placement Worldwide, another major distributor of sponsored videos, says: "Sponsored visual communication is probably one of the oldest forms of marketing/public relations around. From the first days of sound-on-film in the late 1920s, companies like Ford, Caterpillar, John Deere, International Harvester, and Sears produced 20 to 60-minute long movies that they would take out and show to target community groups.

> *In the late 30s Sears produced films in cooperation with 4H on how to make gardens grow. Chrysler showed films of their cars being driven across Africa and Australia. Of course the message there was, 'It takes a-hell-of-a-car to do things like this.' Companies would send out an operator and a projector to a co-op meeting and show the film on the side of a barn. They would show it against a sheet in a church basement. Film was a novelty that drew people together, and companies knew it.*

According to Swanson, World War II gave the sponsored film its impetus, turning it from a direct one-on-one marketing, public relations or promotional vehicle to a mass medium of public relations communications: "I'm talking about the sponsored 16mm film. During World War II, 16mm film came into its own when all schools, communities, and churches became equipped with 16mm projectors for training and information purposes. This meant that corporations could now provide their film-based messages directly to these target audiences which represented a demographic profile which could be isolated."

Today, according to the *Wall Street Journal*, "64,000 of the 110,000 public and private schools in the U.S. have shown at least one of (Modern Talking Pictures) 3,600 titles from 120 corporations to students over the last year and a half" (Ryan, 1994). Clearly, sponsored videos provide an opportunity for an organization to state its case in an educational setting which teachers and college instructors have access to a pool of visual material to draw from to supplement textual material. Says Ed Swanson,

> *Sponsored video communication is a medium widely used in public relations. However, it's not an option public relations practitioners think of immediately when they are looking to reach out to targeted audiences.*
>
> *A sponsored video can capture and hold an audience—take them from beginning to end in a logical, consistent manner time after time. Video takes people places they can't go. It shows them things they normally can't see—all the way from inside the human body to a nuclear power plant.*
>
> *At one time in my career, my company was dealing with over 600 different public relations accounts, each of which had a motion picure that would reach anywhere from 5,000 to 10,000 U.S. schools per year, and would be on 300 to 400 television stations. With the changeover to video, a good news/bad news situation developed.*
>
> *The good news is that video makes it possible for corporations to communicate visually in more places than ever before. That's never going to turn around and go the other way. Whether the format is video, CD-ROM, a hologram, or something yet to be invented, in fifteen years you'll still be communicating visually.*
>
> *The bad news is that there is a perception that video is inexpensive and easy to do. Therefore, the overall quality of the materials being produced is not great from a filmmaker's perspective. That seems to be correcting itself, but it has taken a long time. Communicators have practically lost sight of the fact that McLuhan was correct—the medium is the message—particularly today with a sophisticated, ususually perceptive younger generation. The visual interest and style of your video says just as much about who you are, how you think, and how progressive and aggressive your company is as the informaltion you wish to convey.*

Regardless of the format, Swanson believes—film, VHS, CD-ROM, or some other form of computer-driven interactive video—there is still no better way to reach the youth market and the business-to-business market. Using video to attract attention to supporting print is a powerful combination.

Linear Videos

Rarely does any organization, for-profit or nonprofit, lack access to at least one VHS videocassette player. The distribution opportunity is clear: if an organization has a product or service story to tell and this story can be effectively visualized, the public relations practitioner must have a VCR to show it on.

In the following sections we will examine several examples of linear video programs that have been successfully used for community public relations purposes. *No Day at the Beach,* produced by the Metro Toronto Community Services, deals with the impact of AIDS on the community. *Children Are Too Young to Die* was produced by the New York City Housing Authority to help reduce the incidence of children playing in elevators and dying. *Discover Your Own Song* concerns drug problems in suburban and rural areas in the South.

No Day at the Beach

Video is an effective medium for communicating the impact of social problems. *No Day at the Beach,* a 14-minute award-winning video on AIDS produced by Metro Toronto Community Services, is just such a program. Paul Downey, manager of the Media and Communications Unit for Metro Toronto Community Services (Canada), explains the purpose of *No Day at the Beach* as an attempt to "sensitize people to how it feels to have AIDS. It's not only a fatal disease, but carries a lot of stigma with it. We wanted to dispel the stereotype that this is a gay disease or that only gays are getting it. An actress was used in the program because a lot of people who are hemophiliacs have gotten AIDS through blood transfusions. We didn't want to make the video homophobic or just present drug users and get involved with a lot of issues that weren't necessarily relevant to the subject."

Toronto was apparently the first municipality in North America to come up with an employee policy on AIDS, and the video was created as part of that policy. In 1986, a worker gave mouth-to-mouth resuscitation to a person whom he thought had AIDS. Other workers were upset about this incident and there was a work stoppage. The problem was sorted out through an educational process (bringing in medical opinions and doctors). The video was created to educate people about the policy in conjunction with half-day and three-day seminars (adapted from Marlow, 1992). The program—distributed to 30,000 government and agency employees in the Toronto metropolitan area—has been shown in conjunction with a training tape and the seminars. Says Downey: "*No Day at the Beach* is about how it feels to get AIDS: How are you going to tell your mother? How are you going to tell the people at work? When you're out from work for a long period of time, there is a point where you have to explain to somebody what's going on and that means communicating confidential information."

Children Are Too Young to Die

The New York City Housing Authority was troubled by children who either died or were injured while playing in elevators. They wanted to produce a film to help reduce the problem. According to producer/director Marc Cerutti "There have been no deaths from kids playing in elevators since *Children Are Too Young to Die* came out. It has had a major effect. The program is based on a recreation of an actual event: a kid plays on top of an elevator, gets his arm cut off, people try to save him, the cops go to the mother. A little later the program goes into things kids shouldn't do, like holding an elevator door open, trying to force the door, and sticking one's head through the window of the elevator door."

Cerutti pointed out that the program idea came from Detective Sgt. Peter Cestare of the Elevator Vandalism Squad. "He is the one who has to go to the parents and say, 'Your kid is hurt.' He's the one who gets the call in the middle of the night when a kid gets hurt and has to go and get the kid out of the shaft. He was the one who said, 'We need some education on this, I've seen too many kids get killed.'"

The program has been so successful, Cerutti believes, because at the heart of it are very realistic, dramatic situations: "I think the problem is something people can relate to immediately. To someone not aware of the problem, the program is interesting in and of itself because of the compelling execution and filmatic style. A lot of the people in the program are real people, real cops, so it has that 'real' feel" (from Marlow, 1994).

Discover Your Own Song

Through research, the producers of *Discover Your Own Song* found that the suburbs as well as rural areas in the South were having drug problems. Statistics showed that there was a bigger problem in the rural areas than even in the urban areas.

According to producer Don Corley,

The vice president of South Central Bell Corporate Affairs, Howard Palmes, wanted to do something about the drug culture within the schools. We discovered there are thousands of drugs tapes. However, from the research we also found a new process going on in the schools that could help change the drug culture—so-called "peer listening" and "peer counseling." This is something new in the schools, but we felt it would not be met with open arms by school administrations.

This process actually makes the kids the listeners. They listen to the other kids problems, although they are not actually counseling them. That might make it look like the kids were in control too much. We didn't find any tape that dealt with the drug problem in quite this way, so we developed a story line showing what peer counseling and peer listening could do in the school system. And this was before Beverly Hills 90210.

The program is set up as a drama, Corley explains. One of the characters—on the teetering point of good or bad behavior—has to make a choice.

Through a series of events he meets people in a peer listening group that he is supposed to make a video of for a class assignment. Because of the conflicts he runs through we see him being pulled in different directions. Said Corley, "This character is into making rock videos. It is his hobby, his career. He has his own band and the band image is pulling him both ways. He is a fifteen year old directed by push-pull on both sides. He has an argument with his mom and goes through all the typical things a fifteen year old goes through. When the video ends, we don't know exactly which direction he will actually go in, although we have a good feeling that he'll choose the right way. In this case, the kids in the audience can relate and watch it through. It is very soap opera-ish in style. It is realistic for the kids."

Producer Corley pointed out that it wasn't any one thing that made the program a winner: "The theme, the work that went into it, the direction that we wanted to go in, the music, the sound effects," he lists. "We tried to keep the audience in mind. It was very realistic. Up and down the line we tried to create a class operation. Script conferences went on and on between Atlanta and Birmingham. Coproducer Cindy Kirkpatrick got on the phone with a teenage consultant. We would go back on little nuances and so on. I had a TV monitor on location with me. I had worked with teens for about twenty years. So as the teens were doing different things, I would speak over the director's shoulder to suggest how other teens might work and how the other boys might work with each other" (adapted from Marlow, 1994).

Public Exhibits

Very much in keeping with John Naisbitt's "high tech/high touch," as we have increased our reliance on so-called high technology in our lives, our participation in public events has also increased. Witness the increase in people attending sporting events (despite a neverending stream of such event programming on radio and television), traveling to places they have seen on television or heard about on the radio, and business travel to professional meetings and trade shows (despite the increasing availability of teleconferencing facilities). There is apparently also a trend towards the rebirth of malls where people congregate not only to shop but also to visit with each other. All these public environments (sports stadiums, bus and railroad stations, airports, malls, trade shows) present a public relations opportunity.

According to figures supplied by the Trade Show Bureau (Denver, Colorado), in 1994 there were 4,316 trade shows in the United States. This compares to 3,289 in 1989, or a 31 percent increase in five years. Forty-four percent of these shows are open to the trade only, 40 percent are open to the trade and the public, and 11 percent are open to the public only. From another perspective, the average number of attendees at a trade show is 9,977 compared to 54,462 at a consumer show (Trade Show Bureau, 1994, pp. 14, 16).

Museum and trade show exhibitry is an enormous industry in the United States. Museums and public exhibits are thus a natural environment for an organization to convey a community-oriented message. However, according to various industry groups (including the Trade Show Bureau, the Association of American Museums, the American Society of Association Exhibits, and several others), no one knows for certain what the size of the business is in the United States in terms of dollar volume. There are no numbers for the use of electronic technologies, although even casual observation and anecdotal evidence clearly lead to the conclusion that electrovisual technologies—such as linear videotape, multiscreen video (as in videowalls), interactive videodisc, multimedia, and virtual reality—are increasingly being used as part of public exhibits. The Internet, too—particularly the World Wide Web—will become an integral part of a museum's means of information dissemination.

Clearly, museums and public exhibits sponsored by for-profit and not-for-profit organizations also account for a major public relations opportunity. According to the American Association of Museums, there are approximately 8,000 museums in the United States, many of which contain exhibits that are interactive in nature.

The following are three examples of public exhibits utilizing electrovisual technologies. "Energy Update 2001" is an example of the successful use of electronic media by a regional utility to support its "energy diversity" message; the case of Motorola demonstrates how an electronics manufacturer utilized interactive electronic media to educate the public about science in support of its electronic technology orientation; and the "American Abstraction 1930–1945" exhibit shows how a major public museum can effectively use electronic media to support the message of an art exhibit.

"Energy Update 2001": Behind the Scenes

The use of and need for energy has been increasing in the United States and throughout the world. Major gains have been made in using energy more efficiently, and these improvements in efficiency have helped by the continuing electrification of our society. In fact, one of the clearest trends in all industrialized nations is the growing reliance on electric power. To provide the general public with an overview of what an "all-electric" life might be like in the next century, American Electric Power created "Energy Update 2001," the simulation of a news broadcast in the year 2001. This exhibit was installed in Theater I of American Electric Power's three-theater Cook Energy Information Center in Bridgman, Michigan.

In this exhibit an audience of seventy people are seated in a theaterlike setting and are brought up to date on energy resources in the year 2001 in 20 minutes by Energy Update's two android news anchors: Jared and Velva. At the beginning of the presentation, even before the house lights come down, the audience hears the program director talking with the engineer in charge of the satellite feeds, the program announcer, and one of the on-location reporters. As they settle into their seats, they are integrated into the exhibit by appearing on the three Mitsubishi 35-inch monitors of the exhibit as a live Panasonic camera pans them just prior to showtime. During the program the simulated broadcast goes live on location, via satellite, to Alaska, California, the Midwest, and the East to see and hear reports on our natural resources (geothermal, hydro, solar, wind, oil, natural gas, coal, and nuclear), how we need to conserve them, and the important role these resources will play in our energy future.

The audience also visits (via satellite) a family of the future right in their own computer-driven "Smart House." Here the audience learns what a Smart House is and how it works; how the parents can remotely control the internationally linked flat-screen wall TV, entertainment systems, the thermostat, the phone, power, security systems, and the videotext; the audience also views and hears the features and benefits of the family's electric car.

The edited videotapes were transferred to optical videodiscs by 3M. The end result is the creation of a simulated "live" program going out over the airwaves to a national viewing audience. The "theater" audience "sees" what the program director sees via the two "preview" monitors. All three screens work in perfect synchrony.

"Energy Update 2001" serves two purposes. First, it updates Cook Energy Information Center visitors to the uses of energy (in the year 2001), the potential of energy resources in the future, and the importance of conserving energy today for tomorrow. Second, it tells visitors what kind of energy resources will be available in the year 2001 (and beyond) and what their applications will be ("Energy Update 2001: Behind the Scenes," 1991).

Motorola: The Simulated Exploration of Electronic Knowledge

The audience for Motorola's public exhibit includes students and Motorola employees who visit the Motorola Electronics Museum in Schaumburg, Illinois to get a sense of what the company does. The museum is open by appointment, and Motorola uses it very aggressively as an educational resource on the kinds of technology at the core of its business. The exhibit's objective, therefore, is to provide information on basic concepts of electronics.

According to Glenn Corey of the Chedd-Angier Production Company, "The basic concepts of electronics are a dry subject. It was our responsibility to try to find a way to make it something that people would be engaged by and motivate visitors to the museum to spend 10, 15, or 20 minutes involved with the various activities in the museum. Our goal was to deliver accurate technical information as engagingly as possible. The content deals with the basic laws of electronics, magnetism, and information about individual and electronic components. The exhibit is an electronics textbook presented with the opportunity for each individual to explore under his or her own steam."

The physical environment visitors encounter at the exhibit is important in engaging their interest. Says Corey:

> The environment of the basic interface is a cube. Each face of the cube is activated through a touch screen. It takes you into a different set of experiences related to a particular aspect of electronics. Because we are working out of a hypermedia setting, there are extra things we can do with the cube. The cube has fifteen sides. There are five presentations on three sides of a cube.
>
> Basically a chapter of the electronics textbook is included in the contents, but we wanted to make sure that there would never be just text versions of the particular laws of physics. We always wanted people to play and find out information rather than delivering a pre-prepared package. At the Motorola museum there are five of those workstations set up in an informal area. When Motorola brings in students, you set them up at a machine and let them go at it.

Corey explained how the material was organized:

> There is about 25 minutes of video and linear graphic material laid down on the disc. I forget the actual number of megs of the video graphic overlays, but it was a gigantic piece of work—the biggest of its kind, I think it is fair to say. We have tons of material, particularly graphic material that had to be compressed and decompressed to make it work. The exhibit basically runs on a souped-up Mac platform. There were some special things that we did to increase memory and storage, but nothing outrageous."
>
> In the exhibit we actually give the visitor the opportunity to rub a video balloon. Activity goes on the touch screen. You touch more and more vigorously, and graphically a charge builds up on the balloon corresponding to the amount of rubbing done on the balloon either attracted or repelled. Because we had fifteen of these cubes, they all had to be filled with activity which were similarly unusual and technically difficult to create.

Corey believes that interactivity is vital to the experience. The interactive material gives visitors control over what they see and how they see it, via a touch-screen menu (adapted from Marlow, 1994).

"American Abstraction 1930–1945: The Artists Speak"
The Smithsonian attracts people from all over the United States and the world. The prime visitors for the traveling exhibit for the National Museum of American Art located within the Smithsonian are well-educated people interested in the arts in general who may or may not have knowledge about abstract art.

The interactive video "American Abstraction 1930–1945: The Artists Speak" was developed for use in conjunction with an exhibit on American abstract art held at the National Museum of American Arts that also traveled to museums in many other cities. Its objective was to introduce to museum visitors in a very personal way five of the artists represented at the exhibition, in order to demystify abstract art for visitors and to further interest in the exhibition.

According to Lee Cioffi, producer/manager of the video: "The curator, Virginia Mecklenburg, thought it would be really useful to have an interactive video playing right in the exhibition space itself so that visitors who came in to see the exhibition would also be able to use the interactive video right there. What we found is that people would use the interactive video and then go back in the exhibition to look for those particular works and compare them to others. It was provocative in that way."

Producer Cioffi also described how the material was structured: "The video itself was divided in a number of ways. It had portraits of the five artists. We went to each artist's home and/or studio and did an interview. We also filmed them working so we could see the process. Each artist had quite a record of their work going way back to the 1930s. So as a third part of the taping experience, we brought out paintings or sculptures from each of the decades from the 1930s right on up through that year. Then we had them speak about each piece as we taped it. It was very interesting because their styles have evolved and it was a nice talking point for them to trace their lives while referencing their art."

Visitors who used the program were able to choose from the main menu listing the five artists and another section called "The Times," for a total of six submenus. Under each artist in the submenu were various themes they spoke on, a segment showing the artist at work, or his or her portfolio. So the user was able to interactively slelect a portion of the program at will. Under the separate section called "The Times," each artist spoke about the press, politics, and war from the 1930s to the mid-1940s as well as the American Abstract Group, which they were all part of.

Cioffi described the software and hardware and the mechanics of producing the interactive videodisc presentation:

> *The exhibit runs on an IBM PS 2 model 30 computer with IBM info Windows and a Pioneer disc player. It uses a level III touch screen interactive program. Because it is interactive, it is not intended, of course, to be seen in a linear way. Actually there was almost a full 30 minutes of video on the disc and we purposely designed it so that it would be video intensive. In other words, the underlying program design is very simple, just one main menu and six sub menus. The point was to have as much motion footage as possible, showing the artist at work and hearing them speak about their lives.*
>
> *The curator…actually watched a lot of people using [the exhibit] and she determined that the average user time was probably about 15 minutes. There were a number of people who not only went through the whole program, but actually would come back into the exhibition at their lunch hour several weeks running, use it again and go around and look at the exhibition.*

In contrast to other interactive programs at the Smithsonian that are intended to deliver quick information, Cioffi's program had a longer user time.

Videoconferencing

As we have seen in Chapter 2, the use of satellite and teleconferencing technology has grown dramatically in the last several years. Both for-profit and nonprofit organizations are using the technology for a variety of internal and external public relations purposes. One example of using teleconferencing for community relations purposes is provided by the National Alliance for the Mentally Ill (NAMI).

The National Alliance for the Mentally Ill (NAMI)

NAMI is a national grassroots family and consumer support and education organization built for education advocacy surrounding serious mental illnesses. Most of its members either have a severe mental illness or are the relative of someone with a serious mental illness. These are long-term, debilitating illnesses that impair function and many of the people afflicted with them end up on the street or in prison because the service delivery system is inadequate. Because NAMI has 1,100 affiliates and 140,000 members nationwide, its community education is centered around what these serious mental illnesses are and what NAMI can offer people dealing with these disorders in their lives.

Farrell Fitch, director of communications for NAMI, describes how the organization employs satellite technology to reach people in the educational community:

> *Because we are nonprofit, we do not have a very sophisticated program of electronic media, unfortunately. But we have done three interactive video teleconferences for college campuses in which we engaged campuses with a program based in Washington with experts and people who suffer from severe disorders. The second part of the program had incoming questions from campuses all over the country. Each conference lasted 2 hours with a set piece of 45 minutes.*
>
> *The first Conference reached 175 campuses; the others drew between 100 and 175 campuses each time. Campuses, particularly community colleges, were very anxious for this program because it provided a resource that they couldn't otherwise afford. And basic information about these disorders is very hard to come by if one lives outside of a major metropolitan area. We had as coproducers the National Institute of Mental Health, so we had the leading experts on depressive illness. We had the director of the National Institute of Mental Health as a panelist. We also had young people who had experienced depressive illness, who could talk about what symptoms they displayed while they were in college. We always try to pair doctors and patients, whom we call consumers, so that people will see the real impact of these disorders. So while you can watch all kinds of brain pictures and get lists of symptoms, it makes a big difference when somebody who has had the disorder is talking about it.*

Farrell described the advantage of using videoconferencing technology to reach audiences:

> *This interactive video provided us an opportunity to reach campuses all across America, Alaska, Bermuda, Canada, with a consistent science-based message. One of the biggest problems in the mental illness field is that the information is not always science based and it is not always consistent. And this afforded us a terrific opportunity to get the leaders in the field to discuss a very common disorder—depressive illness—minus the myths and mythology.*
>
> *We also produced and distributed a 17-minute video for high school students called* Straight Talk about Mental Illness. *I hope we can continue to use a combination of these two techniques increasingly because I think they are very effective. Since NAMI's major goal is to get science-based information into the hands of people who need it, this is one sure way to do it. The video for high schools has received very positive feedback and it's been seen by over 200,000 kids. The one sure way to get science-based information out is through electronic media. It is not then subject to interpretation; it is delivered right into the hands of the people who need it.*

Knowledge transfer is a big problem in this field. There is so much basic and important research on these brain disorders being done at research centers all over the country which never reaches treating physicians or families and people effected. One of our biggest jobs is to make sure that when people and/or families of consumers go into a physician's office, they are better prepared than the physician—that they've got the best, latest, most current information. I certainly am an evangelist on these interactive video teleconferences because there is such a small group of scientists working in this area.

Reaching Out: Via the Telephone

There are various other electronic means of communicating with people in the community and government organizations—by using the telephone.

Fax on Demand

According to the Center for Strategic Communications—a tax-exempt nonprofit organization based in New York City that informs and educates nonprofit managers about how to take advantage of the evolving communications environment and extend limited resources through strategic communications planning—callers using fax on demand simply enter their fax number and documents are sent automatically to their fax machine (CSC, May/June 1994, p. 1).

With fax on demand:

- Individuals call the fax on demand number and listen to an audio message that asks them to input a document number.
- Callers input the document numbers they wish to receive.
- After callers enter and verify their fax number, the documents are sent automatically.

The Center for Strategic Communications points out that fax on demand is like a database. Information is timely because the system delivers it immediately upon request and documents can be updated as soon as they are revised. Its ease of use is a result of near-universal access via phone and fax technology that people are comfortable using. To update, staff members can simply fax documents into the system from one or several locations. The system is cost effective because it delivers only what has been requested. Because the information has been specifically requested, it is more likely to be read. Since the staff doesn't have to spend time answering information requests, they have more time for program activities. Information retrieved from a fax-on-demand system is printed at the receiving end, so the supplier's postage, printing, and paper costs will drop.

An organization can set up a fax-on-demand system with either a regular toll phone number or an 800 number. It may give everyone access to everything, or it may restrict access to certain documents by assigning personal identification numbers (PINs) to callers. CSC cautions, however, that an organization should have a sufficient volume of calls to make the service worthwhile. To evaluate the system's usefulness, consider: How often do people currently request information? Are you able to promote the service? Does your audience have access to a fax machine? Most fax-on-demand services charge on a per-minute basis that includes the incoming call as well as the time needed to fax back the information. Most services have a monthly minimum—usually $1,000—as well as a setup fee (CSC, May/June 1994, pp. 1, 2).

Smart Routing with 800/900 Toll Numbers

The Center for Strategic Communications suggests the use of smart routing—using 800, 900, and toll numbers—so that callers can dial a single telephone number and automatically be switched to any one of hundreds of locations (CSC, July/August 1994, p. 1).

The advantage of smart routing is that local chapters of a nonprofit organization—for example, volunteers or even several organizations in a coalition—are available to callers as if they were in a single place. By leveraging decentralized resources, an organization can streamline access while promoting a single number in all its materials, thereby cutting its costs and prioritizing local chapters with material they can use without modification.

The organization lists a single smart routing telephone number. The call is answered by a central computer switching system that is programmed to route calls to the appropriate site in various ways:

- The caller's phone number can be used to route the call to the nearest location.
- Callers can enter their zip codes via touch tone and the call can be transferred to the caller's congressional representative in Washington.
- Calls can be routed to different offices depending upon the time of day as a way to extend office hours—the organization can serve callers from 8 A.M. until 8 P.M. Eastern time, for example, because the office in California stays open until 5 P.M. Pacific coast time.
- Volunteers' phone numbers are captured when they are "on call" and calls are directed to them.
- A simple menu option can be used so that callers can identify the information they're looking for and can be transferred to the specific location that can provide that information.

CSC points out that the primary benefits of smart routing are:

- You can save on overhead costs because you don't have to bring everyone under one roof. Staff can stay where they are—often in offices across the state or across the country—and volunteers can work from home so that the organization won't have to put in extra phone lines or find extra office space.
- Collecting or updating information can be done from any local site and calls that require a live person can be answered from the staff person's workplace.
- Since a single phone number is used, people don't have to be transferred several times before reaching the appropriate resource person, nor will they have to make multiple calls to access the information or service they want.

With smart routing, neither the organization nor the callers need special equipment. Simple phones will do because the "smarts" of this routing system are owned and operated by telecommunications companies that maintain the system and update it according to your specifications. There is a setup fee for the service to cover the cost of programming; a minimum cost is approximately $1,000. Once the system is set up, callers are billed a per-minute charge, just like long distance. Access can be provided via 800 numbers, 900 numbers, or toll numbers (CSC, July/August 1994, pp. 1, 2).

Guidelines

This chapter has described the use of linear video, interactive video, and telecommunications for large-group community relations, educational community relations, public exhibits, and government relations. These electronic public relations applications have certain production and management elements in common. The reader is encouraged to review the guidelines at the conclusion of Chapter 1, which apply equally to the electronic vehicles discussed in this chapter.

Chapter 8

Reaching Consumers

In the 1980s, organizational communicators and public relations professionals extended their use of electronic media to consumer audiences in the home with product, service, and investor information. This new territory opened up because a confluence of several technologies—cable television, satellite communications, home video—suddenly allowed much wider access to consumers at home.

Unfortunately, over the years pitifully little has been reported in either the trade or consumer press on the use of electronic media for consumer and investor communications. There is some evidence, however, that since the early 1980s electronic media have increasingly been used to reach consumer in the home. Two studies by D/J Brush Associates (Brush & Brush, 1986, 1988), for example, reflect the "apparent" modest use of videotape for external communications purposes. In a 1986 study, that identified twenty programming categories, community relations, government/labor relations and security analysts relations were ranked thirteenth, nineteenth, and twentieth, respectively. However, the 1988 corporate video industry study reports "more and more video programming being aimed at outside audiences such as customers, community groups and the general public."

Audiences and Outlets

Today, electronic public relations programmers have two distribution channels through which to reach consumers and investors in the home: (1) via cable channels in select communities, and (2), via the home VCR or CD-ROM. To reiterate part of Table 1 (Chapter 1), there are now 11,351 cable systems in the United States—many with access channels available to profit and nonprofit organizations.

Over 76 million television households own 135 million VCRs, and the number of multimedia players (CD-ROM) players is in the millions and growing.

The Benefits

Since the early 1980s, one central reason has been given for the use of electronic media for external communications generally and consumer and investor relations specifically: they are effective. For example, producers have indicated that executives in action, growth trends, production operations, and product demonstrations can be presented far more clearly in video form. Further, partly because we are so conditioned to television, some things can be shown more graphically in motion than in print. Programmers have also reported that video makes organizational people real: "There's always a suspicion that the people in the printed report are actors." One producer said: "Video provided a realism audiences could feel." Still other programmers have indicated that video presents huge savings compared to print and that speed of duplication provides for effective and efficient access to specific audiences.

Consumer Relations

The distribution channel that has turned organizations on to consumer and investor relations is the home VCR. More than 80 percent of American households have VCRs, for a total of more than 135 million VCRs, and the number is growing by nearly 15 million units a year (Kingaard, 1995). Clearly, the VCR is likely to become an ever more important part of the U.S. media environment as new generations of increasingly technologically proficient consumers become even more comfortable with the technology.

The home video environment is a natural outlet for public relations programming. Organizations are using home video networks to distribute product demonstrations, financial information, and community relations oriented programs. Direct marketers have discovered video can deliver higher response rates per dollar than other media. Just 5 million of these videos were sent to consumers in 1988. By 1994, the figure was 65 million, a 1,300 percent increase in six years. In 1995, it is expected to climb another 20 percent to 80 million (Bartholomew, 1995).

For example, the Merck Corporation produced a video and booklet entitled *Every Man Should Know about His Prostate*. The video explains in simple terms how the prostate works; how it can gradually enlarge in men over forty; and how this condition, known as benign prostatic hyperplasia (BPH), may cause bothersome urinary symptoms that can gradually affect men's lives. A booklet also provides important information about the prostate and the problems that can arise when it enlarges, plus a glossary of terms. Other examples include demos of exercise machines, hair products, and cars.

Investor Relations

Many firms are also using the home video electronic environment to disseminate information to stockholders and potential investors. This includes a cornucopia of videos on initial public offerings, investment opportunities, and annual reports in electronic form.

Emhart

The first reported use of electronic media for investor relations occurred in 1980. In that year the Emhart Corporation, headquartered in Connecticut, used the medium (together with satellite and cable television technology) to beam the annual meeting video by satellite to 100 communities in eight states. They estimated reaching at least 2,000 of its 28,000 stockholders out of a total audience of 1.1 million. Emhart also reported shareholders could borrow a tape to play on their home VCRs.

Emhart's application caused quite a stir, and there was much talk in corporate television and public relations circles that this so-called "innovative" programming application would be widely adopted. There was also much talk (and some activity) in the 1980s about using cable-access channels to distribute internal and external programming not only to customers and the community at large, but to employees as well.

In retrospect, the use of cable television for these corporate television programming applications has been given more credence in the breach than in actual practice. Some companies, both large and small, do use cable-access channels to distribute programming. But the use of satellite and cable technology to distribute annual meeting programming in the hopes of reaching a majority of stockholders remains a rarity.

Oracle Corporation

Lately, however, the advent of CD-ROM technology and the growing number of personal computers with CD-ROM ports presents an opportunity for an organization to distribute financial information in print *and* in CD-ROM format. One such example, and perhaps the first on record, is the CD-ROM annual report created by the Oracle Corporation.

The $3 billion Oracle Corporation, with headquarters in Redwood Shores, California, is a leading supplier of information management software, such as the Oracle7 family of software products for database management. Kathryn Buan, manager of investor relations for Oracle, described the development of the company's CD-ROM *Annual Report*:

> *As a leading-edge technology firm, we thought it was important to be one of the first, if not the first, to put our annual report on CD-ROM. As people become more and more interested in the use of CD-ROMs, more and more people in their home and offices are using CD-ROM technology. Even our customers have moved to CD-ROM. Our software distribution is moving more and more to CD-ROM distribution. Our customers want it. It takes up less space. It's much more reliable. For a shareholder, future employee, or potential customer perspective, I think it promotes our image as a leading-edge technology company.*

Buan described the structure of the CD-ROM's content:

> *As a product itself, it takes the scope of what an annual report does and stretches out the realm of possibilities in terms of how you can communicate with customers, prospective employees, and shareholders. Not only do you get to read over the financials and read about different new products, but you actually get to navigate through what ends up as a virtual company visit.*
>
> *As you open it up, you hear the president's statement about Oracle. Then you meet each member of the management team. Following that, you can get an overview of the major product areas, services business, and highlights of major events during the year. Finally, of course, you can navigate through any of the financials.*
>
> *The most important part of the CD-ROM report is that it is fully interactive. At any point you can navigate through any of these topics. You can rewind it, fast forward it, go back to it again, you can skip over certain parts. We think this is very important, particularly since we're moving into the interactive television realm in the technology industry.*

Buan compared the CD-ROM version of the annual report to its print counterpart:

> *On a hardcopy annual report you can't completely capture the character of the management team. In our financial statements there's an interactive portion where we've highlighted special areas of interest such as geographical revenue breakdown or historical revenue growth, or margin improvement.*
>
> *In this year's CD-ROM report you can double-click on those items with financial statements and you get a voice over of the chief financial officer talking about those particular financials. If you double-click on geographical rev-*

enues instead of just seeing the percent of domestic revenues reported for the year, a three-dimensional bar chart pops up and shows you four years of historicals. Then the CFO says, "As you can see, the last four years has seen an interesting turnaround in our domestic revenues."

The first CD-ROM annual report, says Buan, was an experiment. Oracle published 5,000 to 6,000 copies, distributed them, and ran out within a week because demand was so great. For the next year's report, Oracle is still working out how many they're going to order. Oracle hopes to distribute the CD-ROM to all interested shareholders, all potential customers and clients, new recruits, and internally—which could mean somewhere between 10,000 and 20,000 copies.

Buan analyzed the costs of producing the CD-ROM annual report: Overall production she estimates at $200,000 to $300,000—$200,000 with using existing video, more if new video is produced for the piece. She points out the big cost difference between Oracle's first CD-ROM and their current one:

First, the last one we put together quite rapidly. It looks great despite the fact that it was done so quickly. (It took a couple of months.) That was too tight. Definitely you should budget more time to do it than that.

It was a great idea that came up two months before an event and we wanted to do it for the event and that's why we had the time constraint. This year [1994] we've probably spent three to four months on the new one. Even that's still tough. A lot of it has to do with scheduling and finishing up video clips for the CD-ROM.

I think the biggest difference is that you can navigate through it. Navigation was a big issue in the last one. In the last one you could actually navigate by choosing one of the three major sections to visit: you go into the media server area, the product services area, or the financials area. [However], it was tough to navigate through it when you're in those three areas. We worked on that a lot for this next version. In this version you can begin any of those sections and skip back to the main menu at any point. You can also fast-forward and reverse while you're watching the video roll through.

We also used better development tools. That's key. We're using our own development tools—Oracle Media Objects—for this version. [It's MacroMind Director]. It probably costs about the same when you take out the cost of the videotaping. We did a lot more video shoots in this next version. So if you add that on, it's going to be a little bit more.

Buan reports that the response from stockholders was very positive. Excitement about the CD-ROM report also made the print annual report more popular. The CD-ROM at this point can't replace the print version because not enough people have CD-ROM capability, even though the rate of growth of home and office place CD-ROMs is growing. A print annual report is still appropriate for communicating financials.

Gaining management support for the CD-ROM project was not difficult at Oracle, Buan reports. Oracle, after all, is the second largest software company in the world.

"It was obvious we have to continue to move forward in technological and communications advancements," says Buan. "This represents that kind of move for us."

Is a CD-ROM in Your Investment Future?

John Beardsley, president of the Public Relations Society of America and head of his own firm, commented on the viability of the CD-ROM as an investor relations communications vehicle:

> The CD-ROM has come down so much in price that it is going to become as ubiquitous as the fax machine and the floppy disk drive on computers. As more and more of us get computers, more and more of us are going to have CD-ROMs. We're going to use them for entertainment as well as for work, especially when you have a recordable CD, not just a Read Only Memory, but one you can record on. You can hold vast amounts of data. That's the true advantage of the CD—they hold so much data. You can put the entire contents of an encyclopedia in a CD-ROM.
>
> You want to use a CD-ROM judiciously, I think. It could include everything—sound, moving pictures, video, words, commentary from the CEO. There was movement a decade or more ago to create annual reports on videotape. It never really took off because nobody would stop producing the printed annual report. [That was] because in those days not many people had VCRs. Now just about every household in America has a VCR. Yet the difficulty of a VCR is that it is not randomly accessible. You have to look at it in sequence.
>
> The advantage of a CD-ROM containing an annual report and 5000 other documents that pertain to the company—along with videos—is that it is randomly accessible. You can go to the president's message and you even have hypertext. When the president in his letter says, "Our ratios of net earnings to total debt were such and such," you can click on an icon and be right at the balance sheet, especially the part of the balance sheet he's talking about. You want to compare the figures. Or there can be side-by-side presentations. The president can be talking about something, a window opens up, and there are the graphs illustrating what he's saying. You can do so much with the CD-ROM.

The imperative from the SEC is that every shareholder has to receive the annual report.

Guidelines

Clearly, this electronic public relations programming category is akin to marketing. More broadly speaking, this application resembles the television commercial: audiences are select in a sense, but in another sense audiences potentially can number into the hundreds of thousands as opposed to a few hundred or a few thousand.

Here is the single guideline for marketing to consumers via the electronic media: *Quality is the only rule that counts.* Whatever the audience or external communications environment, the quality of the product must be superior.

Let's take a look at the example cited earlier: the use of cable television to disseminate information to shareholders. This programming is viewed in stockholders' homes. Other than a retail outlet environment, the home is perhaps the most media-competitive environment of all the contexts discussed. The kind of programming described above is in direct competition with the very best broadcast and cable television and Hollywood has to offer. It also competes with the telephone, the newspaper, the radio, the home computer, video games, and every other activity that takes place in a home. If the programming is not of the highest quality, it will not be watched. Moreover, if it is less than high quality, it will be regarded as irrelevant.

Of course, the home is not the only environment in which external communications programming could be viewed: such programming could also be shown at a community meeting, in a government official's office, at a press conference, or a stockholder's meeting. Is the competition for attention in these other environments any less than the home environment? No.

Of all the applications (with the exception of marketing and sales promotion), audiences for external communications programming have very little, perhaps no, vested interest in the programming—either in the message itself, who is in it, or who is disseminating it. Therefore, the quality of the program must be of sufficiently high value to either catch an audience's eye (while the dial is being turned) or keep it if they stay tuned. Whenever the vested interest level is low, the quality must be high (Marlow, 1992, pp. 152–153).

Chapter 9

Reaching Employees

When Sony commercially introduced the three-quarter inch videocassette to the United States market in 1971-1972, the use of videotape as an organizational training medium (initiated in the late 1950s through mid 1960s) expanded to become an employee and management communications medium. The highly portable (and standardized) three-quarter inch videotape format spawned a multitude of organizational video networks (one estimate is 12,000). Dun & Bradstreet's *MarketPlace CD-ROM* lists over 10 million organizations in the United States (mostly for-profit). The Electronic Industries Association estimates at least 50 percent of American businesses own one VCR.

Since the early 1970s, there has been a burgeoning use of electronic media for internal employee and management communications, such as orientation, employee benefits, and employee news.

Audiences and Outlets:
General Employee Communications

In the early 1970s, top management first became highly visible in corporate video programming. Today top executives not only appear in these programs, they are the stars. This use of the medium seems to have satisfied management's desire to reach all employees not only at headquarters, but also in field locations as well.

The growing interest in videotape as a means of employee communications in the 1970s and into the 1980s was reflected in the results of a survey conducted by Ketchum MacLeod & Grove Public Relations at the International Conference of the International Association of Business Communicators (IABC) in 1980. The IABC, which at that time possessed an international membership of 6,800 organizational communicators, encompasses a wide spectrum of businesses, government agencies, and nonprofit associations. IABC membership includes company publication editors, audio/visual producers, press and shareholder relations specialists, and other communication specialists, artists, photographers, typographers, and managers of communications programs.

The survey revealed that a majority of the respondents were using videotape for employee communications in various forms. The medium's ability to visualize a subject, its adaptability to large or small groups, and its flexibility were factors mentioned by respondents as positive attributes of the medium. The use of videotape for "employee orientation" was also cited by many. In numerous cases, tapes explaining company programs and benefits to new employees were produced for long-term use and updated when benefits or programs changed. Videotapes were also used for employee motivation and to explain general news about the company, such as promotions, new acquisitions, and new product lines. The category also included employee news, safety information, and special events, such as an open house or anniversary.

As Chapter 2 described, satellite technology and videoconferencing came into increasing use in the 1980s. Together with video networks, so-called business television networks along with local area networks (LANs) and E-mail created organizational communications systems that have enhanced internal public relations activities. Not the least of the consequences is that middle managers have become less relevant to the internal communications process.

The Benefits

Since the late 1960s, managers and producers have given two central reasons for the use of electronic media for employee communications: cost effectiveness and communications effectiveness. For example, users have indicated that it costs too much—in time and money—to bring all managers and supervisors together at one location and that such meetings are not always practical. In other words, videotaped employee communications messages enable employees to participate in such meetings with executives from company headquarters, even though the experience is somewhat vicarious. Still other company managements have expressed the opinion that videotaped messages gives employees "a closer look at top executives," "helps relate field to home office," "provides a good opportunity to get the whole picture," and "gives an overall view which would otherwise be difficult to grasp."

So strong is the feeling about videotape, for example, for employee communications that managers and employees have made such flat statements as, "All corporate employees should be made to see the tapes," "I had never seen an annual shareholders meeting before and found it interesting and informative,"

"Especially enjoyed pictures of other plants," "Employees would enjoy hearing more about the various products and companies," "More on shares and stock for employees," and "Will probably increase my savings and investment plan as a result of viewing the tapes."

The benefits of using videotape for general employee communications are the same as those for management communications and marketing: videotape has speed, credibility, immediacy; it brings the event, the person, the place to the employee. Following are some examples of how companies have used electronic media successfully for employee communications purposes.

Blue Cross/Blue Shield: Everything's Fine

In a program entitled *Everything's Fine: Adult Children of Alcoholics,* a production of the video division of Blue Cross/Blue Shield of Massachusetts (Boston), Ed Asner narrates a 16.5 minute look at the impact of alcoholism and other addictions on family members throughout their lives.

The award-winning program's objectives were (1) to identify the personality types who emerge from dysfunctional families; (2) to understand that the behaviors appropriate for survival in a dysfunctional family may make adult life much more difficult; (3) to explore the impact of adult/child behavior in the workplace; and (4) to help employees understand that family alcoholism doesn't have to be tolerated.

According to Patricia Frieden-Brown, manager of Vital Video (Blue Cross/Blue Shield's internal video production unit): "One of the reasons we did *Everything's Fine* was that we did some research and found that not only could we use the program for our own internal Employee Assistance Program, we could also sell the program to external audiences across the country."

"What makes this program work," she says, "is the drama, the fact that people can relate to it. It took a year to make from beginning to end and about nine months to script. The hardest thing in the scripting process was that as we were doing the research, we began to understand what the audience didn't understand. We quickly got beyond what the audience didn't know, but we had to hold ourselves back. We had to decide that this was an introductory program, the elementary program. This program was to help understand the concept of being an adult child. The program is not a how-to program, how-to steps of how to get therapy or go through therapy. It's basically an awareness program."

Everything's Fine shows five children playing together as a mock dysfunctional family. Later the five children are seen as adults and how they now act in various abusive ways: alcoholism, workaholism, drug abuse. In between the various scenes, Asner talks about how child feelings (suppressed in order to maintain the dysfunctional family's balance) can be destructive in adulthood.

"I've never had anyone see this program and not be affected by it in one way or another," says Brown.

> *To produce this kind of program you have to think continuously about the end user and be careful not to get too involved in the passion of the subject. When I was writing this program, I had to keep in front of me not what I wanted to tell the audience but what that person needed to know. So you keep the program condensed and understandable. And you keep it in a format so that the audience is able to receive the information. So you have to put your feelings and beliefs aside and do your research and stick to what that research says.*
>
> *Also, no matter how painful, keep your clients down to one thought or one point that an audience will walk away with at the end of the tape. Not two, four, ten points, not fifteen different audiences that the videotape could possibly be addressing. But one particular audience. After the tape is made, then you can look at it and say, "Can it be modified?" But people come in and they say, "We can use this as a marketing tape and a training tape." You have to ask, "What's your primary purpose? What's your primary thought?" and stay with that.*

Catch the Spirit of Innovation: BASF

To encourage its carpet fiber industrial and commercial salespeople to sell more carpet, the BASF Corporation produced a 6.5 minute sales performance incentive program entitled *Catch the Spirit of Innovation: BASF Fibers 1990 Incentive Program.*

Initially sent out to BASF's carpet fiber regional sales offices, the video was first shown in Dalton, Georgia and Williamsburg, Virginia. The program dealt with specifications, rules, regulations, and other information pertaining to BASF's 1990 incentive program: for example, how many yards of carpet they had to sell of a particular BASF product and what they would win after they reached certain sales goals.

According to Big Picture principals William Orisich and Michael Pieprobon, the award-winning program was effective because "it contains just about every production technique ever invented in film. We had live action, we had stop-motion, we had go-motion (animating an inanimate object), cut-out animation, rotoscoped animation. It's several minutes of sheer mania, a fun piece to look at. Visually there's no way you can look at the program and not get sucked into it. It's nonstop. The program was mostly graphics, although we did have some dramatic live–action sequences, like an old Bogie, detective-style scene."

The $75,000 program was originated in 16mm and 35mm film and edited on tape. According to Pieprobon, "From a corporate and industrial viewpoint this is a little unusual. Film seems to be going through a big comeback phase right now. Five or ten years ago, our corporate clients were a different generation. Now the people who are just entering the purchasing end of corporate communications have reached a point where they're initiating corporate communications. That generation has grown up sitting around watching MTV and it's a much more visually sophisticated generation that is buying corporate communications right now."

Big Picture's approach to producing corporate television programming is simply, "The sky's the limit." Says Pieprobon, "Just a few years ago we all had such a sense of corporate do's and don'ts, what was considered mainline, what was considered radical. That has changed drastically in the last two or three years. When we approach a corporate project, the sky's the limit. The BASF program is the kind you would never see produced four or five years ago."

What has made the difference? Pieprobon believes that corporate communications purchasers today truly understand television. "They are not only open to newer, fresher ideas," he says, "they're demanding them."

Programming Guidelines

The three areas of concern users have articulated can be translated into the following programming development guidelines, as follows:

Orientation programs should orient, not overload. Managers and subject experts have a natural tendency to try to get everything into one video. Of course, this just doesn't work. Shorter is usually better than longer. The same is true with employee orientation programs. These kinds of programs should give the new employee a direction; after all, that's why they call them (or should) orientation programs. If there were any way of informing a new employee about everything he or she needs to know, it would have been done already. The fact is, it takes time for an employee to become fully oriented to a new organization and this reality should be taken into consideration in designing an orientation video.

The first step is to decide what a new employee really needs to know for the immediate future. Next, translate this content into a style of presentation that allows for the most efficient delivery of that information. A talking head, such as a personnel relations subject expert, doesn't hack it. It is better to have the program introduced (no more than 60 seconds) by someone from top management, followed by a 10 to 12 minute graphic orientation to the company's operation, personnel, plants, products, customers, and so on.

Employee benefits videos should impart central benefits, not every detail. Whatever goes for orientation programs, ditto for benefits programs, which present potential legal problems. If a benefits video conveys a legally inconsistent point, it could spell trouble for the employee benefits department and the program's producer, which is partly why benefits videos should only convey the central features of the company's array of benefits programs. This is a perfect example of how video and print work in tandem. The video is the open door for the employee to the benefits information; the print version provides the all important details, details that, in all likelihood, will change over time.

Further, benefits videos should be produced as a library: one on insurance, others on major medical, dental, retirement, long-term disability, savings programs, and so on. It might be worthwhile to produce a program that generalizes all the benefits programs, a sort of orientation to the company's benefits. Again, as always, shorter is usually better than longer. Don't dwell. Don't get cute. Visualize everything. Present the information in as stylish but straightforward a manner as possible.

The production quality of the employee communications program should be a reflection of the executives and subject experts appearing in it. This guideline is a direct reflection of the fact that historically the application has included a host of top management on-camera participants. While it is true that this kind of talent creates an inherent audience interest in the program, however, it is also true that top management should not be made to look foolish with poor camera angles, bad lighting, sloppy audio, unflattering sets, lack of rehearsal, no teleprompter, an uncomfortable interviewer, and so on. The reverse is not true, either: lower executives appearing in the program should not be given lower production values. Production values should always be as high as possible.

What makes the difference? The "general employee communications" application by definition can mean a management involvement, usually on camera. Role playing, sales training, skill training, marketing and sales promotion, and external communications programs do not necessarily mean an appearance by top management; at least the practice of the last twenty years seems to support this perception.

Thus, at the very least, every effort should be made to make the executive look as comfortable in the video environment as possible. Lighting should be flattering, but not obtrusive. The director should be comfortable working with top management and not intimidated by rank. At all times, the director must be in charge without becoming a video production dictator. Tact is required throughout. Use makeup judiciously. Whatever it takes, the executive must look good in the final product. He or she must look comfortable, relaxed, credible, articulate, personable, and human.

This result is not always achievable. Some top executives just aren't good in front of the television camera. If this is the case, find another method for getting them into the program. Perhaps an interview approach would be better than a direct to the camera presentation. Sometimes a narrator is useful to bridge statements by the executive; this is especially relevant when reporting on the happenings at an annual meeting. Keep the executive's remarks as brief as possible. A top executive draws a certain amount of initial respect when first appearing on camera, but that respect will fade very quickly if the presentation goes beyond the limits of an audience's patience or believability.

Integrate material shot on location with material shot in the studio as much as possible. Rely on graphics wherever possible: whenever an executive talks about statistics, product, places, events, or abstract concepts, show it graphically. When, however, the executive is communicating personal anecdotes or is "speaking from the heart," keep him or her on camera. Mixing the two styles can be very effective.

Do not fall into the trap, however, of being coerced into using a top executive just because someone said to do it. There must be an inherent production reason for including the executive in the program. If none can be found, then don't do it. A benefits program doesn't necessarily have to include a member of top management for the program to be effective. An orientation program, on the other hand, can be very effective if it is introduced or even narrated by a top company executive.

The program's production style should fit the content intended to be conveyed. The use of top management in a general employee communications program must be carefully decided: if the executive doesn't belong, he or she doesn't belong. Make the choice early. When the audience tells you it was wrong (i.e., boring, unbelievable, too long, a waste of time), it's too late.

Prepare talent before shooting begins. Whether professional or nonprofessional, on-camera talent needs to be prepared. In the case of professionals, this could take several forms. First, if a program is prescripted—such as an orientation program, company benefits series, or employee retirement information—at the very least actors and actresses should be familiar with the script. Preferably, the on-camera professionals should have a copy of the latest version of the script days if not a week or two before production begins.

Second, on-camera professionals should be given an opportunity to have an overall understanding of the program. A read-through with all the actors and actresses present is helpful; a scene-by-scene rehearsal is mandatory. All in all, on-camera talent should be given every opportunity to become familiar with the content of the program and the producer/director's concept of the program. After all, it takes everyone a while to warm up. Preparing on-camera talent before the crew arrives and is ready to shoot ensures a more efficient production, a more efficient editing session and, in the long run, a more effective finished program.

Nonprofessionals should be given the same considerations, regardless of the content of the program. At the very head of the process, a pre-interview with the executive should take place: what that person wants to talk about, in what order, how the ideas can be best presented. This step should take place before the final script is created. Very often, this executive presentation will be edited several times before it is satisfactory, not only to the on-camera talent, but from a television point of view. Don't be surprised if copy is edited at the time of the shoot itself. Be flexible. An electronic lens-line teleprompter will make the job of editing the copy that much easier.

A rehearsal of the nonprofessionals' part in the program should be accomplished some time before actual production, if possible. Here the major problem is inherent: the nonprofessional—top executive, subject expert—is by definition a television nonprofessional. Depending on the inherent video acuity of the nonprofessional, television coaching may be very useful here. An outside professional can be very effective, if one is accessible.

Ensure the use of the program in the field. As with the sales training application, one way of ensuring that the program will be shown in field locations is to gain support for it from field management—department managers, regional managers, supervisors, plant managers. Whatever the situation, some level of management at the field location must be aware of the program and must be motivated to show it in the proper context.

Program screenings can be accomplished in various ways. One way might be the creation of a special "video day" and announcements of the program's availability through signs in employees areas: elevators, bulletin boards, the local house organ, announcement boards, flyers, table cards in the cafeteria, memos to the staff, and so on.

The timing of the program's showing is also important. For example, several showings of the program may be required: for regular staff, for part-time staff, for day workers and night workers.

The physical viewing environment can also play an important part in ensuring that the program is viewed by a broad audience. It may be necessary to show the program from a rolling cart physically transported to all the areas in a location. Often the program will have to be brought to the audience (as in an assembly-line situation) when workers cannot leave their work environment. Or a combination of viewing locations, fixed and portable, may have to be used. In some companies a master antenna system has been built with one central video player and several monitors located in employee areas (such as the cafeteria, various work stations, meeting rooms) with the program played continuously at various times during the day.

A local manager's participation in program screenings can also help ensure the proper viewing environment. For example, if the program is shown during a staff or safety training meeting, a discussion of the program's content led by the supervisor or functional manager can help guarantee that the program's content was conveyed effectively. In some cases, showing a program several times may enhance its effectiveness.

Employee News: The Electrovisual House Organ

Perhaps no other use of videotape for corporate communications purposes attracted more attention from the consumer and trade press in the 1970s and 1980s than *employee news*. This may be because employee news most closely resembles so-called commercial electronic journalism.

Senders and Receivers

Most management users of video for employee news programming are public affairs or corporate communications departments. Audiences for this kind of programming are usually employees at headquarters locations, regional offices, or all employees companywide (domestic and international). Employees have the opportunity to view this kind of programming on portable viewing equipment (in a variety of locations) or in special viewing rooms and, occasionally, even at home.

Quarterly employee news programs have been shown in cafeterias with the program running continuously throughout the noon hour. Most employees catch it going to or from lunch. In some cases, this practice has evoked negative reaction—the program disturbs the noontime repose of those who prefer not to listen to or watch it. In one company this problem was solved by building a little theater around the television set in one location and by putting the set in an alcove in the other location. Thus the sound was not directed straight into the main lounging areas.

In other companies, the television news program is updated weekly and generally runs on the monitors for two days, usually between 11:30 A.M. and 2 P.M., the hours the cafeteria is open for lunch. Still other companies have placed monitors in heavily trafficked areas just outside the company cafeteria. Many employee news shows are also available to night-shift workers.

Companies have also put their employee news shows on one-half inch players on rolling stands in some unusual places—not just offices, but switch rooms, garages, work sheds, and coal yards.

Why Video?

There are primarily two reasons that corporate managements use television for employee news: (1) they are effective communications, and (2) they improve employee morale.

Since the first reported use of video for employee news by Smith Kline & French in the late 1960s, corporate managements have indicated (and experience seems to corroborate) that using video for employee news purposes is more communications effective than using film and, in some cases, more communications effective than using print.

In the early 1990s, it seems somewhat absurd to be considering film as a viable alternative to video for employee news purposes (or any other corporate television network programming application, for that matter). But it must not be forgotten that only in the mid-1980s did it become clear that film was flat in terms of its growth as a corporate communications medium. This seems to be true of external communications and, to an even greater extent, internal employee communications. Film is simply too slow and now relatively too expensive a medium to be considered economically viable for employee news purposes. Only because videotape specifically and television in general are fast turnaround technologies, with characteristics of immediacy and personal intimacy, do television employee news shows exist at all.

The inherent technological and psychological characteristics of videotape and television allow corporate managements to communicate information in a way that is quite different from the content and style of the print employee news format. A statement from top management in video is a very different communications environment from the same statement in print. When the chief executive officer makes this statement on video, it is more alive, more direct, more personal, more credible. The television camera does not lie. It sees all. People "feel" people via television. Rightly or wrongly, television does communicate on an emotional, visceral level.

On the other hand, television is not very good at communicating details or facts that can be reviewed at will. Home video and interactive videodiscs notwithstanding, television (and hence, videotape) is not like a print piece that can be studied, analyzed, gestated, and reviewed at the viewer's discretion. The truth is that in all contexts it is a mixed media world: print and television must work side by side in a multimedia communications environment. Thus, the perception of corporate users that video is more communications effective than print must be understood from the point of view that video does *some* things better than print, but the reverse is also true.

In terms of employee morale, the advent of employee news television programming parallels the development of other electronic communications devices that have permeated the corporate culture in the last two decades. The most prevalent of these devices is the computer; others include such telecommunications devices as fax and teleconferencing. The result is that organizations have become flatter, structurally speaking, and more fluid in terms of communications flow. In turn, employee morale as an issue facing management has changed.

Employee news television programming is but one example of the changes in employee-management relations in the last decade or so. It provides employees (at least ostensibly) with the view that there is a more open employee-management communications environment. Following are some examples.

Directions: AT&T

Between 1983 and 1989, AT&T (Basking Ridge, New Jersey) produced a quarterly and then a bimonthly employee news program for its 300,000 worldwide employees—from the chief executive officer to the mail clerk. According to executive producer Christopher Newton of Corporate Television, who joined the program in early 1987, "Even though our goal was to reach 300,000 employees, the distribution problems were large. We actually only reached 60,000 employees."

This award-winning 30-minute program, titled *Directions,* focused on people for its content. Says Newton,

> *AT&T has a lot of business units: long distance telephone service, switches for telephone companies and computers, fax machines and on and on and on. The problem was always to find stories that would be of interest across that wide spectrum. We tended to focus on the human side of the company more than the technological side. The goal of* Directions *was to build employee morale. It was never seen as a news vehicle per se. It was seen as a vehicle to help the employees feel pride in the company. And it began at a time after divestiture when morale at the company was pretty low. The program was always seen as a way to celebrate our heroes.*

Each 30-minute program usually consisted of five segments. "We differed from the typical employee news program in that we never used an on-camera corporate host. We used a voiceover announcer with a credible news voice, not a slick announcer type." What made this program an award winner? Says Newton:

> It was clearly our ability to truly build employee morale. Anyone who saw it said, "My God, what a company that is. And they sure have great people working for it." For example, the last program opened with a classic AT&T-to-the-rescue kind of a story. It looked at the aftermath of Hurricane Hugo on the coast of North Carolina in 1989 by telling, with some very dramatic, powerful footage that we bought from a local news station, the story of the hurricane and the impact AT&T service had on some of the businesses, the hospitals, police stations, those who had managed to stay open because their phone service had stayed up during the hurricane.
>
> After that, we did a techy kind of a story: a new computer called the Pixel Machine, a high-graphic supercomputer used primarily for scientific purposes to imagine four-dimensional realities using abstract math. And this segment had terrific graphics.
>
> Another segment was the "Goodbye" segment. This was the final edition of Directions. It's no longer being produced. We said goodbye to our audience. We showed them a selection of their favorite stories over the years.

The program was produced almost exclusively by freelance independent producers with strong news documentary reels and a "feeling for people," working with Newton and a coordinator. Each producer supervised the production of individual segments. Newton supervised the production of the last segment.

Directions, however, is no longer being produced because of distribution problems. "The main lesson that I learned from the experience with Directions," says Newton, "is that it's not the quality of a program that makes or breaks a program. Directions was a terrific program. We simply could not break the distribution barrier. We reached about 60,000 people. That's a lot of people, but it's only about 20 percent of the employee body and we really couldn't justify our existence on that basis. We just never found a successful way to reach an audience that's far flung around the world.

Kaleidoscope: Georgia-Pacific

Kaleidoscope is Georgia-Pacific's (Atlanta, Georgia) award-winning employee news program distributed to 300 locations. It is primarily designed for salaried employees, as opposed to hourly employees such as millworkers, plant personnel, and line personnel. All employees though, can have access to the program, including taking a copy home. Out of Georgia-Pacific's 66,000 employees, about 15,000 to18,000 view the program. Approximately 75 percent of the distribution is on VHS, with the balance on three-quarter inch videocassette.

According to Don Blank, director of operations of Georgia-Pacific Television:

> *The program covers general company news. It's in a* PM Magazine *news magazine format. All the wraparounds in the* PM *format with the talent were done at Georgia-Pacific locations. We did wraparounds at one time on a Georgia-Pacific sailing ship. Then one or two of the stories are light entertainment stories about G-P activities. For example, one time we had some employees dog sled racing. Another time a bunch of employees built a plywood submarine for the Plywood Submarine Races held in Florida that the National Geographic covered.*
>
> *There is at least one major, feature Georgia-Pacific informational story, and that can range from financial information (if it's quarterly report time or there are some year-end financial figures) to a big acquisition, to maybe a major plant expansion (a new machine going in) or a new marketing plan. There is also a secondary main story, shorter in length. If there is time in the episode, we might put in some news updates. We try to hold each program to 20 minutes. Occasionally they drift to 24–25 minutes.*
>
> *Everything in the show is news oriented. It might not be today's hot news, it might be news that occurred in the last two months that the employee hasn't gotten any in-depth information about. Or maybe the employee does know about it, but here's some video interpretation of it.*

Blank feels the style of the production is what makes the award-winning program effective. The graphics treatment, the way the talent were handled for the wraparounds, and the feature story production techniques that went into every story were essentially highest quality:

> *What made it network quality was camerawork, editing, use of music, use of the talent, graphics, graphics animation. A lot of the people here have a broadcast background. Because our video operation runs as a profit center, we market our services to the outside. So we are working in broadcast programming for cable companies and networks; we're also working in commercial production, national and regional television commercials, we're working in high-style image videos for companies all around the country as well as basic corporate video for other people. So we have very broad exposure, and because of that type of work I have been able to attract essentially top people.*

Blank offers two pieces of advice for producers involved in employee news programming. The first is to communicate information that the people either need to know or want to know, or both:

If you just load it up with a bunch of fluff stories about fun things, if you orient it like PM *or* Entertainment Tonight, *well—corporate employees get plenty of that at home. They don't need to get any more BS. They are watching your video because they* do *want information about what's going on in your company.*

In our case, and I'm sure this applies to a lot of companies, we are multidivisioned. The guys out in the Building Products division want to know a lot about what's going on in their specific division that's not happening in their general area. They also want to know what's going on in the Paper division because they don't know anything about that division. Because they have no exposure to that, they're really interested. Same thing happens in reverse with the Paper division guys. I don't care how much production value and style and pizazz you put into it, if you're not giving the information these people want to have and don't stay on top of knowing what they want to have, your program will fail because nobody will be interested in it.

Blank's second piece of advice is to aim for the highest productuon values possible. If you can afford it and have the facilities or have the money to buy it on the outside," he says, "the more broadcast production style you put into the show, the better it will be received because you are indeed competing for the attention of people who watch broadcast television."

Blank believes that the Unites States has become such a television society that a corporate video has to be almost as good as what was on NBC last night because viewers have become very sophisticated in their expectations. Unlike the days of industrial films, the more style a corporate video has, the better accepted it is. The better accepted it is, the better the retention will be of the information that the program is trying to communicate.

Programming Guidelines

Users have indicated twelve guideline rules for employee news videotapes, as follows:

The employee news show must be viewed in the larger context of overall employee communications. Just as no single communications medium can help solve all communications problems, so too a television news show cannot solve all employee communications problems. Before management decides to produce an employee news show, it must first define its overall employee communications objectives.

There are various ways managers can help solve communication problems: the print house organ, bulletins, personal letters from management, interpersonal communications, periodic meetings with middle and top management, company social activities, and so on. The question of immediate concern here is: Is there a real need to communicate via television?

There is no substitute for personal contact. This is true of employee news, training, or management communications. However, one-to-one contact is not always possible. Print, of course, has been the mainstay of employee communications. Moreover, print has distribution advantages. The employee house organ, for example, can be distributed to all employees individually. So what will television add to the employee communications effort?

Video can add personality, a sense of immediacy and timeliness. For example, in one company when the chairman of the board and the president appeared on the news shows, several employees stated that this was the first time they had ever seen top management! It might not have been in the flesh, but it was better than nothing. Video as opposed to print and film, also provides the viewer with a sense of being there. It can also be timely. Perhaps one of the best examples of this timeliness was when Chase Manhattan Bank introduced a new president. The in-house video crew taped the news conference, edited the material that night, and distributed the edited program the next day to many of Chase's headquarters employees.

Video is a visual medium and can give depth to graphics that print cannot do. Video also provides more of a "live" experience for the viewer than print. For example, the excitement of an intramural baseball game is much better conveyed on video than in print.

Because video can make company people, places, and events come alive, video employee news can help contribute to employee morale and employee understanding of the corporation as a total entity. These communications programs can be defined in terms of objectives, audiences, and desired results.

The program that will defy analysis, at least from the point of view of measuring meaningful results, is the video employee news show. This is not to say that an employee news show is not worth the effort, but it may be the last application of video as a communications medium in the corporate context, not the first, because of the difficulty of measuring results and proving to management the return on investment.

The employee news show should be the last application of video as a communications tool, not the first. The previous guidelines suggested that management first take a look at the broader problem of overall employee communications problems and objectives before considering using video as an employee communications tool. This long view can be put into an even larger context of the broad communications problems of the corporation, such as marketing and sales, external communications, training and management communications. Video is not merely the tool of public relations, or corporate communications, or personnel, training, or marketing. Video and its attendant programming network is a corporatewide resource, similar to telecommunications and computer processing.

Moreover, video can be an expensive medium at first blush and should therefore be viewed in as large an applications context as possible. While the employee news programming application may have great merit in itself, if the programming network is devoid of other programming applications (e.g., training, internal marketing communications, and so on), the employee news application by itself will probably *not* sustain the capital and operating expense required.

Define the objectives of the program. It follows that if video is going to be used for employee news communications, the program should have a well-defined set of objectives. Will it be used to "improve employee perceptions" of company benefits, or keep them "informed" of government regulations or legislation affecting the company's activities? Or will it be used to "enhance employee understanding" of the various facets of the company's operations; to "show employees how the company provides advancement opportunities"; to "announce" major policy changes, salary increases, new officers, new activities, new products; or to describe how the company baseball team won the intramural championship?

Of course, all these objectives could apply. But management must also define when it will know that the news show has achieved even a modicum of success. Will it be measured by the number of viewers? Will it be measured by feedback mechanisms such as questionnaires distributed on a periodic basis? Will it be measured by the look on employees' faces as they watch themselves or their coworkers on the tube? Whatever the method, management must be clear about what it expects from the program and how it is going to measure success or failure.

Producing a video employee news show is a full-time job. Hire people who know what they are doing. An employee news show is perhaps the most difficult corporate network programming to produce, for several reasons. Often events do not occur on schedule, or a segment will be scripted after the fact, or executives or employees are not available when the production crew is available. Corporate video employee news production crews frequently have all the same problems commercial electronic journalism crews have. The scale of content and logistics may be different, but the central problems are all the same.

Look for someone inside the organization to act as a producer. Or hire someone from the outside who has experience in this area. Or hire a consultant to train the in-house producer (if necessary). Familiarity with the organization is crucial to producing a news show. You need to know whom to see, what to say and what not to say, and where to go for help.

Creating an employee news program on a weekly, monthly, or even quarterly basis requires a high level of concentration and focus. It is a rare individual who can write for the print house organ one minute and then turn around and produce and write for the electronic house organ the next. Hire someone who will work on this corporate television program full time and you'll get the results required.

Define the programming mix before you start producing. An employee news show has a myriad of content possibilities. The list can include (but is not limited to) company benefits, department profiles, personality profiles, company involvement in community affairs, management policy statements, preventive health care segments, the company bond drive, United Fund announcements, driver safety, income tax tips, and so on. Esoteric program segments won't go over very well. As one user put it, "Stories designed for a general audience receive the greatest recognition." Whatever the content mix, the major criterion for the selection of stories is that they support the program's objectives.

Develop a production style that squares with the program mix. There are a variety of production styles and formats for an employee news show: news stories, features, entertainment segments, person-on-the-street interviews, graphics, titles, music, on-location material, in-studio material. Whatever the choice of style, it must fit the program's objectives and content.

Several core rules of production style seem to apply universally, however. One is that only those stories that are well suited to television coverage should be included in the program. This implies that the program segment, in addition to concentrating on people, should also concentrate on the activity being covered. Like it or not, employee news (next to marketing and sales) is the closest application to broadcast television, and broadcast television highlights action.

This production style rule implies also that the program be produced with as much quality as possible. Because the application resembles electronic journalism news in many respects, audiences will unconsciously expect a broadcast quality feel. This does not mean, however, that the production style of *NBC News* should be exactly imitated. On the contrary, as indicted later, imitation is not necessarily the order of the day. What is important is that whatever the content of the program, the available equipment, and available video professionals, every attempt should be made to strive for the highest quality possible in scripting, videography, editing, and all other aspects.

The employee news show is the hardest corporate video application to carry off successfully. Results are hard to measure. Content and production styles are hard to define. Be wary.

A corporate version of Walter Cronkite or Barbara Walters does not belong on a corporate television employee news show. Do not try to imitate the commercial electronic journalists—with a studio setting, an anchorperson, and broadcast news commentator style. The style of the program should reflect the general style and environment of the specific corporate culture. Use that style and environment; it will be more credible.

Keep the program length to no more than 10 minutes. Employees do not have forever to watch a corporate employee news program, and since viewing is not mandatory the length of the show will have an effect on the survivability of the program. Moreover, the length of the program will have a direct effect on its cost. Each minute of finished programming will translate directly into the amount of time required to research each segment, arrange for shooting the segment, shooting the segment, reviewing rough production footage, scripting, preparing graphics, special audio effects, special graphic effects, postproduction time, and duplication. Basic rule of thumb: shorter is probably better than longer.

Base hardware needs on programming mix decisions. Too many companies have made the classic mistake of buying video production hardware before they had determined what their software needs were. This caution is especially relevant for employee news programs.

For best results, an employee news show is most effective when it is shot on location rather than in a studio. Portable equipment is available, so there is really no strong need to shoot an employee news show primarily in a studio. The decision to purchase production and postproduction equipment depends on the volume of employee news shows to be produced on an annual basis, how many other kinds of video programs are or will be produced, and the availability of external production and postproduction facilities. Experience has shown that (other than for reasons of security and proprietary content), if a company is producing less than twelve programs a year, external resources are more cost efficient. Beyond twelve programs, it may pay to purchase production equipment but edit at an outside facility. Beyond twenty-five to thirty programs a year, it may be time to invest in a modest editing system.

Provide an adequate distribution system. Once you know who your audience is and where they are, you will need enough video monitors and playback units to reach them. Without an adequate distribution system, you will not reach your intended audience. Video employee news shows differ sharply from print house organs in this respect. Whereas the printed document goes directly to the employee, either to the desk or to the home, the employee has to go to the video employee news show. Even though some companies may be using cable television to reach the employee at home, nonetheless there is no guarantee that the employee will actually watch the program.

With this inherent distribution problem, employee news shows should be given adequate publicity to let employees know what will be on the show and where they can view the information.

The cost of the employee news show should reflect its objectives. Keep things in context. If the objective of the employee news program is to have it viewed by all 30,000 or 100,000 employees every quarter, then an expenditure of $50,000 to $75,000 per 20-minute program may not be excessive. On the other hand, if the program is to be viewed every week by corporate headquarters personnel only, then the cost of the programming should be less. The difference between the two programs will more than likely be in the kind of content covered and where the segments will be shot. For a corporatewide program, travel for the sake of production is probably appropriate. For a corporate headquarters–only program, production requirements will be significantly different.

Keep costs in line with objectives and audience distribution. Sophisticated production editing techniques may be required, and this usually translates into more production dollars. Rule of thumb: the farther the audience from corporate headquarters and the deeper into the organizational hierarchy the program is distributed, the more sophisticated the production and editing techniques that will be required.

If the company is located in a big city, television employee news shows may not work. Employee news shows do not seem to survive in the long run when they are produced by a large company in a big city, like New York.

The major reason why employee news shows have mostly not survived in New York is that employees in the Big Apple are provided with too many distractions, such as shops and restaurants. However, in smaller communities there is less distraction from the outside during the workday, which in turn gives the employees news show a greater opportunity for a viewership.

The video employee news show has been around since the early 1970s. And while there have been failures along the way, employee news remains a viable corporate programming network application. Communicating effectively with employees is one of the more pressing problems facing today's corporate manager because employees are more sophisticated, more discriminating, and less homogeneous, demographically speaking. They are more concerned with the quality of their work lives. Used judiciously, intelligently, and rationally, employee news programming distributed via corporate television networks can be an effective and efficient means of contributing to successful management-employee communications.

Chapter 10

Reaching Managers

Audience: Executives Get into the Act

One of the major uses of videotape and other electronic media in the organizational context is management communications to organizational middle management and supervisors. Few would argue that this use of video is not advantageous as a means of helping to satisfy management's internal communications needs.

The Benefits

Using videotape for the distribution of management communications videos to a corporate network has several advantages. First, the medium has *speed*. Videotaped messages can be shot, edited, duplicated, and distributed in days to a domestic and/or international employee audience. This is not to say that all programs produced at this rate of speed will have the professional look or depth of content of a *Nightline*. There are differences in content, of course, and more importantly there are vast differences between the number of people working on *Nightline* and (potentially) a management communications video—probably on the order of 50 to 1. Yet once an organization has a corporate video network in place, it can be an extremely effective and efficient means of communicating.

A second advantage is that the video medium has *credibility*. Rightly or wrongly, television today is perceived as the medium for news. If you're seen on television, you gain exposure, if not credibility. Today's corporate communications environment virtually demands that executives use the television medium as one major means of communicating with employees. Executives may not be able to shake hands with everyone in the corporation, but video is the next best thing.

Third, videotape's look of *immediacy* (as opposed to the look of film and even high-definition television) gives the viewer the impression the executive presentation is live, present and directed at the viewer. Film's look is more of something or someone not live or present. Videotape, therefore, gives an employee the feeling (whether real or not) that the executive is actually there, making a personal connection. Following are two examples of organizational management communications.

Management Perspectives: Hewlett Packard

Hewlett Packard started a management-to-management communications show in 1986 called *Management Perspectives.* According to Brad Whitworth, manager of employee communications in HP's Corporate Public Relations Department: "It's pretty flexible in format. It comes out about four times a year. It can be anything from a one-on-one with the CEO and president to a panel discussion with a number of top managers. The intended audience is at least first-line supervisors, middle managers and up within Hewlett Packard; which is a pretty broad audience. You're looking at at least 3,000 to 4,000 people; maybe more than that worldwide."

Hewlett Packard has 70 plant sites and 120 sales offices in the United States, and another 200 sales offices and factories in Europe and throughout the Far East and Latin America. In bringing these farflung elements together, Whitworth reports:

> *One of the most successful programs is our annual recap of the General Managers' Meeting. We bring in the top 190 managers from around the world for two days of sharing best practices, hearing what last year was like, and what the year ahead is shaping up to be. The audience hears a little bit about the directors and top management concerns.*
>
> *What we do is to find a way to take some of the presentations and boil them down into 20 to 30 second soundbites combined with one-on-one interviews with some of the key people who were there and have general reportage of the event. We produce this pretty much as a tool for the managers who were able to get to this meeting; they in turn can use this tape along with notes to share what they were exposed to with their employees. If nothing else, we are encouraging managers to make sure they are talking to their people: giving them a tool for some consistency of message so that we know a baseline of information is made; and at the same time not taking away from them the honor communicating what they learned.*
>
> *We aim for about 15 to 20 minutes maximum length; that's about how long we can keep someone's attention. More in-depth presentations, panel discussions, and customer interviews have gone on for as long as 30 minutes.*

The biggest piece of advice Whitworth has for others producing management-to-management videos is to make sure that whatever they do fits in with the culture and other existing communication channels:

> *We didn't start this program in a vacuum. We've had a management newsletter for a while and there was a clearly defined niche for this newsletter: to try to warn people about things that were coming down the pipe and describe the things that will affect managers in the next six months or so. In that print process, for example, we will talk about the formation of a new workforce; we'll talk about a piece of legislation that might be moving through the governmental body.*
>
> *As part of the early warning system, we felt the video counterpart could deal with things on a more real-time basis. The implications of some major pronouncements. Something like that General Managers' Meeting. So instead of a newsletter to tip people off to things that might be happening, the video program was positioned properly as a tool that helps explain some of the changes as they arrived, once they are there. So the best advice is: figure out what your objectives are; its mission; how you position this video tool—because it can serve a variety of purposes.*
>
> *We have an internal rate card. Most of them are in-studio kinds of things. Usually studio charges and tape duplication run us about $10,000 to $15,000. If I had to pay an outside vendor, my hunch is I'd have to pay about double that.*

Whitworth himself usually acts as the moderator and host. He also writes the scripts, though much of this depends on the format of individual programs. For panel discussions, he gives panelists an idea of the questions he is going to ask so that they can prepare their answers in advance. "But it tends to be very loose," he adds.

> *We can always go back and do little editing. During something like, for instance, our General Managers' Meeting, I'm sitting there taking mad notes of the things we're going to use—the soundbites from people standing behind the podium, which are few and far between, and then where I'm going to have to supplement by grabbing this person for an interview and that person for an interview and then what information is best conveyed by the host of the program. So I'm writing my voiceovers; I'm figuring out what questions to work into an interview; I'm also picking the soundbites to use. Graphics are all done in postproduction.*
>
> *We've always had the capability for doing the production, but we are off in the distribution—making sure someone at the far end can pretty much guarantee the thing will be used. And we're at an advantage over other places because*

we have a communications manager at most of our major sites. Rather than sending a tape to a manager and assuming that he or she is going to get every-one together to watch it, we get the program into the hands of the deadline-oriented/action-oriented communications manager and say: "Please make sure it is seen by this audience." That seems to increase the viewership levels tremendously. It's nice to have people who are action oriented at the distribution end. (Marlow, 1992)

Keeping 400 Executives Informed: At Ford

About every three years, roughly 400 of Ford's top executives from around the world are brought into a high-octane week's meeting where they are immersed in the strategic issues facing the company and then are sent back to their respective jobs.

The problem for Ford: how to keep these 400 top executives up to date on various issues facing the company on a global basis. According to Ray Anderson, manager of the management communications Planning Department of Ford's Corporate Public Affairs, "That's why my function was set up. To keep this top 400 informed. Which in reality is about 2,000 people, well below 1 percent of the company's salaried employment." Anderson communicates with these managers via video and newsletters:

Typically, a video involves the chairman, the president, and maybe the chairman of Ford in Europe, addressing different aspects of an issue. Maybe it's a strategic issue. I've done communications on what our position is on the environment globally. One of the things we try to get is a consistent thought or a mindset.

We produce this programming as needed. For the first quarter or six months, I didn't do a management communications video because we were focusing on getting Harold Poling established as the chairman. Then this summer, I went back into business. Then I'll back off and maybe do something like the state of the company—where do we stand right now?

Right now I'm not doing any communicating because of the [Gulf] war and the impact that it's having; if we come out with some kind of management communications, say, on quality as an issue, that's going to look awfully frivolous compared to what's going on in the world economy and the war in the Gulf."

The 30 to 60 minute programs are distributed to a worldwide audience, places where Ford has major operations like Taiwan, Australia, the United Kingdom, all of Europe. The English language is not a problem for these managers because most speak English. But, says Anderson, *you have to be aware of different meanings of certain words like "redundant." It means something entirely different in the United Kingdom than it does in the United States. So with words where I am aware there are going to be problems during the interview, I'll say, "Let's go back in and put it in this tone." I use a video guide to explain terminology.*

You can't do this kind of programming effectively if you don't have the cooperation of the company's top management. Because you can have doors shut to you and it does absolutely no good. So if you don't have buy-in at the top level, then you're going nowhere. (Marlow, 1992)

Anderson attempts to get a sponsor for a subject; the president of the company, for example, might be focusing on one topic and Anderson will work most closely with him. He reports that he's never had any kind of censoring, which he believes would be disastrous. (Marlow, 1992)

Programming Guidelines

At a minimum, producing a management video should involve:

1. A statement of the program's objectives
2. A definition of the intended audience
3. A definition of the ultimate distribution of the program
4. A preproduction, production, and postproduction schedule
5. A definition of any graphics, film footage, or slides that may be needed
6. A proposed budget
7. An outline of the program's content in the order in which it is to be presented
8. A listing of those members of management who will participate in the program both in front of and behind the camera (e.g., subject experts)
9. A rehearsal schedule

While items 1–6 are de rigueur for any video production, items 7 and 8 present special considerations for management video communications (Marlow, 1992).

Preplan the program. Doing this helps to preclude the error of putting too much content into one program.

The more successful management video programs are those that stick to a few specific subjects. Thus, having the opportunity to see a version of the program in the planning stage gives management and the producer a chance to cut the program down to size. Tapes not planned in this way tend to be longwinded and disjointed, leaving an audience confused by a mass of information. The objective is to create understanding through succinctness and clarity.

The organization of the program's content is equally important. Pre-outlining the program gives management and the producer opportunities to create logical transitions between subjects. All audiences appreciate a logical flow of information, even if it is not obvious. Management will also appreciate a logical sequence because it will be easier for them to perceive and absorb the total program. Moreover, they should carry over this understanding of the total program into the rehearsal and final production stages. The end result should be a more relaxed, genuine, and hence communications-effective management performance.

Preplanning has a positive impact on the time and cost of the production. A well-planned video program involving management should take less time and, thus, less money to produce than an ill-conceived and unplanned program. While all video programs need preproduction planning of some sort or another, preproduction planning is of even more concern when management is involved.

The prime reason for this emphasis on planning for management videotapes is: management's time is at a premium. In the long run, the more time spent in preproduction planning will mean less time management has to spend "under the lights," comparatively speaking. Overall, the preplanning process should take at least 60 percent of the time involved in producing the program. In some cases, the proportion of time devoted to preplanning may be even higher.

While it should not be the producer's intent to make television production look as easy as falling off a log, the process should be as free of unnecessary distractions as possible. Moreover, corporate network programmers who have produced management video programs have learned that management looks to the professional for expertise and guidance as well as constructive criticism. This need or desire may not be articulated verbally or directly, but it is nonetheless there. Therefore, the producer must take the initiative by conveying to management the need for preplanning.

A relatively smooth production process can be a short-term benefit of good preplanning. The longer-term benefits are less obvious, perhaps, but crucial to the growth of video as an internal communications tool. If management understands that it takes a certain length of time and effort to produce a successful video, they will, over a longer period of time, gain a greater understanding of the problems inherent in video production. Hence, participation by management in the preplanning stage, together with the subsequent steps involved, can create a positive environment for the development of future programs, especially if the process is approached in a professional and structured manner. Through this process, management should begin to understand video production is bigger than a breadbox, but smaller than a Cadillac—to produce an effective video program involves more than just setting up a camera and lights, but less than producing the Super Bowl.

Involving management in the preplanning phase can also help management understand what it takes to get the most out of video as a communications medium. Preplanning a management video program can do much to preclude wasting management's (and your) time during an actual shoot while at the same time creating an end product that is both communications and cost effective.

Rehearse. Between the initial stages of planning the production and the actual shoot is a vital step that, when applied, goes a long way towards satisfying everybody's objectives. This step is the rehearsal.

Some will say, "Why is there any need for management talent to rehearse? After all, they know what they're talking about, and as corporate executives it is presumed they enjoy some measure of verbal acumen?" An underlying question is, "Do the rigors of video production require anything more of executive talent beyond their own experience with, and understanding of, communications?" Management personnel are, by their very position, corporate spokespersons. They are to corporations what the President of the United States and his Cabinet and staff are to the federal government. Thus, *who* is communicating is as important as *what* is being communicated; moreover, the manner in which the content is communicated is crucial to communications success. (And, as some critics have observed somewhat cynically, the manner or "style" of the communication is perhaps more important than what is being said.)

Some executives are better communicators than others (likewise Presidents of the United States). This observation notwithstanding, it is still true that any well-intentioned and well-planned message can become garbled if the person delivering the communication fumbles, mumbles, and stumbles. The rehearsal preceding the production shoot can help reduce the chances of this occurring.

There is another reason for using the rehearsal as a preparation technique. Increasing numbers of corporate managers are realizing employee audiences are an important constituency for the corporation's articulated views on so-called public issues, such as equal employment opportunity, wage and price controls, environmental problems, government regulations, management/labor relations, and so on. Thus, internal employee audiences can be a prime source of support for top management's positions on these issues. In a very real sense, top corporate management video programs can be extremely valuable communications tools.

Ideally, then, management should view internal video communications in the same light as external broadcast communications, such as appearing on the *Today* show. After all, before and after working hours, all employees become part of the external public. No audience (employees included) wants to sense that the talent (i.e., executive) is uncomfortable in front of the camera. Many corporate executives who are unfamiliar with the television medium are uneasy in front of the camera during the first few productions; on the other hand, those executives who have planned and rehearsed their programs come off looking more at home.

Another reason for rehearsing a corporate executive is to familiarize him or her with the video production environment. Many executives have had the experience of conducting meetings, giving speeches, or making presentations to small groups of people, but talking into the glass eye of a television camera or being interviewed by someone else while "under the lights" can be a very unsettling situation, especially to the video novitiate. Thus, rehearsing allows the executive the opportunity to become accustomed to the video environment in addition to fine tuning the content and organization of the information to be communicated.

Without a rehearsal, the corporate executive is put on the spot. Every mistake on camera is exacerbated by the frightening newness of the video production hardware and all the terminology, hot lights, cues, stops, and starts associated with video production. The moment the uninitiated corporate executive steps in front of a television camera without the benefit of planning or a rehearsal, that executive undergoes a severe test of his or her self-esteem. Simply imagine if the roles were reversed: you are the executive, and he or she is the video producer. You may be prepared mentally for what you want to say, how you want to say it, and the order in which it is to be said, but more than likely you will be completely unprepared emotionally for the experience of being on camera.

For both mental and emotional reasons, everyone needs a period of transition from the unknown to the known before the filming. In the case of a video communication involving executives, the rehearsal (and the preproduction planning preceding the rehearsal) provides that transition. Considering, then, the frequency with which managements are using video to communicate to employees—and considering that more and more managements are communicating their views on public issues via video and not all managements have a natural flair for communicating via video—it seems clear the rehearsal is a necessary part of the video production process.

E-Mail: Siemens Corporation

Without a doubt, E-mail has become a way of life for many organizational employees, and in some organizations employees have become rooted to their computer screens with E-mail activities. Nonetheless, E-mail saves time and trees, and has created organizationwide communications webs that can be used to great effect by managers and employers alike, as witness the example of Siemens Corporation.

Siemens Corporation U.S. is a $7.3 billion electrical electronics firm, the subsidiary of a European-based company that does about $50 billion globally in sales. Sales were about $7 billion during 1994. It has about 46,000 employees, more than seventy manufacturing facilities, and 10 percent of sales are put back into more than twenty research and development facilities around the country. About 14 percent to 15 percent, or nearly $1 billion, of Siemen's sales are exported. It serves eight primary industries, including telecommunications, information systems, transportation, industrial automation, electronic components, medical systems, and lighting and power engineering.

Kevin Kimball, director of public relations for Siemens Corporation in New York, described how his organization uses E-mail:

> *From an internal perspective, we have seven regional offices around the country. What we've done is establish five public relations offices where we have a critical mass of businesses: Cupertino, California; Chicago, Illinois; Iselin, New Jersey; Atlanta, Georgia; and Boca Raton, Florida.*
>
> *We have two offices which we consider media centers or media critical mass: New York City and Washington, D.C. Each regional office has two basic responsibilities: to provide public relations support for the Siemens businesses in its particular area and to serve as the Siemens corporate spokesperson to the media in their area. These public relations people, fourteen total, are scattered throughout the seven offices. These people have to be specialists in terms of the particular industry or company in their area but generalists when it comes to Siemens overall. Therefore, it's very important that we communicate as one and that we communicate internally with each other. And we rely on electronic mail.*
>
> *For instance, today we are putting out an announcement about a new device that will be used in the automobile industry to alert motorists when an object is in their blind spot while they're driving, to prevent or help prevent collisions. We're announcing this device to both the national press and the regions where we have offices. This is a Cupertino-driven announcement, but that Cupertino office has to communicate to our other six offices. The way we orchestrate this is through electronic mail.*

Videoconferencing: Teamwork Day 1990

As described in Chapter 2, using satellite technology for various forms of video-conferencing is another electronic means of internal public relations. Following is an example of how the Xerox Corporation used this electronic medium.

To communicate Xerox's corporate commitment to quality and to showcase the accomplishments of the Xerox teams, Xerox produced an employee communications teleconference that received an award as Outstanding Direct Broadcast Satellite Application from the International Teleconferencing Association in 1991.

Teamwork Day started in the early 1980s and grew into a large event celebrated in many different locations. The live broadcast originated from three separate locations: Rochester (New York), Los Angeles (California), and Dallas (Texas). It went live to those three locations as well as to seventy-one downlink sites. The program audience was estimated at over 15,000 people, including Xerox employees, external customers, and suppliers in the United States. Because Xerox used satellite technology, they could go through their Leesburg, Virginia facility to send the signal to London for a European audience.

According to producer Joann Kildow:

> *The presentation consisted of our continuing quality improvement process, our dedication to customer satisfaction and the processes of quality. Top-level executives did the presentations. The whole presentation was on quality. This was the year before we won the Malcolm Balridge Award.*
>
> *In 1989, we did a two-way satellite broadcast between Rochester and Los Angeles carrying satellite signals back and forth. We went to seventy downlinks under the same network in district locations. As it grew in popularity, the Xerox people at local venues started bringing in customers to show off the quality process and the celebration of teamwork and quality.*
>
> *The event grew to a three-city event among Rochester, Dallas and Los Angeles in 1990. Each one of these venues had a featured speaker, a featured team and some local events. We basically threw satellite signals back and forth for about ninety minutes.*
>
> *1990 was a special year for us because David Kearns was retiring as Xerox CEO. Xerox was touting present and former company employees involved with community and Kearns was presented with an award. There was really good bantering between him and a couple of the other executives in other locations. They were basically throwing friendly barbs at each other from 3,000 miles away. It was a nice touch. There was good energy, good reaction from the audience, standing ovations, and a lot of visuals.*

The three origination locations were convention centers, with large facilities and a large audience capacity. At the seventy-one downlink sites, the audience was smaller. To handle the technical complexity of the event, Kildow managed the Xerox education network in partnership with two other media groups. Design teams in all three cities had a committee going all year to plan these events. Even with downlinks installed in seventy-one sites, the planners had to bring up links to all three origination locations, which meant uplink trucks and satellite time to deal with. Each of the live one-hour shows had video clips of different successful teams in the field, so it was necessary for the production team to go on location and take video clips to reinforce messages that are being made.

In addition to planning, Kildow recommended intensive rehearsals, in part because of all the technology involved. "Some of the problems often are just getting visuals for executive speakers to support their messages. Also, there are last-minute changes and scripting. We do a full rehearsal the day before, so it gives us an opportunity to catch any new things that might have been dredged up. We always do a full rehearsal both technically as well to make sure all the scripts are intact. If we don't have the actual presenter, we have someone stand in for that person."

Kildow recalls Teamwork Day 1990 as "an exciting, complex event: three locations and going back and forth among the three locations. It was also a big event, a fun thing. It is something we do on an annual basis and obviously we are very proud of being a quality company and winning the awards and it's a great time for us to share what we have accomplished during the year and bring our customers and suppliers in to work with us."

The Impact of Electrovisual Media on Management Communications

Videotape, teleconferencing, E-mail, computer networks—all these electronic media have had a direct impact on the nature of management communications.

Introduced virtually within a decade of each other—the computer in 1946, videotape in 1956, and the satellite in 1957—today all three communications technologies are used singly and as part of networks in American corporations. As with the ubiquitous telephone, it appears these technologies have acted true to Marshall McLuhan's contention that "once a new technology comes into a social milieu it cannot cease to permeate that milieu until every institution is saturated" (1964, p. 177). In recent times these technologies have also dramatically impacted the shape of American corporations and institutions.

The Evolving American Corporation

Since 1987, American corporations, particularly large ones, appear to be shrinking. The *New York Times* for example, reported that "big companies are continuing to cut [jobs]—a trend that promises to keep the pace of [the economic] recovery slow....A recent survey of more than 800 companies by the American Management Association found that one in four companies is planning work force reductions by the middle of 1993. That is the highest level since the research group began its survey six years ago. Examples of job cutting companies included IBM (25,000 jobs) and General Motors (18,000 jobs)" (December 17, 1992, p. 1).

In other words, American corporations seem to be getting thinner, not just in terms of numbers of employees, but also in terms of layers of management. Is there a correlation between the saturation of American corporations by electrovisual media—such as the computer, satellites, and videotape—and the apparent evolving general organizational structure of these corporations? Has the advent of electrovisual media changed the nature of the relationship among top management, middle management, and lower level employees? Has the burgeoning use of electrovisual media changed both the formal and informal organizational structure of American corporations in the last forty years?

The answer to both questions appears to be yes. Since the late 1950s and continuing to the present day, electrovisual media have altered—sometimes blatantly, sometimes subtly—the relationship between American corporate managers and employees. The relationship between American corporate executives and various internal and external publics is becoming far more fluid and dynamic as a direct result of the increasing use of electrovisual media, as opposed to the bureaucratic/militaristic model formerly typical of American corporate organizations.

Moreover, American corporate managers, particularly middle managers, are far more vulnerable to layoff today than ever before because of the communications patterns that have been created as a direct result of the increasing use of electrovisual media. This vulnerability is evidenced by the tens of thousands of corporate employees (particularly middle managers) who have been displaced in the last five to six years.

Technology Diffusion

The very brief review of videotape, teleconferencing, and the computer as management tools in the corporate context in Chapter 2 shows clearly that once these media became standardized and portable—as with the videocassette in 1971 (Marlow & Secunda, 1991, p. 19), and microcomputers in 1975 (Rogers, 1986, p. 25)—American corporate managers began to use these media for a growing variety of communication purposes.

The use of videotape in the nonbroadcast context, for example, has clearly gone far beyond original expectations. In the early stages, a handful of individuals and organizations enthusiastically adopted the medium. Today is there any organization that does not take the VCR for granted, even though it has taken decades for the medium to become truly part of the "corporate communications" landscape?

The adoption of videotape in the nonbroadcast (or corporate context) over a period of thirty-five years very much parallels the observations of Gabriel Tarde, who "observed that the rate of adoption of a new idea usually followed an S-shaped curve over time: At first, only a few individuals adopt a new idea, then the rate of adoption spurts as a large number of individuals accept the innovation, and, finally, the adoption slackens as only a few individuals are left to adopt" (Rogers, 1986, pp. 72–73).

Only a few individuals and organizations adopted videotape in the late 1950s. It wasn't until the early 1970s, when Sony introduced the standardized and highly portable three-quarter inch U-Matic videocassette, that the innovation became more widespread. And while the so-called nonbroadcast television market has grown from a $207 million industry in the early 1970s to a more than $5 billion market in the 1990s, the rate of growth has slackened in the last five years, suggesting strongly that only a few holdouts are left. If we liken the technology diffusion history of videotape to a stone dropped into a pool, the diffusion of the technology in the early stages can be described as the first ripple in the water and in the later stages as the larger ripples. From the beginning, videotape distribution took place primarily in centralized or regional areas: the distribution area for a program was constrained. Following the introduction of the three-quarter inch videocassette, the distribution area of videotaped messages extended beyond centralized and regional areas to include all company locations, domestic or international. With the introduction of the one-half inch videocassette and growth of the home VCR market, companies extended their distribution of videotaped messages into the home.

The same analogy can be made of the use of the medium in the corporate hierarchy before and after 1971—that is, before and after the advent of the three-quarter inch videocassette. Before 1971, top management was conspicuous in its absence from direct use of the medium. After 1971, this pattern was reversed; the presence of top management in videotaped messages to employees or external audiences is concurrent with the introduction of the three-quarter inch video-cassette. Once a cost-efficient distribution medium was available, top management appears to have taken immediate advantage of it.

The adoption of teleconferencing and computing technology shows a similar pattern of growth to that of videotape and Tarde's S-shaped curve. Moreover, the economics of teleconferencing and computing technologies also seems to fit the classic pattern: as the number of adopters increase, the unit price decreases, which, in turn, stimulates the adoption of the technology by even larger numbers of adopters.

The Breakdown of Hierarchy

Top management's use of the videotape medium, particularly after 1971, implies a significant change in management style, organizational structure, and communications. Before 1971, with top management reportedly absent from the use of videotape as a communications medium, the typical organizational structure of the times—a hierarchical bureaucracy based largely on a military/industrial model—was intact. Top managers were invisible. They remained in their boardrooms talking among themselves and communicating with their immediate subordinates who, in turn, communicated corporate policies to lower-level subordinates, until ultimately "orders" were received by workers at the line level.

Even the term *line management* implies a militaristic model, a characteristic that media and culture analyst Marshall McLuhan might have dubbed mechanistic. Economic historian Harold Innis might interpret this kind of organizational model as monopolistic in terms of the communications flow—that is, communication flows from the top of the organization down until the workers at the bottom line of the so-called organizational chart get the message.

Videotaped messages, especially those in which top management appear, implicitly subverted the typical hierarchical organization chart. Not only did top management become visible (though not in the flesh), they were also communicating directly with line workers, in effect bypassing the bureaucratic authority (and communications monopoly) of middle managers.

This practice is particularly reflected in the use of the medium for employee news. Many employee news programs are produced by workers not even in middle management, employees not that far from the bottom rung of the organizational chart. In many instances, they have chosen the content of employee news programs, providing higher level-managers with an upward flow of information about employees and the company's operations that without videotape might have gone uncommunicated. Overall, the videotape medium, based on the reports of users, seems to have contributed, by implication, to the creation of a communications environment that runs counter to the bureaucratic/militaristic hierarchy typical of the post–World War II era.

Teleconferencing seems to have produced similar consequences. Ironically, the growing use of so-called "business television" (the video side of teleconferencing) is a throwback to the old days of live broadcast television. In this instance, a live performance (with perhaps some canned videotaped sequences) is beamed via satellite to one or more locations (perhaps domestic, sometimes international). Some organizations have permanently installed business television facilities. J. C. Penney, for example, was one of the earliest users of business television. Today, it "broadcasts" daily programs from its Dallas headquarters to its buyers to inform them of developments in product, prices, and policies. In a very meaningful way, this business television network circumvents J. C. Penney's middle management. Top policy decision-making management reaches the retail level in an electrovisual instant.

The computer and computer networks have also contributed to this corporate revolution. Today, tens of thousands of low-level clerks (defined by *Megatrends* author John Naisbitt as *the* job that defines the labor landscape of the second half of the twentieth century) have access to mounds of information that heretofore went unshared. They also have communications access with other clerks in a multitude of other organizations. On the other hand, computers and computer networks have also given top managers greater access to up-to-date information, with the result that their span of control is wider and dynamic. As a result, the role of middle managers as carriers of information to and from top management and lower management and employees has become deflated.

In sum, over a thirty-five year period the videotape, teleconferencing, and computer media seem to have contributed to the creation of a communications flow that has reordered the multilevel corporate organization to the potential detriment of middle management's role and authority. During this time the communication environment has become more holistic, open, and free flowing in contrast to the more rigid, closed, manual print-oriented organization reflected in the bureaucratic/militaristic organizational hierarchy.

These observations tend to support Harold Innis's (1951) contention that new technologies have a bias toward either time or space. The videotape, teleconferencing, and computer electrovisual media clearly are space biased: they transcend the physical boundaries of nations, transcend the organizational boundaries of departments, management levels and programming distributors. Innis's further observation that new technologies have the capacity to upend monopolies also seems to find support in the evidence. By implication, because these media can transcend organizational boundaries, they have the potential for breaking up the informational monopoly created by hierarchical conceptions of the corporate management culture.

The Future Structure of American Corporations

"The typical large organization, such as a large business or a government agency, twenty years hence will have no more than half the levels of management of its counterpart today, and no more than a third the number of 'managers.'" So states Peter F. Drucker in *The New Realities*. "In its structure, and in its management problems and concerns," he continues, this corporation of the future "will bear little resemblance to the typical manufacturing company, circa 1950, which our textbooks still consider the norm....the business, and increasingly the government agency as well, will be knowledge-based, composed largely of specialists who direct and discipline their own performance through organized feedback from colleagues and customers. It will be an information-based organization" (1989, p. 207).

In other words, as well as shifting decision-making authority, organizations will continue to *flatten* structurally. Marc S. Gerstein and Robert B. Shaw seem to concur with Drucker's prediction. In a chapter entitled "Organizational Architectures for the Twenty-First Century," they state that "the 1990s may witness the beginning of the end of the traditional organization. A century dominated by a single type of organization—the machine bureaucracy—is slowly giving way to a new era. Driven by…eight forces [including technology]…organizations are being forced to reshape themselves to survive and to prosper" (1992, p. 263). Gerstein and Shaw conclude that "information technology has begun to revolutionize organizational design by providing alternatives to hierarchy as the primary means of coordination. Information systems, common architectures, shared databases, decision support tools, and expert systems facilitate the coordination of behavior without control through hierarchy, thus enabling the creation of autonomous units linked together through information" (1992, p. 263).

Thomas W. Malone and John F. Rockart also point to the limitations of traditional hierarchies: "Central decision makers can become overloaded and therefore unable to cope effectively with rapidly changing environments or to consider enough information about complex issues. Furthermore, people at the bottom may feel left out of the decision making and as a result be less motivated to contribute their efforts" (1991, p. 133). Malone and Rockart also surmise that "what appears to be happening is a paradoxical combination of centralization and decentralization. Because information can now be distributed more easily, people lower in the organization can now become well enough informed to make more decisions more effectively. At the same time, upper-level managers can more easily review decisions made at lower levels. Thus, because lower-level decision makers know they are subject to spot-checking, senior managers can retain or even increase their central control over decisions" (1991, p. 133).

Is it a mere coincidence that the mechanistic, militaristic, bureaucratic style of American corporate management and organizational architecture typical of the manufacturing organization is evolving into a more fluid, dynamic "information-based" system at the same time that many of the world's leading nations have apparently come to the conclusion that war (at least on a large, mass scale) does not pay? Or, to put it in even more economic terms, that a military style of management and organizational architecture just does not flow to the bottom line as it once did? Is it a mere coincidence that, a generation after the introduction of three major electrovisual technologies (the computer, videotape, and satellites), the shape of American corporations appears to be changing? It is reminiscent of the forty years that Moses and the emerging Jewish people wandered in the desert, allowing the old slave mentality generation to die off and the new free men generation to enter the promised land. But as contemporary events are reminding us, the promised land of technology is not without its pain.

Because of the accelerated flow of information, electrovisual technologies have gradually contributed to the obsolescence of the traditional social contract between employer and employee that provided an employee with opportunities, advancement, and stability in return for company loyalty and hard work.

Implications for Public Relations

The impact of electrovisual media on the organizational hierarchy—in effect, the breakdown of hierarchy—has meaningful implications for public relations practitioners. To be successful, public relations practitioners must accept the concept that the old world view of the organization as a bureaucratic/militaristic model is anachronistic. Electronic technologies have not substantially changed what we do—we still talk, write, communicate—but rather how we do it. This includes the speed with which we perform these actions.

As a result, the linear, step-by-step view doesn't work anymore. A more simultaneous perspective must be harnessed. For public relations practitioners, this means having greater flexibility and nimbleness. To work successfully with product and service organizations on one hand, and journalists, community groups, government organizations, and consumers on the other will require a broader perspective.

In *TechnoTrends: Twenty-four Technologies that Will Revolutionize Our Lives* (1993), Daniel Burrus describes this new shifting focus in corporate culture, management, human resources, price vs. speed, information, computers, manufacturing, globalization, cultural barriers, national focus, law, logistics, television news, the environment, and electronic data interchange. Corporate culture alone, Burrus predicts, will shift from

> *status quo, industry performance, incremental innovation, expansion, sameness, corporate groups, new technology as cost, cost/growth/control, bottom line of last quarter*

to

> *rapid change, individual action, fundamental change, consolidation, redirection, partnerships, new technology as necessity, quality/innovation/service, global market share. (1993, p. 348)*

Heightened awareness of these changes in organizational culture as a direct result of the application of electronic media is a necessity for public relations professionals. As the next chapter spells out, as we approach the millennium electronic media have moved everyone from the simple to the complex, from the mass market to the one-on-one market. Marketers and public relations professionals alike must "think globally, act locally." Today we have the unparalleled opportunity to disseminate information to many or to a few anywhere on earth.

Chapter 11

Reaching Individuals on a Global Scale: Welcome to Cyberspace

The Cyberspace Audience

Much has been written about the Internet and its use for marketing and public relations—several thousand articles in the United States and Europe from early 1994 to early 1995, according to the Reuters News Service. Clearly, the Internet is here to stay as a communications medium, and there is high interest in it as a marketing and public relations medium.

The Internet has also been called the new anarchy, the Wild West of the late twentieth century, the information superhighway, and *cyberspace,* a phrase coined by science fiction writer William Gibson in a novel written over ten years ago. The Internet was born in 1968 when the U.S. Department of Defense created a computer network among seven universities for the purpose of facilitating the sharing of information among academics at these various institutions.

The paradigm of virtual instant access to information on a global basis is yet another milestone in the process of democratization initiated by the Greeks around 700 B.C., when their culture developed the ancestor of the modern alphabets of the Western world. An alphabet is, in fact, a series of standardized, digital representations of analogic sounds. It can be argued that this significant development in the history of Western communications technology led to the Renaissance, Gutenberg's invention of the printing press, the Industrial Revolution, and (leaping forward to today) increasing global economic interdependance. It can similarly be argued that in this century communications technologies (such as satellites and computers) led to the demise of the former Union of Soviet Socialist Republics. Because electronic technologies transcend geographic and political boundaries, they have changed the shape of the global world order. The Internet is in that chain of electronic technologies.

So what does the Internet mean to public relations professionals? Before written history, the storytellers of yesteryear (today we call them public relations practitioners, journalists, novelists, playwrights, songwriters, performers, actors, television producers, filmmakers, advertisers, comedians, clergy, and politicians) were older men and women sitting around the campfire telling the stories of the tribe to an enraptured audience. Today, our campfires are primarily print and electronic based and our tribes geographically global. And they still seem to be enraptured.

The Internet is only the latest electronic medium among a chain of electronic media starting with the telegraph in the mid-1840s. This network of computer networks—made possible by developments in personal computers and telecommunications hardware and software—gives a user access to textual and graphic material in various ways. On-line consumer services, such as CompuServe (the oldest), Prodigy, and America Online, provide access for a monthly fee. By mid-1995, all provided access to the larger worldwide Internet. The Internet can also be reached by going through an internet access provider, also for a monthly fee. The World Wide Web—which allows a user access in a multimedia form—is also part of the Internet.

Who's on the Net?

What is the size of the Internet, and who's there? No one source can provide a definitive answer, but a gathering of data can provide an outline of the Internet's growth and who's using it.

One way of gauging the Internet's demographics is by counting the number of domain names. A *domain name* is a key component of an Internet address used for electronic mail and other data services on the global computer network. For example, the author's E-mail (domain name) address is emabb@cunyvm.cuny.edu. Another example, America Online, now the largest on-line service with 3.5 million subscribers, has aol.com as its domain name.

In recent years, more than 118,000 Internet domain names have been assigned to businesses, educational institutions, nonprofit organizations, and network service providers (Peter, 1995). Of these, about 102,000 are commercial domains, 8,990 are nonprofit organizations, 5,694 are network service providers, and the balance (2,030) are education domains.

In August 1995 alone, more than 14,000 businesses and individuals applied for new domain addresses (according to Network Solutions, Inc., which handles Internet registrations under contract to the National Science Foundation). This does not mean to say that there are 118,000 organizations on the Net. On the contrary, many organizations have applied for multiple names; therefore, the actual number is lower. By contrast, according to Dun and Bradstreet there are over 10 million organizations in the United States. In effect, it appears there is a substantial way to go before all organizations in the United States sign onto the Internet.

Another way to guage the Internet's demographics is by looking at the number of people subscribing to on-line services, such as AOL, CompuServe (the oldest), and Prodigy. The investment firm Goldman Sachs estimates that by the end of 1995, over 9 million paying consumers will have access to the World Wide Web (the fastest growing segment of the Internet) through on-line services. They expect this to grow to more than 14 million by 1996 and 22–25 million by 1997 (Philo and Boswick, 1995, p. 2). These numbers contrast to the 97 million television households in the United States (the rest of the world notwithstanding).

The similarity between the growth curve of the Internet as a potential advertising, marketing, and public relations medium to the early days of cable television is obvious. It is not a matter of *if* the Internet will become a source of advertising revenue, but *when*.

A few organizations have performed on-line surveys of users. In its Third World World Web User Survey (April 10–May 10, 1995) of Prodigy users, the Georgia Tech Research Corporation found the following demographics from 13,000 questionnaire responses:

- The mean age is 35.
- Of the respondents, 15.5% were women, 82% male, and 2.5% chose not to say.
- The overall median income is between $50,000 and $60,000.
- Of the respondents, 80.6% were from the United States, 9.8% from Europe, and 5.8% from Canada and Mexico.

The survey also found that 41 percent of Prodigy subscribers report using their Web browser (e.g., Netscape) between 6 and 10 hours a week.

The character of Internet users can also be surmised from a recent Yankelovich Partners survey (September 1995). According to the survey, between the end of the third quarter of 1994 and the end of the first quarter of 1995, the penetration of on-line usage of all commerical and noncommercial services doubled to the current level of 14 percent of all American adults. That still leaves another 85 percent to go!

The Yankelovich survey did find that so-called "cybercitizens" differ disproportionately from adults in general in being more likely to be

- men—57% versus 48% for adults in general
- younger—38% under 30 versus 26% for adults in general; average age of 35 versus 43 for adults in general (this squares with the Georgia Tech survey)
- better educated—33% with a college degree versus 19% of adults in general; 57% with some college versus 43% for adults in general
- single—39% versus 25% of adults in general

The Yankelovich survey found that on average, cybercitizens are on line a little over 30 minutes a day. Within the past year, 22 percent of all cybercitizens also report having made some kind of on-line purchase.

All these numbers need to be put into the context of an SRI International survey of World Wide Web users (June 7, 1995) which rightly points out that there are really two Web audiences: "The first is the group that drives most of the media coverage and stereotypes of Web users, the 'upstream' audience. Comprising 50% of the current Web population, this well-documented group is the upscale, technically oriented academics and professionals that ride in a variety of institutional subsidies. Yet because this group comprises only 10% of the U.S. population…their behaviors and characteristics are of limited usefulness in understanding the future Web." In effect, a significant portion of the U.S. population, the rest of the world notwithstanding, has yet to sign onto the Net!

According to Survey-Net (www.survey.net), by the end of 1994 more than 10,000 companies were offering information and services for sale over a combination of Internet and value added network providers. Their ranks are expected to swell to 100,000 in three years and a million in five years, when Internet connectivity approaches the ubiquity of the fax. The authors of this on-line document state that by 1995 the Net will link 25 million users in over 130 countries. Millions more send E-mail through the Internet via gateways provided by the on-line services, AT&T, MCI, and other leading proprietary networks. "The Internet," the authors say, "provides connectivity between far more points than any alternative, and does so at very low cost. Anything less is at a competitive disadvantage." (Neches, Neches, Postel et al., 1995).

As an indication of the scale of the Internet's use as a marketing and public relations medium, Edward Roche (1995) reports that as of mid-June 1995, more than 80,000 companies were using the Internet for distribution of critical company information such as press releases. As a final point, all this information ("Who's on the Net?") was gathered directly from the Internet itself!

All for One or One for All

The Internet is *the* communications medium for the balance of this century. In a very unvirtual way, the Internet provides an opportunity for marketers and public relations professionals to reach either all audiences on the Net or simply one individual, if that is their choice. Moreover, cyberspacers can communicate with each other about products and services, if they wish. The Internet is also developing an audience that may not be reachable by so-called more traditional means. It is true that more people don't read *Time* magazine than do. The Internet may be the way to reach the audience that doesn't on an individual basis, and on a global scale.

The challenge of the Internet for public relations practitioners is finding where specific audiences are and identifying ways to communicate with them directly in cyberspace. While there may be more initial work involved in defining the audience and their location, the end result can be effective and efficient.

The Internet has also begun to change the nature of journalism. An extreme example is *Omni* magazine's March 1995 announcment that it would be dropping its print version and converting entirely to an on-line presence and a CD-ROM version. As newspapers and magazines are moving onto the Internet, so are merchants. New magazines (or *zines*, as they are called) are being created. Advertisers are creating information-based home pages on the World Wide Web.

Public relations practitioners have to go where the audience is, and the audience is on the Net! If the public and journalists are using the Net, so too must public relations practitioners.

The Benefits that Accrue to Explorers of New Territory

Here are some of the advantages the enterprising PR person will reap by boldly venturing into Internet territory.

Leapfrog the competition. The Internet and online services are here to stay, and marketing and public relations on the Net will only increase in importance. By starting with an Internet presence—a Gopher site or a Web site—an organization can experiment with Net marketing *before* Net marketing becomes a critical success factor. The best time to learn the ins and outs of the Net is before competitors arrive, before they are watching and matching every move you make.

Experiment and learn about a key new medium. Successful Net marketing and public relations require skills and approaches that take time to master and are idiosyncratic in each business case. By getting involved early, an organization can precede its rivals along the necessary learning curve. This may be impossible if the competition is quickly moving to the on-line world.

Get asset insurance. Providing a no-cost, limited-access Internet presence should preempt and minimize the piracy of an organization's content. It can also protect an organization's valuable brands and preempt competitors wanting to enter the market. This highly desirable goal may be accomplished by determining the most popular data or content, boiling it down, and making it available free of charge from the Net. Doing this will draw interested parties to an organization's site and build a foundation for the near future, when the organization can sell product and service securely over the Internet. It will also encourage other sites to link to an organization's pages.

Attract new kinds of clients and tap new revenue streams. Once commercial transactions are available over the Internet, an organization can be positioned to serve new, currently unserved, or underserved markets. An organization can sell these markets the moderate value content they desire over the Internet, conveniently and at reasonable cost. Heavy industry users and analysts will continue to access a direct-dial professional service for its extensive database and powerful search and analysis engines.

Doing Business on the Internet

As the comprehensive, excellent (and accessible through the Internet) Electronic Frontier Foundation's *Guide to the Internet* points out, companies are already doing business on the Internet: "Back in olden days, oh, before 1990 or so, there were no markets in the virtual community—if you wanted to buy a book, you still had to jump in your car and drive to the nearest bookstore. This was because in those days, the Net consisted mainly of a series of government-funded networks on which explicit commercial activity was forbidden" (EFF, 1994).

Today, much of the Net is run by private companies, which generally have no such restrictions, and a number of companies have begun experimenting with on-line "shops" or other services. Many of these shops are run by booksellers, while the services range from delivery of indexed copies of federal documents to an on-line newsstand that hopes to entice you to subscribe to any of several publications (of the printed on paper variety).

Many companies also use news groups to distribute press releases and product information. Still, commercial activity remains far below that found on other networks, such as CompuServe, with its Electronic Mall, or Prodigy, with its advertisements on almost every screen. In part that's because of the newness and complexity of the Internet as a commercial medium. In part, however, it is because of security concerns. Companies worry about such issues as crackers getting into their system over the network, and many people do not like the idea of sending a credit card number via the Internet (an E-mail message could be routed through several sites to get to its destination). These concerns could disappear as Net users turn to such means as message encryption and "digital signatures." In the meantime, however, businesses on the Net can still consider themselves something of Internet pioneers.

The EFF *Guide* describes various marketers on the Net, including the following:

- The World in Brookline, Massachusetts currently rents space to several bookstores and computer-programming firms, as well as an adult toy shop.

- Msen in Ann Arbor provides its Msen Marketplace, where you'll find a travel agency and an "Online Career Center" offering help-wanted ads from across the country. Msen also provides an Internet Business Pages, an on-line directory of companies seeking to reach the Internet community.

- The Nova Scotia Technology Network runs a Cybermarket on its Gopher service. There you'll find an on-line bookstore that lets you order books through E-mail (to which you'll have to trust your credit card number) and a similar "virtual record store." Both let you search their wares by keyword or by browsing through catalogs.

- AnyWare Associates: This Boston company runs an Internet-to-fax gateway that lets you send fax messages anywhere in the world via the Internet (for a fee, of course).

- Bookstacks Unlimited: This Cleveland bookstore offers a keyword-searchable database of thousands of books for sale.

- Counterpoint Publishing: Based in Cambridge, Massachusetts, this company's main Internet product is indexed versions of federal journals, including the *Federal Register* (a daily compendium of government contracts, proposed regulations and the like). Internet users can browse through recent copies, but complete access will run several thousand dollars a year.

- Dialog: The national database company can be reached through Telnet at dialog.com. To log on, however, you will have first had to set up a Dialog account.

- Dow Jones News: A wire service run by the information company that owns the *Wall Street Journal*. As with Dialog, you need an account to log on.

- Infinity Link: Browse book, music, software, videocassette, and laser disk catalogs through this system based in Malvern, Pennsylvania.

- The Internet Company: A service bureau, this company based in Cambridge, Massachusetts is working with several publishers on Internet-related products. Its Electronic Newsstand offers snippets and special subscription rates to a number of national magazines, from *The New Republic* to *The New Yorker.*

- MarketBase: You can try the classified ads system developed by this company in Santa Barbara, California by using Gopher to connect to mb.com.

- O'Reilly and Associates: Best known for its Nutshell books on UNIX, O'Reilly runs three Internet services. The Gopher server at ora.com provides information about the company and its books. It posts similar information in the biz.oreilly.announce Usenet newsgroup. Its *Global Network Navigator,* accessible through the World Wide Web, is an on-line magazine that lets users browse through interesting services and catalogs.

The Internet Mall™: Shopping on the Information Highway

An Internet Mall is available on the Internet. Maintained by Dave Taylor (taylor@netcom.com), the Electronic Mall is organized into seven "floors": The first floor features media; the second floor, personal items; the third floor, computer hardware and software; the fourth floor, services; the fifth floor, clothes and sporting goods; the sixth floor, furniture; the top floor, a food court and garage.

In December 1994 alone, the Electronic Mall welcomed over fifty new shops, including the University of Chicago Press, the Project Mind Foundation, Crescent Productions, Hobart Galleries, Witney and Airault 20th Century Decorative Arts, Optical Brokers, the Hometown Railroad Station, the Speak-to-Me Catalog and the Hometown Coin Shop, Desert Treasures, Elaine Coyne Galleries, flowers from FTD Internet, Flower Stop, or Blue Ribbon Orchids, Harlequin Graphics, Creative Solutions, CDs from Edinburgh Multimedia; and up-to-date mining information from Robertson Info-Data, Doorstep Delivery, Stopwatch Video and Film, WORDNET Foreign Language Translations, Travel Ukraine, and Soxcess, as well as Rolling Hills Golf, Elwell Emporium, Godiva Online, Republic of Tea, Salsas, Etc! The Spice Merchant, Rowena's, and, to find the right plate, Classic China.

In March 1995, the Internet Mall announced that it passed the 1,000 mark of companies signed on. The criteria for being on this list are that the company must be on the Internet, must have products that they sell and customers must be able to order through the Net directly, either by Gopher, WAIS, the World Wide Web, or E-mail. Excluded from this list are Internet service providers themselves, contract technical support from companies, consultants, franchise, or other similar marketing and sales schemes.

As an electronic "informational" outlet, the Internet Mall provides a hybrid public relations/marketing opportunity. Clearly, the Internet is a source of information; information is to a meaningful degree what public relations practitioners provide. On the other hand, Internet sites such as the Mall are places where consumers of one kind or another make initial purchasing decisions.

Financial Information Services

Public relations professionals working in the financial services area are now having to deal with a plethora of financial services cropping up on the Internet. As Jayne Levin, editor of *The Internet Letter*, writes in the *Washington Post*:

> *The Internet is making room on its global web of 23,000 computer networks for a panoply of services aimed at helping people learn how to invest and manage their money.*
>
> *From stock quotes and investment tips to annual reports and small-business advice, investors and entrepreneurs are finding a wealth of information on the Internet. There even is access to a database of filings the Securities and Exchange Commission requires of publicly traded companies. Theodore D. Raphael of Falls Church, referring to an academic paper that he found on the after-tax performance of mutual funds, said: "Without the Internet, I never would have seen that article. Not a chance." But Michael Greenberg of Houston, who recently has begun exploring the financial resources on the Internet, still is more comfortable getting information from newspapers and television. "Some of the Internet discussion groups do not have enough traffic from informed professionals to get my vote," he said. "I still prefer the Wall Street Journal…and the Nightly Business Report."*

Levin describes the free, investment-related services that have come on line in 1994:

- *The Financial Economics Network (FEN)*. FEN is an Internet discussion group where subscribers swap information via electronic mail on banking, accounting, stocks, bonds, options, small business, corporate finance and emerging markets. FEN's subscriber base has grown so rapidly—about 10,000 people joined FEN in one month—that cofounder and Clemson University finance professor Wayne Marr said he is exploring taking FEN private and possibly making it a fee-based service.

- *The SEC's Electronic Data Gathering, Analysis, and Retrieval System (EDGAR) system.* EDGAR is a database of SEC-required filings by publicly traded companies. The EDGAR Internet project is sponsored by the National Science Foundation (NSF). Carl Malamud, an NSF subcontractor and president of the Internet Multicasting Service, said about 14 gigabytes of data—the equivalent of 14 million pages of information—were sent out in March. About 31,900 documents are available, each with a digital signature to guarantee authenticity.

- *Microsoft Corp.'s financial database.* Microsoft...unveiled a public database containing financial information about the company. The computer software giant is the first company to offer such a service. You can download Microsoft's 10-K annual and 10-Q quarterly reports and recent press releases.

- *The Los Angeles Times,* as an experiment in electronic distribution, is making Market Beat available for a limited time. The investment column is delivered free via E-mail three times a week.

- *FEN delivers Holt's Stock Market Reports,* also by E-mail, to subscribers. The daily report provides a market summary of twenty-nine indices and averages, including the Dow Jones Industrial Average and the Standard & Poor's 500-stock index. It also lists the most actively traded stocks and changes in foreign currency prices. (Levin, 1994)

For public relations practitioners dealing in the financial media area, these Internet financial services mean that Internet users have access to mountains of information directly, at their fingertips 24 hours a day, seven days a week. Public relations professionals need to become aware of these Internet sites and find ways to link with them.

Magazines, Newspapers, and News Organizations On Line

Public relations professionals must deal with their journalistic counterparts in the electronic realm for no other reason than magazine, newspapers, and news organizations are creating a presence in on-line services. For example, according to *Netguide* (mostly), the following publications have already put themselves on the "Net" either as content or as a database:

American Banker (database), *American Quarterly Magazine*, Associated Press, *Banking News, Billboard* charts, *Boardwatch, Books in Print, Boston Globe, Business Week, Byte, Cadalyst, Career, Chicago Tribune, Commerce Business Daily, Computer Shopper, Computer World, Congressional Quarterly, Consumer Reports, Digital Review, Discovery*, Electronic Frontier Foundation, *Entrepreneur, The European* (newspaper), *The Financial Times, Forbes, Fortune, The Guardian, The Independent, Information USA, Kiplinger's, Los Angeles Times, MacUser, MacWeek, Macworld, Mobil Travel Guide, Modern History Review, Money, Ms., The Nation, National Geographic, National Review, New England Journal of Medicine, The New Republic, Newsday, New York Times, Online Access, PC, PC Week, PC World, Pen, Penthouse, Popular Mechanics, Psychology Today, Publish, Publishers Weekly, Rolling Stone, San Jose Mercury News, Time, USA Today, Wall Street Journal, Washington Post, Wired, Worth*, Ziff magazines, *Women's Day.*

The Electronic Newsstand

One company, The Electronic Newsstand, is providing an Internet opportunity (via Gopher and the World Wide Web) for magazines, newspapers, periodicals, even public relations professionals, to have a presence. Founded in July 1993 to provide the Internet community with easy access to a wide range of interesting information furnished by the world's leading publishers, The Electronic Newsstand is a site that users can browse—free of charge—through many publications and have their interest stimulated by a variety of subjects. The Newsstand provides a window on the world of computers, technology, science, business, foreign affairs, the arts, travel, medicine, nutrition, sports, politics, literature, and many other areas of interest. Every Newsstand publisher provides the table of contents and several articles from each current issue. The Newsstand, which archives previously featured material, is also searchable by keyword.

Single copies and subscriptions to the printed versions of any of the publications on The Newsstand can be ordered via E-mail or an 800 number (1-800-40-ENEWS). The majority of titles are not offered electronically—yet. However, if an electronic version of the publication is available, then it will be noted in the subscription offer. All of The Newsstand publishers guarantee prompt delivery and complete satisfaction. Access to The Electronic Newsstand is free and available via Gopher or Telnet.

The Electronic Newsstand was developed by Cambridge, Massachusetts–based netResults, which describes itself as "Your Marketing Gateway to the Information Superhighway." According to netResults' Internet commentary: "What does this mean to marketers? It means you can immediately utilize a powerful communications media to interact with your current customers and to make your product information accessible to millions of potential customers. You can:

- offer vast amounts of product literature, efficiently and clearly organized
- update product listings and prices daily (or even hourly)
- receive orders and respond to customers via electronic mail
- allow customers to easily retrieve technical reports and specifications
- conduct interactive forums and conferences with customers
- easily distribute corporate news (philanthropic, educational, financial)
- link branch offices anywhere in the world through electronic mail—or use the system for in-house communication."

The Newsstand delivers articles from the world's leading magazines, newsletters, and book publishers and gives each publisher an E-mail address to receive orders and communicate with customers. In its first six months, the Newsstand was accessed more than 2 million times—or some 25,000 people a day. During its first week of operation, it was accessed by Internet users more than 2,000 times per day. By fall 1994, the Newsstand was accessed by users more than 40,000 times per day and sells magazine subscriptions all over the world.

News Organizations

Individual publications notwithstanding, news organizations have created a real presence on the Internet, according to The Journalism List created by John S. Makulowich (verbwork@access.digex.net) of The Writers Alliance, Inc. The Journalism List identifies and describes briefly a number of resources targeted to the journalism community. These resources include news groups, mailing lists/discussion groups, and information accessible via WAIS (an information retrieval program that accesses a variety of databases using simple English queries), anonymous FTP, Telnet, Gopher, and the World Wide Web. It includes sites that cater to journalists—for example, NASA's SpaceLink, where users can FTP (File Transfer Protocol) media kits.

Under "Journalism" in the World Wide Web Virtual Library (makulow@trainer.com) as of September 1995, entries include:

1. Virtual Library Sub-fields, and Specialized Fields (5)
2. Associations, Clubs, Guilds, Institutes, and Societies (20)
3. Awards, Grants, Prizes, and Scholarships (2)
4. College and University Departments (3)

5. Courses, Studies, and Surveys (8)

6. News Bureaus, Organizations, and Services (30)

7. Not Elsewhere Classified (10)

8. Other Resources and Services (35)

9. Related Fields (2)

In various ways, news organizations and publications are using their Internet sites to interact one on one with potential subscribers. Depending on how the publication has constructed its Internet site, the site can become a means for gathering valuable demographic information. The Internet site can also become a venue for communicating useful information to a potential subscriber. This is electronic public relations.

Public Relations Applications

It does not take long before a new communications medium—such as on-line services via the Internet—becomes a vehicle for commercial purposes. According to Bill Lutholtz (Corporate Communications, Indianapolis Power and Light) a long-time Internet user (he manages the Internet's PRFORUM Listserv list and is also an assistant systems operator with the PRFORUM on CompuServe), public relations practitioners have found several ways to use the Internet. Among them Lutholtz lists:

- media relations—electronic distribution of news releases, E-mail responses to reporters' inquiries
- issues tracking—via the various news wires and newspaper databases
- electronic clipping services—to track story appearances in national and international media
- competitive intelligence—checking up on what the competition is doing
- marketing communications—via World Wide Web and Gopher sites (such as Bell Atlantic, Digital Equipment, and the like)
- research—for writing articles and speeches
- government affairs—using some or all of the above
- employment opportunities—using the Internet to recruit new employees, or to look for a new job for yourself
- professional affiliations—with organizations such as the Public Relations Society of America, the International Association of Business Commun-

icators, the American Marketing Association, and other groups that have
established varying degrees of on-line presence on the Internet

- clip art—for desktop publishing of company newsletters
- technical support—for computer questions
- mailing list information—such as address and phone numbers of the
  members of the U.S. Senate and Congress, addresses of newspapers, and
  so on
- the Electronic Water Cooler—for the solitary consultant who doesn't
  hang out at a *real* water cooler anymore
- E-mail delivery—of files to clients, faster than express mail (Lutholtz,
  November 10, 1994)

Christina O'Connell elaborates on these themes:

*The Net is not just a snappy fax machine approach: News groups, forums, and
list servers can give PR pro's considerable access directly to your customer base.
Bringing your message, in your own words, to these audiences can be extremely
successful…if you know what you're doing! Hype, sales pitches, rehashes of
stilted press releases don't cut it online, but ongoing availability to your
customers, providing a genuine resource to appropriate audiences does.*

O'Connell offered this example:

*As corporate communications manager for a computer hardware company, I
initiated a broad online campaign which included daily monitoring of appropriate CompuServe forums, participation in discussions which involved our product line, E-mailed product info when requested.*

*One area where we were really successful was the promotion of new memory
products. At the time, Apple was introducing several new PowerBooks, each
with different memory configurations. Our company manufactured PowerBook
memory boards. In a section of America Online which focused on PowerBook
topics, I posted messages explaining the new configurations, giving advice on
how to identify "in spec" memory boards and what to do if you were sold out of
spec boards. These messages were not pitches of our product but rather consumer-oriented posts on the lines of, "No matter who you buy memory from,
here's what to ask when ordering…"*

*The results: increased sales (folks trusted us since we "knew what we were
talking about" and they "knew where to find us"), great corporate image boost
(as consumer oriented and as engineering pros), a better informed consumer
base (which was valuable to us as "quality manufacturers") and a nomination
as "Service Heroes" for being so helpful. (O'Connell, October 31, 1994)*

Lynn Cox, director of public relations for Digital Express, an Internet access provider, describes one of the discussion groups she belongs to on the Net: "If you're an organization, you can put information out there for other people to see. It's also easier to get quick responses, for gathering information, for surveys, or whatever you want to do." Cox points to the accessibility research materials through the Internet with respect to helping the public relations practitioner to define a target audience:

> *The Internet makes it a lot easier to interact with your public and explain your message or get your message out in a new way that will help people understand better. There are tons of new research tools. You have basically the entire world at your fingertips now. Research is very important. The more information you have readily acceptable, the better a decision you can make.*
>
> *If you can pull up information about a special topic or if you plug in the Philippine Heritage Foundation, maybe they have an information server up, and you're working with that public, if you can have all sorts of information about that public right away, it makes your life easier. It makes it easier to understand how to interact with them best.*

Tech Image Ltd. is a Midwest company that promotes high-tech companies and groups, including Ameritech and IPC Technologies. Michael Nikolich, president of Tech Image, describes many of the other ways public relations practitioners can promote their clients via the Internet:

> *USENET news groups are discussion groups that are accessible via the Internet. These groups cover every topic imaginable—from collecting tropical fish to photography. One of our clients is an association of Amateur Radio operators. We monitor all USENET news groups that cover Amateur Radio, plus relevant World Wide Web sites. This helps us provide our client with a steady stream of story ideas. We automate most of our monitoring by using newsreader software. The software automatically tracks stories from the news groups and sends the information to us via E-mail.*
>
> *The Internet is a very powerful medium for public relations professionals. The challenge for public relations practitioners is figuring out how to get access to the Internet and using this medium cost effectively.*
>
> *We monitor news groups as part of our ongoing services to clients. One client, for example, manufactures videographics boards that are used to produce desktop video and multimedia. We track all relevant news groups and send regular reports to the client. This helps them keep informed about the rumors, and also lets them keep a pulse on what people are saying about them.*
>
> *The Internet offers an immediacy that can't be matched by phone calls or faxes. If a negative story starts appearing on the Net, you can do something*

about it immediately. The companies that act the most proactively are the ones that will benefit most from the Internet.

Nikolich also believes in using the Internet for interactive press conferences, which, he says,

are one of the powerful tools you can build into your WWW site. This capability is very similar to the conferences you see on CompuServe and America Online. Before the emergence of online media, you had to physically gather people into a room to announce a new product or service. With an electronic press conference, everything is done digitally.

An interactive press conference makes it much easier for anyone to direct a question to a CEO or spokesperson right from their keyboard. A lot of bands, such as the Rolling Stones, have done interactive press conferences. The Stones actually broadcast a live segment of one of their concerts via the Internet. You'd need an ISDN line to actually hear the clip in real time, but that scenario isn't very far away.

The Home Page on the World Wide Web

Apart from using the Internet for information gathering or posting to forums and news groups, organizations can create a home page to provide Net surfers with marketing and public relations information. Tech Image's Nikolich commented:

Once we've developed these home pages—which might include information about the company, product information—we might have a section of the home page that lets you get wired right into technical support. It might have an area to direct questions that can be sent back to you so you can get automated replies.

We look at this as a kind of adjunct to technical support that's available right now. A lot of companies are downsizing their staffs. The home page gives them a means to communicate in an additional domain where you don't have to have hundreds of people manning the phone. Literally, most of the replies can be done automatically within a home page. On your home page you can have product demos and different types of multimedia presentations that can play automatically to people.

Chiat/Day Advertising has taken a leadership position in employing new technologies for itself and its clients. Dick Hackenberg of the agency's West Coast office describes their foray into the Internet:

We have developed a prototype piece for Nissan that we put on the Net in July 1995. Working with Nissan's Interactive Multimedia Task Force, we created and developed the Nissan Pathfinder Guide to Outdoor Adventure.

It's based on a Nissan Pathfinder print campaign in special interest magazines like Skiing, Outdoor Photography, Off-Road. *It's a content-rich application focused on the adventure, the interest, the excitement you can have with the vehicle rather than being focused on the vehicle itself. It fits into the mindset and the expectations of the Internet user.*

It has a rotating graphics home page, with adventure options. We've developed five adventure choices—watersports, fishing, the Amazon, mountain biking, and the Yukon. You can choose the area you're interested in, link to other Web sites with related information, get information about the Nissan Pathfinder, find your nearest dealer or request a brochure.

The piece will be textual and full-motion. Right now it's based on graphics and text, but it isn't finished. We can easily add full-motion video of the vehicle in unusual places and add sound. It will be a full multimedia effort when we're finished with it.

Asked why Chiat/Day was motivated to explore the Internet, Hackenberg commented: "We believe the on-line service user and the Internet user represent a desirable audience that is likely to be interested in, and hopefully will buy, Nissan vehicles. In the short run, the biggest users of any interactive technology are users of CompuServe, Prodigy, and America Online (AOL). We did a test on Prodigy two years ago that did pretty well. We're now on CompuServe and AOL. What we know of the demographics of the Internet user and of the on-line user is that they are people we would like to interest in Nissan vehicles and who will respond if we approach them in the right way."

Creating an Internet Presence

An organization can create an Internet presence by building a Gopher site or a Web site. Regardless of the choice, an organization can begin by registering one or more domain names to protect key brands and creating E-mail and forum mechanisms to enhance communication with and among existing and prospective users.

Generally speaking, an organization should plan to maintain an Internet site for a minimum of six months to make the effort worthwhile. Creating the organization's Gopher or Web site application involves the following steps:

Design

In general, a business needs to inventory its current marketing materials to determine which ones can be used in developing a Gopher site application. These materials might include a brochure, the corporate logo, direct mail copy that has worked, and perhaps letters from satisfied customers.

Because the Internet is an interactive, computer-based medium, it offers new ways to communicate with customers. An organization should look for ways to involve customers and prospects in its business—for example, soliciting customer feedback and asking for suggestions for new offerings. Look for ways to minimize the impact of this new customer feedback on staff time. Also look for related Net resources that can be linked to the site to increase its interest and value.

Programming the Internet Site

Gopher sites consist of text or data files organized into nested directories and specially constructed *link* files that define the menus. Link files contain an entry for each menu item. Each entry says what kind of file it is, where it is to appear on the menu, what the menu label should say, and where the file is stored.

A Gopher site, for example, might require the following setup work:

- organize client information
- ensure information quality and accuracy
- decide what outside information to include by reference
- choose good names for files, directories, and menu items
- add documentation to each directory
- set up the link files and directories
- create text indexes where necessary

Choosing a Server Site

An experienced vendor to host the site should be selected. The *host* runs the computer system where the site application resides, manages the communications equipment and lines needed to link those pages to the Internet, and regularly backs up all files. The vendor also provides an automatic E-mail–forwarding service to an E-mail address, supports timely updates to the application, and keeps the system running 24 hours a day, seven days a week.

Creating and Installing an E-Mail System

An E-mail system is a company's direct link to Internet users who do not have World Wide Web access. The organization should register its domain name and implement an automatic mail server that will routinely provide information and promotional material to users and prospects.

Testing the Site

Because a Gopher site is part of the corporate image, it should be tested very carefully. Make sure everything about the organization's site works correctly: documents are spell-checked, Gopher links will go where they should, comments are properly forwarded to you, and the E-mail robot sends out the right message when asked.

Ongoing Support and Promotion

The work doesn't stop once the site application and E-mail system are initially implemented. The creative content of the site must be refreshed periodically. It is generally recommended that a site be refreshed at least every month.

To make your presence on the Internet effective, your home page really needs to be kept interesting over time. Many people will visit your home page—it's not uncommon to get thousands of "hits" during your first week of presence on the Internet. Each hit is essentially someone coming and taking a peek at your home page and perhaps looking a little further at your site.

But just having that many people come in doesn't necessarily mean much. You want to begin to attract people to your site on a repeat basis. This all depends upon what you are trying to accomplish with your site. Assuming that what you're trying to do is to develop a relationship, maintain that relationship, and hopefully sell to people over time, you really do need to keep your site interesting over time.

Interesting means that you either make special offers to people over time and vary them or you change the look in the same way that a retail store owner may periodically modify the way a store window looks. You have to do some of that on the Internet as well. Simply rearranging things is not enough. Instead, you need to think about what kinds of new developments and new material your organization has created.

If you're an R&D company, perhaps you have a new research report; if you're an investment advisor, perhaps you have a new study on a particular industry that you think might interest your potential customers. That kind of material can become a highlight on your home page in order to show that there's something new there and give reasons for people to check you out.

You really want to seek links to your sites in some of the malls developing on the Internet. Very much like The Electronic Newsstand, other organizations are creating malls. The Cyber Mall, for example, is attempting to become a virtual electronic mall.

On an ongoing basis, the site should be announced and promoted to news groups and lists, and links should be obtained to, or at least announcements of, the site in appropriate directories and databases. The site should be promoted on CompuServe, America Online, and Prodigy in forums frequented by appropriate audiences. As the on-line services implement full Internet connections for their subscribers, the organization should seek links on these services to your Gopher site.

Guidelines

Christina O'Connell adds a few things to look out for when doing PR on line:

- Pick your audience well—each service tends to draw a different audience. Get the right message in the right place.
- Don't take your message publicity on line without lots of in-house support—your customers will expect immediate answers to E-mail inquiries. You will need a process set up to channel these questions to the right departments.
- Don't try to do PR online unless you are "at home" on line—if you're not comfortable with the on-line community, you're unlikely to be effective. And you have to know how to handle flames and such...rumors hit the Net fast and furious. Make sure your sense of humor and your damage control skills are in top form.
- Remember that your audience is enormous—when answering one person's question, your real readership may easily be 100,000 potential customers, so make sure you have your message together.
- Participate rather than exploit—if you share information, offer your corporate resources, give straight answers, skip the sales hype, your message can become a welcome addition to on-line discussions...but if you see the Net (in its many forms) simply as a new place to push sales, you'll end up as toasted as Canter & Siegel and infamy does not build good corporate image.
- Learn from the on-line community—simply reading news groups can be the most effective market research around, monitor the comments of your target market to learn what features matter, what causes folks to love or hate a product, etc. (O'Connell, October 31, 1994)

Independent consultant and Internet expert Neil Ruggles (also a principal in New York–based Net Marketing & PR, Inc.) offered this advice about promoting a site on the Internet: "The promotion step is really a critical part of the overall process of getting a home page up on the Internet. It follows the actual act of creating, designing, and putting that page on the Internet. Without it, your page is invisible to everyone on the Internet, unlike a physical store in a physical town, where every storefront is going to be visible to anyone walking down the street. Out in Internet space/cyberspace, there are no paths for people to wander along, so to speak, so they just don't find you."

Ruggles described the several ways an organization can approach promoting itself on the Net:

> The simplest approach is to start by putting an announcement of the fact you have opened up your shop, your home page, into a couple of fairly well-known Internet lists which track things on the Internet.
>
> There are a couple of such lists, which get circulated to thousands of people around the Internet to tell them what is happening. People who are interested in new home pages and other kinds of new developments on the Internet subscribe to these lists. In addition to the lists, there are a number of sites around the Internet that are well-known indexes of other things around the Internet. You could look at these as sophisticated electronic yellow page directories. Some are extremely well known, an example being Yahoo at Stanford University, a comprehensive directory of services and places on the Internet that would be of interest to people.
>
> In addition to being on these key lists which announce things, you would also want to notify the people who maintain these various indexes that you exist as a new presence on the Internet and suggest to them proper ways to index your material—where to put you in their directory of services.

Other ways to publicize an organization, according to Ruggles, are to look at both news groups and other kinds of mailing lists that have narrow niche audiences. Says Ruggles: "Look through the news group listings and the listings of the mailing lists and identify which of the niches seem to match the kinds of customers you're hoping to find on the Internet. Then you can begin to participate in both the news groups and those mailing lists either through making a simple announcement of your existence—of the existence of your home page—or perhaps you may want to go to a more sophisticated participation where you actually begin a dialogue with people in that news group, or in the mailing lists you subscribed to."

In any case, he advises, the public relations practitioner should periodically inform those audiences—the people subscribing to certain special purpose mailing lists and people subscribing to the news groups—about everything taking place at the company site.

What Are the Implications of the Internet?

Media relations; vendor relations; client relations; local, state, national, and international government relations; customer relations; investor relations; employee communications; research and competitive intelligence; job information; peer-to-peer communications; and professional development—all these marketing and public relations activities are possible on the Internet.

But what does the Internet *mean*? What can we expect from it? In very short bursts, following are some of the explicit and implicit ramifications of the Internet:

- The Internet began as a computer network to share information among multiple locations. Almost thirty years later, the Internet continues to be a superb tool for gathering and distributing information.

- Issue tracking, market and competitor research, public relations, customer service—these are the easy and obvious business uses for the Internet. However, the Internet could well reshape the role of marketing and public relations professionals. With a Web site, an organization can inform a potential customer directly—there is no need for conversations mediated by journalists. In fact, the interactivity of on-line communication has much in common with direct marketing, direct response, personal selling, and sales promotion.

- Increasingly, people on the Internet will know about changing events faster than they can be reported on CNN's *Headline News*. Further, the very concept of news will change. News will be what people talk to each other about on the Internet, not what the *New York Times* or the *Wall Street Journal* decides is fit to print.

- The Internet may redefine the role of newspapers, magazines, libraries, even museums. These institutions have collections of content—databases. The Internet can open these databases to global access around the clock—24 hours a day, seven days a week, fifty-two weeks a year.

- For museums and libraries, the Internet can provide access to material that would take up too much physical display space or that is too fragile to handle. Further, the Net has the potential for removing the geographic basis for these institutions' past success.

- Nonmedia businesses also own content—service manuals, product literature, press releases, research reports, speeches, annual reports. The Internet—as a potential on-line access tool—makes every business a publisher and gives every business a chance to find advertisers willing to buy into its Internet presence.

- Domestic and international travel will be enhanced by the Internet—as *Megatrends* author John Naisbitt says, "high tech/high touch." The more we communicate electronically, the more we will want to visit the people and places we reach and touch via cyberspace. Face-to-face meetings and handwritten notes on personal stationary will become more compelling.

- Electronic media, such as satellites and the Internet, transcend geographic, political, economic, and legal boundaries. With its global reach, the Internet pits national law against international law as never before.

- The Internet will extend the breakdown of hierarchy that American organizations have been experiencing since the late 1980s. Electronic media subvert the communications role of middle managers.

- But the breakdown will extend even further. By enabling direct communication between customer and supplier, the Internet threatens to eliminate or redefine the roles of salespeople, wholesalers, and distributors—literally everyone between the supplier and the customer.

- Car salespeople beware. After browsing a Web site that explains in great detail what the features and benefits of a car are, customers will visit the showroom not to haggle, but to finalize a purchase decision they have made at home via the Internet. Car salespeople may become car order people. And music stores watch out. The Net makes it easy to search for, sample, and order music without ever setting foot in a physical store.

- Let's not forget Bulletin Board Systems (BBS)—where people can talk to each other electronically on the Net. Long the domain of mostly male hobbyists much like ham radio, BBSs are waking up to the Internet. Nearly every important BBS software program is adding graphical and Internet interfaces. They are easy to set up and can be run out of the basement.

- In *Boardwatch* magazine, the BBS bible, author John Dvorak refers to *Hot Wired* magazine's Web site as "hardly different than any BBS you pay a fee to use" (1995, p. 170). Keep an eye on the BBS dark horse in the Internet race.

- The Internet is the antithesis of the mass market medium. Key Internet services—mailing lists, news groups, and forums—involve narrow niche interests. Moreover, customers talk back and can talk to other customers with the press of a button.

- Using the Internet, a product or service-oriented organization can reach prospective customers on a one-on-one basis—but on a global scale.

- So far, businesses have generally been willing to build on-line presences that are isolated from their internal computer systems. The exceptions, such as the Ziff Davis computer magazine database link to CompuServe, have mainly involved database vendors looking for new places to sell their data.

- Information, copywriting, and graphic design skills have sufficed so far for most on-line presences. Expect this to change.

- The next step in on-line services will involve companies trying to connect their on-line presence with their internal computer systems. The home page will become a customer interface to a company's order entry system or to their reservation system. This step requires real computer programming, systems analysis, and design skills.

- The trend toward real programming began with the use of HTML forms—which is a programming language—as well as "image maps," and will accelerate as companies try to connect to databases of all kinds to the Net.

- On-line site *design* is about to become a major strategic and marketing business *decision*. Marketing and communication experts will have to be deeply involved in planning on-line sites. So will information technology experts.

- Finally, presuming cable companies move forward with their plans to connect the Internet to the home via their wide band–width cable, the Internet will increasingly become a conduit for motion video and desktop video teleconferencing. Even if the cable companies stay away, video and audio compression techniques just around the corner assure that multimedia will soon play a big role on the Net.

Chapter 12

The Future of Electronic Public Relations

As the previous chapters indicate, public relations via electronic channels has the potential for significant growth in the coming years. The history of communications media suggests, as economic historian Harold Innis has shown, that communications media are adopted as their economies (or efficiencies and effectiveness) are revealed. And as Daniel J. Czitrom points out in his analysis of the work of Innis and Marshall McLuhan, there is a strong relationship between economics and communications (1982, p. 149).

Print versus Electronic Media: The Economics

There is evidence to indicate that the traditional form of conveying public relations information—print—is losing the cost-effectiveness struggle. A survey by *Media Relations Insider* starts with the following headline:

> *Journalists Say Public Relations Mail Is Spinning Out of Control, Decry Waste of Their Time…and Clients' Money.*

The survey itself states that "on average as much as 34 percent of all journalists' mail from public relations each week is perfunctorily trashed before it is opened." According to the report, "Since the U.S. Public Relations industry produces about 200,000 press releases a year at an estimated cost of about $3,000 per release, including writing and distribution, the survey conservatively calculates the industry's waste due to unopened releases at $204 million annually"(1994, p. 1).

Media Relations Insider further points out the "Seven Biggest Mail Mistakes": (1) misdirected, (2) arrives too late, (3) wrong focus, (4) overwrought mail, (5) overpackaged pitches, (6) no followup, and (7) duplication, triplication. The San Francisco–based newsletter concludes its piece on print-oriented public relations with a look at measurement: "According to a 1993 study by the Delahaye Group in Portsmouth, New Hampshire, 63 percent of marketing/communications professionals predicted that their budgets for measurement would grow in the next five years. In 1992, only 29 percent said so" (1994, p. 4).

As a way of communicating public relations content, print may be giving way to electronic means. Many of the public relations professionals interviewed for this book emphasized that they contacted journalists electronically, particularly via E-mail and the Internet.

The use of E-mail (versus "snail mail," as one interviewee put it) as *the* way to effectively reach a journalism audience is expressed in extreme form by John C. Dvorak, a well-known and controversial commentator on the computer industry. In *Alert,* a newsletter published by Cambridge, Massachusetts–based MediaMap, Dvorak writes in a "Manifesto, An Open Letter to the Public Relations Community,"

> *It's time for the public relations firms and the in-house Mar\Com people to look at the calendar and see that it's the 20th century and about to become the 21st century. There is no justification for their incredible senseless waste of paper that we have in this business. (1994, p. 5)*

Dvorak points out that E-mail is faster: "I get the material 5 minutes after it's sent. E-mail is easier to scan. You can plow through it faster than the arduous letter opening and discarding process. E-mail makes it easier to file quotes or backgrounders or whatever you want to keep. It also makes access easier if you want to put all the material into a database. Finally, it's ecologically sound and saves trees" (1994, p. 5).

At issue is the relative roles of journalists and public relations professionals in the so-called "information superhighway age." This issue was the subject of a roundtable discussion in late June 1994 among representatives of BMW of North America, *Time* Magazine, *Crain's New York Business,* Video Image Productions, New York University, *Brandweek* Magazine, and J.P. Morgan hosted by Amster-Young Public Relations of New York. The primary objective of the session was for the participants to explore how public relations professionals will be delivering and how reporters will be receiving information in the future. There was general agreement that electronic technologies, such as CD-ROM, E-mail, and on-line services "will play more of a role in the reporter/public relations professional relationship in the future," but, according to Tresa Chambers of *Time* Magazine, "Reporters still like to be able to hold a press release in their hands and receive hard news by telephone or fax."

In early December 1994, the New York chapter of the Public Relations Society of America hosted a session on the information superhighway. For the almost 100 public relations professionals present, the immediate issue was: "How can we use these on-line services for public relations purposes?" More important, the discussion among the speakers and participants touched upon the potential for journalists to sidestep public relations agency personnel and reach a subject expert directly through an on-line service, and vice versa—whereby a client deals directly with a journalist through an on-line service (such as the Internet) through E-mail. Clearly, the world is changing. Electronic technologies are once more impacting the structure of the media landscape and redefining the roles of professionals within the media fishbowl.

Predictions

We asked some of the public relations professionals interviewed for this book to comment on the future of electronic public relations and the impact technologies may have on the profession in general and the role of the public relations professional in particular. In general, the experts' consensus was that:

1. Electronic media, such as the Internet, continue to annihilate the concept of a mass audience.
2. Electronic public relations is expanding exponentially.
3. The demand for video news releases is likely to continue to grow.
4. There is a definite trend towards interactive media in public relations.
5. The use of paper will decrease as the digital world expands.
6. Newspapers and magazines will increasingly adopt electronic venues.
7. As more and more journalists go on line or use E-mail, the direct need for a public relations pro as an informational buffer between organizations and journalists may be eliminated.
8. The downsizing of organizational public relations departments parallels the growth of public relations consultants and consulting firms.
9. The public relations industry will experience a change in the backgrounds of people who come into the profession.
10. Public relations is and always will be about human relationships.

Here's what they had to say specifically about each of these points.

Mass Audience versus One on One

The experts interviewed for this book all agreed that one of the major effects of electronic media on the future of public relations is the fact that the inherent characteristics of electronic media annihilate the concept of a mass audience.

As John Beardsley, president of the Public Relations Society of America (also chairman and chief executive officer of Padilla Speer Beardsley, a public relations firm located in Minneapolis, Minnesota) puts it: "You're dealing with many audiences, many constituencies. The technology makes it possible to subdivide and subdivide—until you get to the point where you're almost talking one to one. The mass audience of fifty years ago no longer exists. The technology has changed it entirely. The people are still there; they haven't changed at all. But the ways to reach them has absolutely demolished the concept of a mass audience. No one sits around at the same time of day watching anything on television anymore—with the possible exception of the Super Bowl or some other grand event."

Electronic media have splintered the mass audience. We see this happening in the phenomenon of cable channels dedicated to one topic. With the VCR and pay-per-view programs, audiences watch programming at times of their choosing. Those public relations professionals who keep up with technological changes, however, will be able to take advantage of the multitude of potential venues for a client's message.

A skilled communications manager of the future will not only be aware of all the media options available but will be able to accurately assess which ones to choose. As Karen Amster-Young, president of the New York–based public relations firm that bears her name, puts it, "We're going to face a bigger challenge of delivering the right information to target audiences of various influentials in an efficient manner so that they will be able to make use of it." In this model, the public relations professional takes on a role similar to that of the advertising agency media planner.

Electronic Public Relations Is Still Growing

In a relatively short time, major developments have taken place to harness information, like a raw fuel, and refine it for distribution and daily use. The electronic public relations frontier is consequently wide open, and the experts agree it is growing fast. According to Beardsley, "the future [of electronic public relations] is expanding exponentially."

Partly what is pushing the electronic public relations frontier is the accessibility of electronic technology and the merging of telephone, cable, and computer companies as well as the increasing utilization of E-mail and the Internet by journalists, cumulatively creating the information superhighway. It is helpful to look back at the changes in just the last five to ten years to measure where we were and where are we now. Tony Esposito, group manager of Bozell Public Relations, describes this transition: "So much has changed in the last five years. When I started doing this on a regular basis about eight years ago, a satellite feed for a satellite news release was extremely unusual. A lot of stations were not even set up to capture them....In the last eight years, you're hard pressed to find a station that wants a hard tape because it's so much easier for them to aim the satellite dish and take it down, whether they use it or not."

Demand for VNRs

The demand for video news releases is likely to continue to grow. Factors supporting this growth include smaller budgets at local news stations and the need for professional-looking material. More and more newsrooms are working with smaller budgets and don't have the manpower or the time to go out and shoot all the material they need. Yet they face the dilemma of remaining competitive and global to keep viewers interest.

At the same time, consumers have become more sophisticated and expect a certain level of quality to their news. Therefore VNRs need to be of top quality and credibility, produced with the best production values available and having inherent news value. Greg Albrecht, publicity manager of Walt Disney World, confirms this. "I think there's always going to be a demand for this kind of material. But I think the quality has to improve. The viewers out there are very sophisticated. They're very savvy. And they can recognize when it's quality material and when it's not....There's a big market out there, but I think the companies have to be very sensitive to making sure it's not too commercial. And it has to be quality. Regional television is also looking at how the story is applicable to their market. If you can find a local angle or a local focus, that makes it more palatable and much more interesting."

Other factors will contribute to the growth of VNRs (and hence electronic public relations in general). According to Rebecca Madeira, vice president of public affairs at Pepsi:

> With the proliferation of cable and exploding visual media of communication, there will be lots of opportunity to talk with consumers and with multiple audiences through visual means. Whether VNRs are the way to do it has a lot to do with the intelligence and temperance of the industry. It could easily become something that's banned from newsrooms if they become infomercials and if they are such heavily biased pieces that they serve no purpose other than an advertisement.
>
> If the profession uses this vehicle to provide material and information in as objective a way as possible, with good quality, and it's there as tools for reporters to then build their piece, there may be a real value to it. I think there's a fine line there, and it's important to understand how journalists want and need things.

Another trend is taking a backdoor approach to the traditional VNR. Instead of arranging through their public relations firm for footage of a newsworthy event to be documented on video tape and then to be distributed, corporations are being approached by independent production companies, assuming the role of public relations professional, with the intent of creating and documenting an event to be distributed as a VNR. Jim Schwinn, manager of broadcast media relations at 3M, has been approached with this type of proposal: "What I see as a trend now, in fact, is the emergence of a whole new concept of marketing programs as VNRs. Any number of companies will pitch corporations like ours to get their story on the air in some video magazine format they control. You don't buy air time. What you pay them for and how they make their money is in their 'production fees.' So they produce a piece on your company working in concert with you, to position you however you want, whatever philosophy or goal or product or person you want, and this runs in their show. It's an emerging vehicle."

On the news director side of the equation, David Bartlett, president of Radio and Television News Directors Association, had this to say: "The future is now. I think that there are so many sources of video. There is so much video out there, some of which some people would call some form of a VNR, that no television news organization could probably say that it doesn't use some. Everybody gets material from syndicators, public relations firms, what have you. Sure, this kind of thing has a future, and the future is right now. It's already being used extensively."

More Interactive Media

Apart from linear electronic media, there is a definite trend toward interactive media. Dick Hackenberg, account director for interactive advertising of Chiat/Day in Venice, California, peeked in his own crystal ball to comment on the next five to eight years and his agency's use of interactive media:

> I see more of it for a couple of reasons. One, every forecast I've seen says computer penetration of U.S. households will move, approximately, from 33 percent to 50 percent by the end of the decade. Two, since computers have modems or CD-ROM hard drives today, more and more people will be using an on-line service, the Internet and CD-ROMS.
>
> The trend in computer penetration and the aggressive activity of the telephone companies and cable companies to put some form of interactive television into the marketplace suggests that, four to five years out, we're going to see a lot of people doing things differently with their computers and their televisions.

Suzanne Rothenberg of New York–based Suzanne Rothenberg Communications had a more conservative slant on interactive media, however: "I think public relations is going to get into CD-ROM, I have a feeling that's where publicity is going to go. Newspaper outlets and magazines will be equipped with CD-ROM. You may be sending your press kit via CD-ROM. They can put a disc in their computer as opposed to having all that paper on their desk. But I think it's a long time away before anything like that is universal."

From the Paper Tablet to the Electronic Tablet

Are we looking at a paperless future? When personal computers were first introduced to the marketplace, the hopeful prospect of using less paper was put forward. With hindsight, we can see that what really happened was to create an outlet for more people to create more professional-looking documents on their own, thus causing the printing of more paper.

A paperless future, however, may be possible with the advent of the capacity to move massive amounts of information from point A to point B electronically while incurring very little cost, combined with the public's ecological consciousness about cutting down trees as the major motivators.

Dick Jones, current president of the New York chapter of the International Interactive Communications Society, concurs: "Over the course of the next ten to twenty years, the price of printing paper is going to go up and up. The cost and availability of viewer technology, which is cheap and portable, is going down and down. So clearly it's going to all become electronic except for circumstances when you deem it advantageous to print these things out."

Michael Nikolich, president of the public relations firm Tech Image, surmised: "I don't think we'll be using much paper by the year 2000. Most correspondence will be digital. Ecologically it makes a lot of sense. Why cut down a tree if you don't need to? You can just send something to someone electronically and get it on their desktop. It's cost effective and immediate. If you don't abuse E-mail, it's a way to get someone's attention and a way to be very helpful in real time."

Nikolich echoed Dvorak's position on the use of electronic media by journalists: "What I like about working in a digital environment…is you can save all the pertinent E-mail and you can go in and browse it quickly. It takes a fraction of the time to access an electronic file than it does to physically open up an envelope, read it, and then throw it away. And you don't have to deal with the clutter. The clutter is all on your desktop, neatly tucked into a one file folder. There's an immediacy to it. My theory on public relations is: the easier you can make it for people to use the material, the more likely they will use it."

Newspapers and Magazines Go Electronic

What about newspapers and magazines, if the paperless future proves real? They will probably not go the way of the dinosaur entirely. More likely, they will adapt to the electronic outlets. Already magazines like *Newsweek* offer their content on a CD-ROM. *Wired* magazine offers a counterpart electronic version on the Internet called *Hot Wired*. *Omni* magazine has announced it will dismantle its print version in favor of a CD-ROM and on-line version by the end of 1995.

John Beardsley spoke of a product in development that would allow the downloading of newspapers: "Knight-Ridder, at their research laboratory in Boulder, Colorado, is working on an 8 1/2" x 11" (approximately) notebook display panel which will in effect allow you to download a newspaper anytime you wanted from Knight-Ridder. It would be Knight-Ridder's version of the news, but you'll be able to pull it off the air, wireless."

Another advantage for newspapers and magazines to go electronic is the fact that as the use of electronic transmission increases and paper use decreases, the cost of paper will become too expensive and thus not a cost-efficient medium. In 1995, major newspapers such as the *New York Times* have raised the price of their papers because of the increase in the cost of paper. As a potential result, Tony Esposito points out, newspapers and magazines will "be able to more finely tune...target media outlets to reach the audiences you want."

Journalists Bypass Public Relations Professionals

The increasing use of electronic media by media outlets, and on the practical level by journalists, could have the impact of changing the nature of the relationship between the public relations professional and print and broadcast journalists. As more and more journalists go online or use E-mail, the direct need for a public relations pro as an informational buffer between an organization and the journalist could be eliminated.

Here the advantages and disadvantages of electronic communication needs to be addressed. "The beauty of electronic communication," states John Beardsley, "is that it is fully descriptive, and entirely noninterruptive. In this case, the public relations professional can send an idea via E-mail directly to the journalist. They can discuss it back and forth a bit and if it's of interest, or the public relations pro piques the journalist's interest, then he can send the necessary information, including text and graphics, directly to the journalist very fast and with minimal interruption—the E-mail acts as the phone and messenger/mail all in one."

But now consider the scenario where the journalist is assigned to write about a particular product. A journalist can use on-line services or the Internet to conduct all the research necessary to write the story using bulletin boards and browsing the Internet without necessarily having to contact the public relations firm handling the account for that product. The journalist may even be able to go directly to the company manufacturing the product. Companies who put their information on line or on a home page on the World Wide Web have the potential of being discovered by more journalists than before. Direct contact between journalist and organization potentially cuts out the PR person in the middle.

This concern was expressed by Karen Amster-Young: "What I'm concerned about is reporters being able to bypass public relations people....That's why I think we have to become increasingly information managers. The nurturing of the relationship of those reporters is continuously important. There is a rise in the increase for the need for reputation management. The role of public relations professionals is going to become more and more important. However, I think there is going to be a decrease in the number of people who are required to do that."

On the surface, it looks like gloom and doom for the public relations pro and greater objective access for the journalist. The weak link in this chain, though, is the fact that the public relations pro is needed to give shape to an organization's product or service and give perspective to it. The public relations professional may, indeed, be the one in the best position to counsel an organization on creating a home page for access by journalists.

Companies Are Downsizing/Consulting Is Growing

Electronic media are not only changing the way public relations pros do their job, but also how it gets done. Organizations are cutting their public relations staffs down to a few good people to do the work. This trend has already begun and can be seen in the downsizing of public relations departments in concert with the growth of public relations consultants and consulting firms. Consulting firms are thriving because the work to be done still exists, but companies find it more cost efficient to bring in an outside consultant as needed than keeping someone on staff year round to do work.

Newsrooms, too, have seen significant reductions in staff writers due to a focus on the bottom line. Again, the freelance/consultant is growing here. With on-line services and the Internet, writers can work from home and literally have all the resources they need right at their fingertips.

Clients want a good rapport with their public relations firm, not an impersonal feeling. Karen Amster-Young underscores this sentiment and explains how the smaller public relations firms can stay competitive: "Public relations comes down to relationships between a few people....Smaller firms are more hands on....They need to know that a few good people are going to be focusing on how to work on their business. Small companies like mine are hooking up with other small companies across the country to make sure we have the resources in place that we would need to service an international account. I think the large agency is a thing of the past."

Public Relations Professionals of the Future

Because of the impact of electronic media, the public relations industry will experience a change in the type of people who come into the profession. "In the 1950s," says Michael Nikolich, "most public relations people had a newspaper or trade magazine background. Technology is what's going to totally change the type of person who is attracted to public relations because you're going to have people who are interested in video, computers, and telecommunications. Journalism will continue to be a foundation for public relations, but the profession will require a much more skilled communicator. A lot of it is technology driven." Those "more skilled communicators," however, will be working in an environment where the focus on relationships is a key to success.

Public Relationships

Public relations is and always will be a relationship business. For example, even though an increasing number of journalists want to be contacted electronically, other journalists have not yet embraced electronic technology. Perhaps there are two reasons for their hesitation. The first is human nature: journalists are people. Technology may have changed, but they have not.

Second, it is still important to journalists to have face-to-face meetings or hold a hard copy of a press release or a product in their hands. Electronic technologies aside, people still want access to a product "in the flesh"—to touch it, feel it, see it.

Nikolich expressed the relationship concept as central to the profession: "I keep telling my clients, the message is consistent and will always be consistent: it's a relationship business. It involves establishing a relationship with someone, being able to pick up the phone and talk to you, and being able to come out and demonstrate a product to you. Hands-on is still the way to go."

One potential benefit public relations professionals see from the use of electronic tools such as E-mail may be a better rapport between themselves and journalists. As Kevin Kimball, director of public relations for Siemens Corporation, put it, "I'm hoping [journalists] will be more accessible, there will be more dialogue. I was on the journalism side of the industry before I came over to public relations fifteen years ago. The biggest challenge in journalism is to capture the attention of journalists. To do that he or she needs to get to know what that journalist thinks, how that journalist writes, what subjects that journalist is interested in, how he writes about those subjects. So maybe, these electronic media will somehow bridge that gap and hopefully reduce those [inherent] walls that exist between journalists and public relations practitioners."

Epilogue

The following article, is reprinted in its entirety from an issue of *Knowledge Tools News,* an electronic newsletter of Omegacom, Inc., by James Baar (jimbar@omegacom.com), president/managing consultant and Theodore Baar (tedbar@omegacom.com.), vice president and chief technologist. The article raises some important issues—about the use of the Internet and its impact on the practice of public relations—for public relations practitioners, students of the profession, and clients. What it has to say is food for thought as electronic media, such as the Internet, pervade the civilized world as we move toward the millennium.

Is the Internet the medium that will create a worldwide collective consciousness? Will the Internet and what it may evolve into substantially change the relationships among public relations practitioners, print and electronic journalists, and the public? Will organizations be able to control their public relations image while the Internet increasingly becomes a venue for news?

The Pentium Bug War Ends PR as We Know It
James Baar and Theodore Baar

The real long-term significance of the Great Intel Pentium Flaw Imbroglio is the imminent demise of the current practice of public relations and corporate and government communications as we know them.

Ironically caught unaware of the communications world it helped create, Intel suffered a public relations near-disaster. Intel's arch competitor, IBM, wandered bubba-like into a public relations bog the future depths of which are still to be determined.

Clearly we soon will see on the boneyard of history such communications artifacts as:

- The lengthy, well-spun news release or official statement explaining what "really" happened or why a product "really" is a breakthrough for all mankind.
- The news conference where the news is what the media said yesterday or last week is "really" not the news at all.
- The necessity to convince rushed and often ill-informed journalists and beautiful and much more ill-informed TV anchors that your truth is "really" true.

The Internet is doing to public relations what C-SPAN, CNN Forums, and talk radio are doing to news coverage: When you are there, the messenger is extraneous. And, on the Internet, you are there and you are the messenger as well.

The Pentium Flaw War was the first major corporate war to be fought primarily in cyberspace. The initial, very scattered shots were fired more than five months ago on the Internet; major engagements got underway in October [1994]; and a worldwide battle raged through November and early December.

Little of this was noted particularly in the general or trade media until near the end. And then it was reported as a highly technical problem of limited general interest. Only when IBM found it convenient to drop the equivalent of a small nuclear weapon did most of the major national media take note that something much more than an academic, technically obscure brawl was underway.

Only then did the *Wall Street Journal* shout from its front page:

Chip Shot
Computer Giants' War over Flaw in Pentium Jolts the PC Industry

And, on the same day, the *New York Times* shouted from its front page:

I.B.M. Halts Sales of Its Computers with Flawed Chip

Both stories were inspired belatedly by an IBM announcement that it was suspending sales (sort of) of any of its personal computers that included the Intel Pentium chip because the chip had a flaw.

Well, ho-hum: Except for the IBM announcement, this was old news along the Information Highway. And the IBM announcement was immediately discounted by many of the veteran cyberspace combatants of the Pentium War as highly suspect: something similar to Parliament coming out against slavery in America after Lexington and Concord.

Most great military engagements begin quite casually if not accidentally: A sniper picks off a poacher stealing a chicken. A nervous platoon leader calls in a little artillery fire on a bunker. A lost company stumbles on a tank column.

Back in June, Intel and some of its customers already knew about the bug that was preventing the new Pentium microprocessors to divide accurately out to more than nine or ten decimal places in some cases. Intel did not publish the information. If any messages about the bug appeared here and there in various newsgroups on the Internet for the next few months, they initially attracted little attention.

This was not the kind of consumer problem that causes a lot of excitement at your neighborhood 24-hour store. But this bug was of interest—and in some cases important—to parts of the world technical community engaged in major mathematical calculations: This is a community that also appreciates that such a flaw is not the first nor will be the last in the increasing complexity of computer components and software; exalts technical openness; recognizes quickly when it is being stonewalled; and has a biting specialized sense of outrage and humor.

Prof. Thomas Nicely of Lynchburg College reports that when he began running into a potential flaw in the Pentium in June he started a three-month effort to determine whether the problem was the Pentium or something else. For example, his own calculations; or possibly known bugs in other hardware such as the Borland C Compiler. And in Copenhagen mathematicians developed a T-shirt satirizing the Intel chip logo "Intel Inside" as "No Intelligence Inside" and published memos saying "We knew about it early in June…"

Intel managed to downplay and contain word of the bug for the most part through the next three months. Any callers were told at first that a fix was underway and that the bug affected only very special situations.

Then, on October 30, Dr. Nicely posted a message to "whom it may concern" on the Internet, reporting his findings and his frustrations with getting Intel to pay serious attention to him. In the succeeding weeks, the war between Intel and its users exploded. Each day there were more reports about the bug and Intel's truculence.

The number of the strings of messages on the Internet increased and grew longer as users at universities, laboratories and corporations around the world reported the same bug and its potential variations; discussed their research for possibly more bugs; and reported on their unsatisfactory and frustrating phone calls to Intel.

And here was where the war was really fought. Intel treated each caller as an individual, linear event to be dealt with in isolation; turned around or at least mollified. Intel's position was that this was a routine bug that was being taken care of and was of no major importance to most of its customers. The Intel position essentially remained that there was no need for a general replacement on demand; that the problem was relatively minor; that if a user was engaged in the kind of heavy mathematics that could be affected by the bug then Intel, if it agreed, would replace a Pentium.

Meantime, Intel and its commercial allies continued to promote and sell Pentiums. More than 4 million Pentiums were reported sold.

The words "greedy" and "arrogance" became popular on the Internet among customers describing Intel's position. The Internet discussion was highly technical and profane. It also included useful suggestions for broadening the discussion. For example, participants were provided with the fax number of the *New York Times*. And more and more of the callers to Intel shared their mostly frustrating experiences on the Internet with a worldwide audience of customers. An angry mob—slowly recognized as a major threat by Intel—began to assemble in cyberspace.

Intel CEO Andrew Grove issued a statement on the Internet November 27 seeking to quiet the mob. Instead, the roar in cyberspace increased. Intel's Software Lab Technology Lab director Richard Wirt on December 8 issued a statement on the Internet describing Intel's plans to provide a fix for the flaw. The roar continued and spread and Intel's weakening protests were increasingly drowned out as the users reinforced each other with new data and complaints around the clock around the world.

It was at this point on December 12 that IBM—a reported minor player in the sale of Pentiums, but the developer of a competitive chip, the PowerPC— decided to announce both on the Internet and to the major national media the halting of its shipments of Pentium-based IBM PCs.

The war was now spread to the major national media, where the problem was easily confused with various consumer product recalls, and the Internet, where IBM's move was both discounted as self-serving and used simultaneously to pummel Intel further.

By December 20 Intel had had enough. It agreed to a general recall and apologized for not doing so sooner.

The public relations lessons are clear.

People—particularly customers—are no longer isolated waiting to learn sooner or later what is happening through the third-party media screen and, in turn, relying on the third-party media to screen and sooner or later report their reaction. Even when the third-party media is accurate, this process can take many days.

Through the Internet, people—particularly customers—can tell a corporation or organization exactly what they think and why and share that simultaneously and instantaneously with all concerned around the world. The Internet returns the world to the agora where everyone hears what was said; and everyone hears all comments and reactions; everyone knows who is talking and can make credibility judgments.

The first Intel error was not to spot the issue stirring on the Internet months ago when the commentary was helpful and understanding. At that time and for several months later, Internet commentators could have been embraced and thanked for their efforts; immediate plans for a work-around fix could have been disclosed; and work on a permanent fix could have been described: all in cyberspace among sophisticated customers who well understand the complex nature of the technology.

Intel's second error was not to recognize that because of the Internet it no longer could reason at least semiprivately with customers and advance rational technical arguments. In pre-cyberspace days, that could be effective: the customer is grudgingly mollified until the issue is eventually resolved. But in this case, as its customers shared both their problems and experiences with each other in real time, they fed each other's frustrations; were empowered as a group to demand better treatment; and built mutual strength with each day for new battles to come.

Intel's third error was not to go directly on line with its customers and deal with the issue interactively. Instead, Intel pursued the classic static public relations mode of issuing statements and news releases. These were turned into blackened ruins by Internet flame messages in a matter of hours.

Meantime, IBM by its announcement uncorked the Law of Unanticipated Consequences. The Internet mob really understood the issue; the general public for the most part did not. IBM, with motives already under suspicion, opened the bottle labeled "Doubt about Technology" to the overall potential future detriment of the Information Technology Industry in general.

As more people around the world join the millions already using the Internet for communications, corporations and government will be forced, if they wish to succeed, to function within the new realities of cyberspace: information is shared and sifted by thousands of knowledgeable people; time is collapsed; facts are quickly checked; loss of credibility can be instantaneous; second chances are rare and harder to effect; grandstand plays had better be perfect; and the playing off of one audience against another is far more easily detected.

Above all else, a smattering of obscure messages or even a random one or two can no longer be automatically disregarded as mere technical mumbling. For example, is anyone following up on a recent Internet potential bug message regarding AMD DX-80 chips or another regarding "something about a conditional loop" in the Pentium?

One final cyberspace reality of note: instant corrosive humor is abundant and effective. (If they really are laughing about you, you can't be taken seriously anymore.) This was ably demonstrated by the Internet author who wrote for the delectation of Intel customers and potential customers everywhere a *Star Trek* parody. He called it: "BBUUGGS IINN SSPPAACCEE!!"

Bibliography

Advertising Council. *Inspiring Action and Saving Lives*. Advertising Research Foundation, April 1991.

AdWeek Magazine. *Marketer's Guide to Media*. Spring/Summer 1994.

Angell, David, and Brent Heslop. *The Internet Business Companion*. Reading, MA: Addison-Wesley, 1995.

Baar, James (jimbar@omegacom.com), and Theodore Baar (tedbar@omegacom.com). "The Pentium Bug War Ends PR as We Know It." *Knowledge Tools News*, an electronic newsletter of Omegacom, Inc., January 1995.

Barlow, John Perry. "Forward: A State of Minds," in Rutten, Peter, Bayers, Albert F., and Kelly Maloni. *Netguide*. New York: Michael Wolff [Random House Electronic Publishing], 1994.

Bartholomew, Anita. "Video as a Marketing Tool: Bonanza or Bust?" *Tape/Disc Business*, March 1995.

Banet, Bernard. "What Happened to the Interactive Videodisc?" *Digital Media*, March 23, 1992.

Bergman, Robert E., and Thomas V. Moore. *Managing Interactive Video/Multimedia Projects*. Englewood Cliffs, NJ: Educational Technology Publications, 1990.

Blankenhorn, Dana. "Multimedia Products Aimed at Schools." *Electronic Media*, December 9, 1991.

Brush, Judith M., and Douglas P. Brush. *Private Television Communications: The New Directions—The Fourth Brush Report*. Cold Spring, NY: H.I. Press of Cold Spring, in association with the International Television Association, 1986.

Brush, Judith M., and Douglas P. Brush. *Private Television Communications: The Fourth Brush Report, Update '88*. LaGrangeville, NY: H.I. Press, 1988.

Burrus, Daniel. *TechnoTrends: Twenty-Four Technologies that Will Revolutionize Our Lives*. New York: HarperCollins, 1993.

Caldwell, Kate. "Online PR." Internet communique to multiple recipients of List PRFORUM, November 3, 1994.

Center for Strategic Communications. *New Ideas in Communications*, document 273, May/June 1994.

Center for Strategic Communications. *New Ideas in Communications*, document 281, July/August 1994.

Coe, Steve. "Mixed Blessing of Video News Releases." *Broadcasting & Cable*, June 28, 1993.

Cutlip, Scott M. *The Unseen Power: Public Relations, A History*. Hillsdale, NJ: Lawrence Erlbaum Associates, 1994.

Czitrom, Daniel J. *Media and the American Mind: From Morse to McLuhan*. Chapel Hill: University of North Carolina Press, 1982.

Dataware Technologies. *Guide to CD-ROM and Multimedia Publishing*. March 1993.

Dessart, George. *More than You Want to Know about PSAs: A Guide to Production and Placement of Elective Public Service Announcements on Radio and Television*. National Broadcast Association for Community Affairs, 1982.

Digital Express. *Express Access TM Online Communications Service*. 1994.

Drucker, Peter F. *The New Realities*. New York: Harper & Row, 1989.

Dvorak, John C. "Manifesto, An Open Letter to the PR Community." *MediaMap/Alert*, August 1994.

"Energy Update 2001: Behind the Scenes." *Exhibit Builder*, August 1991.

Federal Communications Commission. *The FCC and Broadcasting*, March 1993.

Federal Communications Commission. FCC Form 303IV, iii.

Federal Communications Commission. *Report and Order Re: Petition to Institute a Notice of Inquiry and Proposed Rule Making on the Airing of Public Service Announcements by Broadcast Licensees*. BC Docket no. 78-251, released October 27, 1980.

Federal Communications Commission. *Reporting and Statement of Policy Re: Commission EN/BANC Programming Inquiry*, FCC 60-970 25 Federal Register 7291, released July 29, 1960.

The Federal Register, vol. 46, no. 36, Tuesday, February 24, 1981, "Rules and Regulations," p. 13946.

"'Flexible' B-roll Packages Produse Results." *O'Dwyer's PR Services Report*, April 1994.

Forester, Tom. *High-Tech Society*. Cambridge, MA: The MIT Press, 1987.

Forrester Research. *Interactive Media Business*. Cambridge, MA: October 1992; December 1992.

Gabriel, Trip. "Public Relations Has Potent Image." *New York Times*, March 17, 1994.

Gerstein, Mark D., and Robert Shaw. "Organizational Achitecture." In David A. Nadler, ed., *Organizational Architecture: Designs for Changing Organizations*. San Francisco: Jossey-Bass, 1992.

Hollowell, Mary Louise, ed. *The Cable/Broadband Communications Book*. Vol. 2, *1980–1981*. White Plains, NY: Knowledge Industry Publications, 1980.

Hughes, Kevin. *Entering the World-Wide Web: A Guide to Cyberspace*. Honolulu Community College, October 1993.

Innis, Harold. *The Bias of Communication*. Toronto: University of Toronto Press, 1951.

International Teleconferencing Association. News releases. June 14, 1993; June 19, 1994.

Internet Electronic Frontier Foundation. *Guide to the Internet*. February 1994.

Jewett, Sally. "Electronic Publicity—Plus 10 Years." *The Publicists Guild Directory*. Publicists Guild: 1991.

Kalish, Karen. "VNR: Guidelines." Washington, DC: Kalish Communications, undated.

Ketchum MacLeod & Grove Public Relations. "Employee Communications Energy." Paper presented at the International Conference of the International Association of Business Communications, 1980.

Kingaard, Jan. "Video Marketing." *Tape/Disc Business*, March 1995.

Laurie, Lynn. "This Year, Software from Santa." *New York Times*, December 16, 1994.

Levin, Jayne. "Internet's Electronic Link to Managing Money: Computer Network Provides a Wide Array of Financial Information and Is Adding More." *Washington Post*, April 1994.

Lewis, Peter H. "Trying to Find Gold with the Internet." *New York Times*, January 3, 1995.

Lieberman, David. "Fake News." *TV Guide*, February 22, 1992.

Lohr, Steve. "Big Companies Cloud Recovery by Cutting Jobs." *New York Times*, December 17, 1992.

Lutholtz, Bill. "Online PR." Internet communique to multiple recipients of PRFORUM List, Digex/Internet access, November 10, 1994.

Makulowich, John S. (verbwork@access.digez.net). The Journalism List. Gaithersburg, MD: The Writers Alliance.

Malone, Thomas W., and John F. Rockart. "Computers, Networks and the Corporation." *Scientific American*, September 1991.

Marlow, Eugene. "Even Though Videoconferencing Will Continue to Attract Attention, Audiographic Teleconferencing Will Be Making Bigger Waves." *International Television*, June 1983.

Marlow, Eugene. *Corporate Television Programming*. White Plains, NY: Knowledge Industry Publications, 1992.

Marlow, Eugene. "The Electrovisual Manager." *Business Horizons*, Bloomington, IN: Indiana University Graduate School of Business, March/April 1994.

Marlow, Eugene. "Sophisticated News Videos Gain Wide Acceptance." *Public Relations Journal*, August/September 1994.

Marlow, Eugene. *Winners! Producing Effective Electronic Media*. Belmont, CA: Wadsworth, 1994.

Marlow, Eugene, and Eugene Secunda. *Shifting Time and Space*. New York: Praeger, 1991.

Mayo, John S. Remarks. AT&T Bell Laboratories Technology Symposium, Toronto, October 13, 1993.

McLuhan, Marshall. *Understanding Media: The Extensions of Man*. New York: McGraw-Hill, 1964.

"Journalists Say Public Relations Mail Is Spinning Out of Control." *Media Relations Insider*, vol. 1, no. 4, April 1994.

Medialink. *Video Public Relations Handbook*. 1994.

Microsoft Corporation. *Multimedia Publishing and Microsoft Multimedia Viewer Publishing Toolkit Version 2.0*. Microsoft Corporation Backgrounder, February 1993.

"Modern Talking Pictures." *Corporate Backgrounder*, 1994.

Naisbitt, John. *Trend Letter*, vol. 11, no. 7 (April 2, 1992).

National Association of Broadcasters. *User's Guide*. NAB, 1994.

National Cable Television Association. *Cable Television Developments*. Washington, DC: NCTA: April 1994.

Neches, Robert, Neches, Anna Lena, Postel, Paul et al. "Electronic Commerce on the Internet." SurveyNet, downloaded September 16, 1995.

"netResults." The Electronic Newsstand. Gopher, Internet, 1994.

O'Connell, Christina. "Online PR." Internet communique to multiple recipients of PRFORUM list, October 31, 1994.

O'Dwyer's Directory of Public Relations Firms. New York: J. R. O'Dwyer Co., 1994.

Peter, Lewis H., "Prime Internet Address Will Now Cost $50 a Year," *New York Times*, September 14, 1995, D1, D6.

Philo, Michael K. Prekh, and Storm Boswick, "CyberPublishing: A New Front in Content Liquidity," *CyberCommerce: On Line and Internet Services*, Goldman Sachs, July 26, 1995, p. 2.

Public Relations Service Council. "Code of Good Practice for Video News Releases." *Public Relations Journal*, December 1992.

Public Relations Society of America. "Public Relations: An Overview." *Public Relations Journal*, vol. 1, no. 3 (November 1991).

Radio and Television News Directors Association. *Revised Code of Ethics*. Unanimously adopted by the RTNDA Board of Directors, August 31, 1987.

Reeves, Thomas, and Stephen Harmon. "What's in a Name—Hypermedia," *Interact*, vol. 3, no. 1 (Fall 1991).

Resnick, Rosalind. "The Microsoft Network: Good News for Online Publishers?" *Interactive Publishing Alert Newsletter*, December 1994.

Rheingold, Howard. *Virtual Reality*. New York: Simon & Schuster, 1991.

Robins, J. Max. "Time Cooks Up Fast Feed for Hungry News Outlets." *Variety*, October 28, 1991.

Roche, Edward Mozley. "Business Value of Electronic Commerce over Interoperable Networks." Discussion paper, Cross-Industry Working Team, Freedom Forum Media Studies Center, July 6-7, 1995.

Rogers, Everett M. *Communication Technology: The New Media in Society*. New York: The Free Press, 1986.

Ryan, Suzanne Alexander. "Companies Teach All Sorts of Lessons with Educational Tools They Give Away." *Wall Street Journal*, April 19, 1994.

Schubin, Mark. "An Overview and History of Videodisc Technologies." In *Video Discs: The Technology, the Applications, and the Future*. White Plains, NY: Knowledge Industry Publications, 1980.

Shell, Adam. "An Easy Guide to VNR Suppliers: Are Client Expectations Too High?" *Public Relations Journal*, December 1990.

Shell, Adam. "VNRs: Who's Watching? How Do You Know?" *Public Relations Journal*, December 1993.

SIMBA Information, Inc. *Multimedia Business Report*. Wilton, CT: SIMBA, June 16, 1994.

Smith, Leslie F. *Perspectives on Radio and Television*. New York: Harper & Row, 1985.

Stone, Vernon A. "TV News Work Force Grows." *Communicator*, April 1994.

Taylor, Dave (taylor@netcom.com). The Electronic Mall.

Taylor, Steven T., and Morton Mintz. "A Word from Your Friendly Drug Company." *The Nation*, October 21, 1991.

Tesler, Lawrence G. "Network Computing in the 1990s." *Scientific American*. September 1991.

Trade Show Bureau Report. Denver: Trade Show Bureau, 1994.

U.S. Department of Commerce. *U.S. Industrial Outlook 1994*. U.S. Government Printing Office, January 1994.

U.S. Internal Revenue Service. *Annual Report*, publication 55. Washington, DC: U.S. Government Printing Office, 1994.

"VNR Update: Facts Versus Fiction." *Public Relations Journal*, December 1989.

WCBS. *Public Affairs at WCBS NewsRadio 88: Your Guide to Public Affairs Programs and Services*. WCBS Public Affairs Department, undated.

WNBC. *PSA Guidelines*. WNBC Programming Operations, November 11, 1994.

West Glen Communications. *Information Kit 1994*. New York: West Glen Communications, 1994.

Yankelovich Partners. www.yankelovich.com. "Cybercitizen: A Profile of Online Users," September 1995.

Appendix 1: Interviewees

Greg Albrecht
Publicity Manager
General Publicity Office
Walt Disney World
Orlando, Florida

Lew Allison
Former Senior Vice President
Hill and Knowlton
New York, New York

Karen Amster-Young
President
Karen Amster-Young Public Relations
New York, New York

Ray Anderson
Manager, Management
    Communications Planning
    Department
Ford Motor Company
Detroit, Michigan

John Beardsley
President
Public Relations Society of America
New York, New York;
Principal
Padilla, Speer, Beardsley, Inc.
Minneapolis, Minnesota

David Bartlett
President
Radio and Television News Directors
    Association
Washington, DC

Don Blank
Director of Operations
Georgia-Pacific Television
Atlanta, Georgia

Ted Bozovich
Office of Employee Plans & Exempt
    Organizations
Field Systems Branch
Internal Revenue Service
Washington, DC

Richard S. Brooks, Jr.
Corporate Communications Manager
BMW
Woodcliffs Lake, New Jersey

Kathyrn Buan
Manager, Investor Relations
Oracle Corporation
Redwood Shores, California

Mark Cerutti
President
Cerutti Productions
New York, New York

Lee Cioffi
Producer/Manager
The National Museum of American
   Arts
Smithsonian Institution
Washington, DC

Steven Cook
President
Steven S. Cook & Company, Inc.
   Public Relations
Washington, DC

Glenn Corey
Producer
Chedd-Angier Production Company
Watertown, Massachusetts

Don Corley
Executive Producer & Manager
Bell South Telecommunications
   (Video)
Birmingham, Alabama

Lynn Cox
Public Relations
Digital Express
Greenbelt, Maryland

Paul Downey
Manager, Media & Communications
   Unit
Metro Toronto Communications
   Services
Toronto, Canada

Tony Esposito
Group Manager
Bozell Public Relations, Inc.
Chicago, Illinois

Farrell Fitch
Community Relations
National Alliance for the Mentally Ill
Arlington, Virginia

Patricia Frieden-Brown
Manager
Vital Video
Blue Cross/Blue Shield
Boston, Massachusetts

Dick Hackenberg
Account Director for Interactive
   Advertising
Chiat/Day
Venice, California

Jim Hampton
Manager, Publicity/Public Relations
Universal Studios Florida
Orlando, Florida

Dick Jones
President
International Interactive
   Communications Society
(New York Chapter)
New York, New York

Karen Kalish
President
Kalish Communications
Washington, DC

JoAnn Kildow
Producer
Xerox
Leesburg, Virginia

Kevin Kimball
Director of Public Relations
Siemens Corporation
New York, New York

Rebecca Madeira
Vice President, Public Affairs
Pepsico
Purchase, New York

Larry Moskowitz
President
Medialink
New York, New York

Christopher Newton
Executive Producer, Corporate
    Television
AT&T
Basking Ridge, New Jersey

Michael Nikolich
President
Tech Image
Palatine, Illinois

William Orisich
Michael Pieproben
Principals
Big Picture

Elizabeth Parkinson
Producer
Edelman Public Relations, Worldwide
Chicago, Illinois

Judy Lyn Prince
Executive Television Producer
Mobil Oil
Fairfax, Virginia

Suzanne Rothenberg
President
Suzanne Rothenberg Communications
New York, New York

Neil Ruggles
Principal
Net Marketing and PR, Inc.
New York, New York

Jim Schwinn
Manager, Broadcast Media Relations
Minnesota Mining & Manufacturing
Minneapolis, Minnesota

Ed Swanson
Executive Vice President
Video Placement Worldwide
Northbrook, Illinois

Joe Tiernan
Editor
Communicator
Radio and Television News Directors
    Association
Washington, DC

Dennis Wigent
Manager, Electronic Communications
K-mart
Troy, Michigan

Brad Witworth
Manager, Employee Communications
Hewlett Packard
Palo Alto, California

Appendix 2: Organizations

ARF
The Advertising Research Foundation
3 East 54th Street
New York, NY 10022-3180
212/751-5656
FAX: 212/319-5265
The Advertising Research Foundation (ARF) was formed in 1936 by the Association of National Advertisers and the American Association of Advertising Agencies to advance state-of-the-art advertising, marketing and media research. The ARF is composed of some 400 member companies, primarily major national advertisers, advertising agencies, research firms, and the media as well as educational institutions and other industry associations.

The Ad Council
The Advertising Council, Inc.
261 Madison Avenue
New York, NY 10016-2303
212/922-1500
FAX: 212/922-1676
The mission of the Advertising Council is to identify a select number of significant public issues and stimulate action on those issues through communications programs that make a measurable difference in our society.

The Ad Council's public service partners include nonprofit or government agencies that sponsor Ad Council campaigns and share their organizational strength and their community-based grassroots marketing power. Hundreds of advertising and communications industry volunteers help to create campaigns.

Nearly 29,000 media outlets across the country donate time and space, making the Ad Council one of the leading Advertisers in America. More than 400 small and large corporations, as well as individuals, support the work of the Advertising Council with their generous gifts.

AICP
Association of Independent Commercial Producers
11 East 22nd St., 4th floor
New York, NY 10010
212/475-2600
FAX: 212/475-3910
The goal of the Association of Independent Commercial Producers (AICP) is to improve the dialogue and working relationship between clients (advertisers and their advertising agencies) and the commercial production industry.
The national AICP represents some 80 to 85 percent of all commercial production in this country and is the only united industry voice talking to and dealing with advertising agencies and their clients, and with the various governmental local, state and national agencies and unions serving this industry.

AIGA
The American Institute of Graphic Arts
164 Fifth Avenue
New York, NY 10010
212/807-1990
Founded in 1914, the American Institute of Graphic Arts (AIGA) is the national nonprofit organization of graphic design and graphic arts professionals. The AIGA conducts an interrelated program of competitions, exhibitions, publications, educational activities, and projects in the public interest to promote excellence in, and the advancement of, the graphic design profession.

Members of the Institute are involved in the design and production of books, magazines, periodicals, film and video graphics, and interactive media as well as corporate, environmental, and promotional graphics. Their contribution of specialized skills and expertise provides the foundation for the Institute's program. Through the Institute, members form an effective informal network that is a resource to the professional and the public.

AMA
American Management Association
135 West 50th Street
New York, NY 10020-1201
212/586-8100
The American Management Association (AMA) was founded in 1923 and has approximately 70,000 members. The AMA provides educational forums world-wide where members and their colleagues learn superior, practical business skills and explore the best practices of world-class organizations through interaction with each other and expert faculty practitioners. AMA's publishing program pro-vides tools individuals use to extend learning beyond the classroom in a process of lifelong professional growth and development through education.

ANA
Association of National Advertisers, Inc.
700 11th Street, NW
Washington, DC 20001
202/626-7800
The Association of National Advertisers, Inc. (ANA) was founded in 1910 and is committed exclusively to serving the interests of companies that advertise regionally and nationally. To meet this commitment, the ANA helps its members make advertising dollars work more efficiently; serves a source of timely and reli-able information; works to keep government from eroding the values of adver-tising; provides advertising-related training and educational programs; and speaks on behalf of advertisers with government and within industry councils. These are the charges that distinguish the ANA from other organizations in the industry, and the guiding principles that have kept the ANA at the forefront of influence and progress in advertising since its establishment.

Center for Strategic Communications
505 Eighth Avenue
Suite 2000
New York, NY 10018-6505
212/967-2843
808/669-4TCN
Center for Strategic Communications (CSC) is a tax-exempt nonprofit organiza-tion that informs and educates nonprofit managers about how to take advantage of the evolving communications environment and extend limited resources through strategic communications planning.

EIA
Electronic Industries Association
2001 Pennsylvania Avenue, NW
Washington, DC 20006-1813
202/457-4900
Electronic Industries Association (EIA) is the national industrial organization of electronic manufacturers in the United Sates whose primary mission is to enhance the competitiveness of the American producer.

It supports and strives to advance the defense of our country, the growth of our economy, the progress of technology, and all interests of the electronics industry compatible with the public welfare. It operates at all times within the framework of law, ethics, and the national interest.

IABC
International Association of Business Communicators
One Hallidie Plaza
Suite 600
San Francisco, CA 94102
415/433-3400
The IABC is a 12,500-member professional association of communication practitioners encompassing the disciplines of public relations, public affairs, marketing, advertising, employee communication, community relations, corporate relations, shareholder relations, and audiovisual communication. It has 119 chapters in Canada, the United States, the United Kingdom, Australia, Belgium, France, Hong Kong, Ireland, the Philippines, Mexico, New Zealand, and southern Africa. IABC has offices in San Francisco and Toronto.

IIA
Information Industry Association
555 New Jersey Avenue, NW
Suite 800
Washington, DC 20001
202/639-8260
Information Industry Association (IIA), founded in 1968, represents more than 500 organizations involved in the generation, distribution, processing, and provision of information products, services and technologies. IIA is home base for businesses offering the innovative products and services that make up the information marketplace.

IIA's mission is to promote, enhance, and strengthen the business environment within which information companies exist, grow, and prosper. Since its inception, IIA has been the only trade association addressing the broad, diverse, and common concerns of this dynamic industry.

INTV

INTV Association of Independent Television Stations, Inc.
1320 Nineteenth Street, NW, Suite 300
Washington, DC 20036
202/887-1970
INTV is the only trade association devoted to representing the interests of local independent television stations, both those affiliated with the Fox network and those that are not. INTV is a nonprofit organization which has been in existence for twenty years and has been recognized for its contribution to numerous key telecommunications issues.

ITCA

International Teleconferencing Association
1150 Connecticut Avenue, NW
Washington, DC 20036
202/833-2549
International Teleconferencing Association (ITCA), an international nonprofit association, is dedicated to the growth and development of teleconferencing as a profession and an industry.

ITCA currently represents over 1,900 teleconferencing professionals from throughout the world. ITCA members use teleconferencing, manage business television and teleconferencing networks, design the technology, sell products and services, advise customers and vendors, conduct research, teach courses via teleconference, and teach about teleconferencing.

ITVA

International Television Association
6311 N. O'Connor Road, no. 110
Irving, TX 75039
214/869-1112
International Television Association (ITVA) serves the needs of video professionals in a non-broadcast setting. It has 8,000 members in 107 chapters throughout the United States.

The association has worked to advance the video profession and to promote the growth and quality of video and related media through providing relevant member services.

PRSA
Public Relations Society of America
33 Irving Place
New York, NY 10003
212/995-2230
Public relations practitioners in business and industry, counseling firms, trade and professional groups, government, education, and health and welfare organizations.

NAB
National Association of Broadcasters
1771 N Street, NW
Washington, DC 20036-2891
800/521-8624
The National Association of Broadcasters (NAB) is the United States' largest, most extensive association that offers a wide variety of services to radio and television stations, as well as organizations that provide products and/or services to the broadcasting industry (our associate members).

NAVD
National Association of Video Distributors
1255 Twenty-Third Street, NW
Washington, DC 20037-1174
202/872-8545
The National Association of Video Distributors (NAVD) is the national trade association of wholesale distributors and manufacturers in the prerecorded home video products industry.

NBACA
National Broadcast Association for Community Affairs
1604 North Country Club Road
Tucson, AZ 85716
602/325-0940
National Broadcast Association for Community Affairs (NBACA) is an organization for broadcast professionals dedicated to strengthening community affairs

programming. NBACA acts as an advocate and resource for community affairs broadcasters seeking professional development by offering seminars, workshops, scholarship, and awards programs.

NCTA
National Cable Television Association
1724 Massachusetts Avenue, NW
Washington, DC 20036-1969
202/775-3622
National Cable Television Association (NCTA) represents cable systems serving more than 80 percent of the nation's 59 million cable subscribers. It also represents more than sixty cable programmers. In addition, NCTA represents the hardware suppliers and providers of other services to the industry.

NCTA's mission is to advance the cable television industry's public policy interests before Congress, the executive branch, the courts and the American public; and to promote the industry's operating, programming, and technological developments. NCTA, working with state cable associations, also represents the industry's interests to state and local policy makers.

SBCA
Satellite Broadcasting and Communications Association
225 Reinekers Lane, Suite 600
Alexandria, VA 22314
703/549-6990
Satellite Broadcasting and Communications Association of America (SBCA) is the national trade organization representing all segments of the home satellite industry. It is committed to expanding the utilization of satellite technology for the broadcast delivery of entertainment, news information, and educational programming. The SBCA is composed of satellite manufacturers, system operators, equipment manufacturers, distributors, retailers, DBS companies, mass merchandisers, encryption vendors, and programmers.

STC
Society for Technical Communication
901 North Stuart Street, Suite 304
Arlington, VA 22203
703/522-4114
Society for Technical Communication (STC) is the largest professional association serving the technical communications profession with more than 18,000

members and 140 chapters worldwide. STC offers high caliber programs that keep both entry-level and veteran communicators aware of the latest trends and technology in technical communication. STC offers innovative services for the educational and professional development of its members.

WIC
Women in Cable, Inc.
230 West Monroe Street, Suite 730
Chicago, IL 60606
312/634-2330
Women in Cable (WIC) was founded in 1979. Its mission is to empower women in the cable industry to attain their personal, professional, and economic goals while influencing the future shape of the industry.

Membership is composed of 2,500 professionals in twenty-three chapters across the nation. These chapters address both national and industry issues and concerns specific to their locale.

WIC Foundation
Women in Cable Foundation
230 West Monroe Street, Suite 730
Chicago, IL 60606
312/634-2330
The Women in Cable (WIC) Foundation was created in 1985. WIC Foundation is a not-for-profit entity designed to address long-range trends and issues impacting the cable industry.

Since 1988, the WIC Foundation has committed its attention to identifying how industry, demographic, and workforce trends will affect the cable business, and suggests solutions and strategies for the industry to effectively plan for the changes ahead. The programs of the Foundation are funded entirely through corporate donations and sponsorship of specific initiatives.

Appendix 3: Publications

Exhibits

Exhibit Builder
Exhibit Builder Box 4144
Woodland Hills, CA 91365-4144

Exhibit File
J.P. Harrington & Associates
1117 Talleyrand Rd.
Westchester, PA 19382

Exhibit Schedule
Bill Communications, Inc.
341 White Pond Rd.
Akron, OH 44313

Exhibitor
Material Handling Institute Inc.
8720 Red Oak Blvd, Suite 201
Charlotte, NC 28217

*Expo—The Magazine for Exposition
   Management*
Sanford Publishing Company
8016 Pennsylvania
Kansas City, MO 64114

Video

In Motion Magazine
421 Fourth Street
Annapolis, MD 21403

Millimeter
826 Broadway
New York, NY 10003

Post
25 Willowdale Avenue
Port Washington, NY 11050

Video
460 West 34th Street
New York, NY 10001

Video Choice
Connell Communications, Inc.
331 Jaffrey Rd.
Peterborough, NH 03458

Video Digest
600 S. Coast Avenue
Lantana, FL 33464

Video Extra
121 S. 13th Street, 2nd floor
Philadelphia, PA 19107

Video Insider
223 Conestoga Road
Wayne, PA 19087

Video Librarian
2219 E. View Ave., NE
Bremerton, WA 98310

Video Magazine
Reese Communications
460 W. 34th St.
New York, NY 10001

Video Maker
Video Maker, Inc.
381 E. Fourth St.
Chico, CA 95928

Video Marketplace
World Publishing Co.
990 Grove St.
Evanston, IL 60201-4370

Video Monitor
10606 Mantz Road
Silver Spring, MD 20903

Video Review
Viare Publishing Co.
902 Broadway
New York, NY 10010

Video Specialist
2630 Coronada Drive
Fullerton, CA 92635

Video Systems
Intertec Publishing Corp.
9221 Quivira Rd.
P.O. Box 12901
Overland Park, KS 62212

Video Week
2115 War Ct. NW
Washington, DC 20037

Videodisc and Opt. Disc Update
11 Ferry Lane West
Westport, CT 06880

Videodisc Monitor
Box 26
Falls Church, VA 22046

Videography
Media Horizons, Inc.
2 Park Avenue
New York, NY 10010-5292

Videomaker
Box 4591
Chico, CA 95927

Worldwide Videotex Update
Box 138
Boston, MA 02157

Photography
Industrial Photography
210 Crossway Park Drive
Woodbury, NY 11797

International Photographer
7715 Sunset Blvd., Suite 150
Hollywood, CA 90046

Popular Photography
1515 Broadway
New York, NY 10036

Photo Weekly
1515 Broadway
New York, NY 10036

Graphics/Animation
Animation
Box 25547
Los Angeles, CA 90025

The Animator
1219 SW Park Avenue
Portland, OR 97205

BRD Report Graphics Artists
Box 1561
Harrisburg, PA 17105

Computer Graphics World
1714 Stockton Street
San Francisco, CA 94133

Technology
American Journal of Distance ED
Rackley Building
Penn State University
University State, PA 16802

Atlantic Tech
2626 Van Buren Avenue
Valley Forge, PA 19482

Channels
Box 600, Dudley House
Exeter, NH 03833

Display and Imaging Tech
Box 786 Cooper Station
New York, NY 10276

Electronic Servicing and Technology
9221 Quivira Road
Overland Park, KS 66212

*IEEE Trans. Professional
    Communication*
345 East 47th Street
New York, NY 10010

*Journal of Technical Writing and
    Communication*
120 Marine St, Box D
Farmingdale, NY 11735

Optical Engineering
1022 19th Street Box 10
Bellingham, WA 98225

Optical Information Systems
Box 160609
Cupertino, CA 95015-0609

Satellite Age
Box 5254
Beverly Hills, CA 90210

*Satellite BUS/Video Publishing
    Corporation*
Box 2772
Palm Springs, CA 92263

Satellite Communications
6300 Syracuse Way Suite 650
Englewood, CO 80111

Satellite News
7811 Montrose Road
Potomac, MD 20854

Science and Technology
Box 28130
San Diego, CA 92128

Sound and Communications
25 Willowdale Avenue
Port Washington, NY 11050

Technical Insights
Technical Insights, Inc.
Box 1304
Fort Lee, NJ 07024

Technology Forecasts
Technology Forecasts, Suite 208
205 S. Beverly Dr.
Beverly Hills, CA 90212

*Technological Forecasting & Social
    Change*
Elsevier Science Publishing Co., Inc.
Journal Information Ctr.
655 Avenue of the Americas
New York, NY 10010

Technology Futures Newsletter
Burrus Research Assoc., Inc.
Box 26413
Milwaukee, WI 53226-0413

Technology Reimbursement Reports/the Beige Sheet
F-D-C Reports, Inc.
5550 Friendship Blvd.
Chevy Chase, MD 20815

Technology Today
Ontario Research Foundation
Sheridan Park, Mississauga, ON L5K 1B3 Canada

Technology Today (Tomorrow Through Research)
Southwest Research Institute, Drawer 18510
San Antonio, TX 78228-0510

Techtrends/Association Educational Comm.
1025 Vermont Avenue NW no. 820
Washington, DC 20005-3516

Telecommunications
Horizon House
685 Canton Street
Norwood, MA 02062

Telecommunications Week
1036 National Press Building
Washington, DC 20045

Telespan Newsletter, The
50 W. Palm Avenue Suite BSS
Pasadena, CA 91030

TV Technology
5827 Columbia Pike no. 31
Falls Church, VA 22041

Marketing
Video Marketing Surveys and Forecast
1680 Vine Street no. 820
Hollywood, CA 90028

Marketer—The Magazine for Marketing Management
Act III Publishing
401 Park Ave., S.
New York, NY 10016

Sales & Marketing Digest
St. James Publishers, Inc.
Box 3061
Boca Raton, FL 33431-0912

Marketing
Maclean Hunter, Ltd.
777 Bay, Suite no. 1000,
Toronto, ON M5W 1A7 Canada

Marketing Action Planner (MAP)
Synectics Network, Inc.
15050 NE 20th Ave.,
Miami, FL 33181

Marketing Communications Report
Pete Silver Association
Box 1702
Gainesville, FL 32602

Marketing Exchange
Financial Marketing Association
2801 Coho St., no. 300
Madison, WI 53713

Marketing New Media
Paul Kagan Associates Inc.
126 Clock Tower Pl.
Carmel, CA 93923

Marketing News
American Marketing Assoc.
250 S. Wacker Dr., Suite 200
Chicago, IL 60606

Marketing Professional Services
Behavior Dunamics
11800 NE 160th St.
Bothell, WA 98011

*Marketing Research: A Magazine of
    Management & Applications*
American Marketing Association
250 S. Wacker Dr., Suite 200
Chicago, IL 60606

Marketing Research Review
High Tech Publishing
10 Ridge Rd., Box 360
Ridge, NY 11961

Marketing Review
American Marketing Assn.,
    New York Chapter
310 Madison Ave., no. 1211
New York, NY 10017-6009

Marketing & Sales Journal
First Information Technology Group,
    Inc.
Box 372
Marblehead, MA 01945

Marketing Science
Institute of Management Sciences
290 Westminster St.
Providence, RI 02903

Marketing Science Institute Newsletter
Marketing Science Inst.
1000 Massachusetts Ave.
Cambridge, MA 02138

Marketing Social
Les Editions Marketing Social Inc.
976 Moneton Ave.
Quebec, PQ G1S 2Y5 Canada

Marketing Treasures
Chris Olsen & Assoc.
857 Twin Harbor Dr.
Arnold, MD 21012

Marketing USA
Market Entry Inc.
149 Raritan Ave.
Staten Island, NY 10304-4017

Communications
Information World Magazine
1060 Marsh Road
Menlo Park, CA 94025

Communications Research Association
10606 Mantz Road
Silver Spring, MD 20903

Corp Comm Digest/Stein Printing
2161 Monroe Drive
Atlanta, GA 30324

Communications News
7500 Old Oak Blvd
Cleveland, OH 44130

Channels of Communications
Box 6438
Duluth, MN 55806

Communications Age Magazine
55 East Jackson Blvd.
Chicago, IL 60604

Journal of Biocommunications
6105 Lindel Blvd.
St Louis, MO 63112

Training Magazine
50 South 9th Street
Minneapolis, MN 54403

Business Communications Review
950 York Road
Hinsdale, IL 60521

Journal of Business Communication
English Building, 608 S. Wright St.
University of Illinois
South Urbana, IL 61801

Communications Week
600 Community Drive
Manhasset, NY 11030

AVC Communication
15125 California St. no. E
Van Nuys, CA 91411-3027

Communicator
900 Palm Avenue Suite BS
South Pasadena, CA 91030

Communications Consultant
323 Geary Street, no. 507
San Francisco, CA 94102

Communication Arts
410 Sherman, Box 10300
Palo Alto, CA 94303

On Communications
Box 880
Framingham, MA 01701

Communication Briefings
Communication Briefings, Inc.
140 S. Broadway
Pitman, NJ 08071

Connections
Burson-Marsteller
230 Park Ave South
New York, NY 10003-1566

Communication Industries Report
Communication Industries Assn.
3150 Spring Street
Fairfax, VA 22031-2399

Pacific Dialogue
Box 1312
New York, NY 10018-0724

Trends In Communication Management
Telemation Management Group, Inc.
315 W. 23rd Street
New York, NY 10011

Professional Communicator
Women in Communications, Inc.
2101 Wilson Blvd., no. 417
Arlington, VA 22201

Special Issues
Standard Rate Data Service
3004 Glenview Rd.
Wilmette, IL 60091

Public Relations
Public Relations Journal
Public Relations Society of America,
    Inc.
33 Irving Place, 3rd floor
New York, NY 10003

Public Relations News
127 E. 80th St.
New York, NY 10021

Public Relations Quarterly
Newsletter Clearinghouse
Hudson Associates
44 W. Market Street, Box 311
Rhinebeck, NY 12572

Public Relations Reports
Communication Research Assoc., Inc.
10606 Mantz Road
Silver Spring, MD 20903

Public Relations Review
Communications Research Associates,
   Inc.
10606 Mantz Road
Silver Springs, MD 20903

Public Relations Society of America
   (PRSA News)
Public Relations Society of America,
   Inc.
33 Irving Place, 3rd floor
New York, NY 10003

Entertainment
Billboard
1515 Broadway
New York, NY 10036

Backstage Magazine
330 West 42nd Street
New York, NY 10036

Cue Magazine
1430 Benito Avenue
Burlingame, CA 94010

Box Office
1800 North Highland
Hollywood, CA 90028

Coming Attractions
550 Grand Street
Jersey City, NJ 07302

Illustrators
27 Madison Square Pr.
10 East 23rd Street
New York, NY 10010

Showtime Magazine
P.O. Box 149
Reno, NV 89504-0149

Film/Broadcast
Hollywood Reporter
1501 Broadway
New York, NY 10036

Broadcasting Magazine
1735 Desales Street NW
Washington, DC 20036

American Film Magazine
J.F. Kennedy Center
Washington, DC 20566

Society of Broadcast Engineers
7002 Graham Road
Indianapolis, IN 46250

Broadcast Engineering
PO Box 12901
Overland Park, KS 66212

National Association of Broadcasters
Box 119
Topeka, KS 66601

Journal Of Broadcasting/BEA
1771 N. Street NW
Washington, DC 20036

Business of Film
22 Tehama Street, no. 2B
Brooklyn, NY 11218

Cable Industry
Cable Reports
Box 1205
Annandale, VA 22311

Cable World Magazine
1905 Sherman Street
Denver, CO 80203

Index

About the Authors

Eugene Marlow, Ph.D.
Eugene Marlow (emabb@cunyvm.cuny.edu) has been involved with the strategic application of print and electronic media for over twenty-five years. He has consulted to dozens of organizations in the media, technology, healthcare, consumer products, and nonprofit sectors. He has produced over 500 video, radio, multi-image, videodisc, and teleconferencing presentations and received dozens of awards for programming excellence from a variety of national and international organizations. He teaches graduate and undergraduate courses in electronic journalism and business communications at Bernard M. Baruch College (City University of New York).

Marlow is the author of *Winners! Producing Effective Electronic Media* (Wadsworth, 1994), *Corporate Television Programming: Applications and Techniques* (Knowledge Industry Publications 1992), coauthor of *Shifting Time and Space: The Story of Videotape* (Praeger, 1991), *Managing Corporate Media* (2nd edition, Knowledge Industry Publications, 1989), and *Communications and the Corporation* (United Business Publications, 1978), as well as many articles on television programming and video technologies.

Janice Sileo, Research Associate
Janice Sileo has been involved in marketing communications and public relations since 1988. She has served as a judge for the International Film and Television Festival of New York and the Quasar Awards. She has been a member of the National Academy of Televsion Arts and Sciences (New York chapter), and is currently a member of the Healthcare Public Relations and Marketing Society and the National Association of Female Executives (NAFE).